Romanticism and the Poetics of Orientation

Edinburgh Critical Studies in Romanticism
Series Editors: Ian Duncan and Penny Fielding

Available Titles
A Feminine Enlightenment: British Women Writers and the Philosophy of Progress, 1759–1820
JoEllen DeLucia
Reinventing Liberty: Nation, Commerce and the Historical Novel from Walpole to Scott
Fiona Price
The Politics of Romanticism: The Social Contract and Literature
Zoe Beenstock
Radical Romantics: Prophets, Pirates, and the Space Beyond Nation
Talissa J. Ford
Literature and Medicine in the Nineteenth-Century Periodical Press: Blackwood's Edinburgh Magazine, 1817–1858
Megan Coyer
Discovering the Footsteps of Time: Geological Travel Writing in Scotland, 1700–1820
Tom Furniss
The Dissolution of Character in Late Romanticism
Jonas Cope
Commemorating Peterloo: Violence, Resilience, and Claim-making during the Romantic Era
Michael Demson and Regina Hewitt
Dialectics of Improvement: Scottish Romanticism, 1786–1831
Gerard Lee McKeever
Literary Manuscript Culture in Romantic Britain
Michelle Levy
Scottish Romanticism and Collective Memory in the British Atlantic
Kenneth McNeil
Romantic Periodicals in the Twenty-First Century: Eleven Case Studies from Blackwood's Edinburgh Magazine
Nicholas Mason and Tom Mole
Godwin and the Book: Imagining Media, 1783–1836
J. Louise McCray
Thomas De Quincey: Romanticism in Translation
Brecht de Groote
Romantic Environmental Sensibility: Nature, Class and Empire
Ve-Yin Tee
Romantic Pasts: History, Fiction and Feeling in Britain and Ireland, 1790–1850
Porscha Fermanis
British Romanticism and Denmark
Cian Duffy
The Lady's Magazine (1770–1832) and the Making of Literary History
Jennie Batchelor
Mary Wollstonecraft: Cosmopolitan
Laura Kirkley
Romanticism and Consciousness, Revisited
Richard Sha and Joel Faflak
Remediating the 1820s
Jon Mee and Matthew Sangster
Romanticism and the Poetics of Orientation
Joey S. Kim

Forthcoming Titles
Romantic Networks in Europe: Transnational Encounters, 1786–1850
Carmen Casaliggi
Death, Blackwood's Edinburgh Magazine and Authoring Romantic Scotland
Sarah Sharp
Seeking Justice: Literature, Law and Equity during the Age of Revolutions
Michael Demson and Regina Hewitt

Visit our website at: www.edinburghuniversitypress.com/series/ECSR

Romanticism and the Poetics of Orientation

Joey S. Kim

EDINBURGH
University Press

Edinburgh University Press is one of the leading university presses in the UK. We publish academic books and journals in our selected subject areas across the humanities and social sciences, combining cutting-edge scholarship with high editorial and production values to produce academic works of lasting importance. For more information visit our website: edinburghuniversitypress.com

© Joey S. Kim 2023, 2025

Edinburgh University Press Ltd
13 Infirmary Street
Edinburgh EH1 1LT

First published in hardback by Edinburgh University Press 2023

Typeset in 10/13pt Sabon
by Cheshire Typesetting Ltd, Cuddington, Cheshire

A CIP record for this book is available from the British Library

ISBN 978 1 3995 1125 4 (hardback)
ISBN 978 1 3995 1126 1 (paperback)
ISBN 978 1 3995 1127 8 (webready PDF)
ISBN 978 1 3995 1128 5 (epub)

The right of Joey S. Kim to be identified as the author of this work has been asserted in accordance with the Copyright, Designs and Patents Act 1988, and the Copyright and Related Rights Regulations 2003 (SI No. 2498).

Contents

List of Figures	vi
Acknowledgements	viii
Introduction: Romanticism, Orientalism, Orientation	1
1. Situating the "Orient" in British Romantic Poetry	16
2. Byron's Cosmopolitan "East"	56
3. The Racialized Poetess	86
4. Disorienting Romanticism: William Blake's Orientalist Poetics	118
Conclusion	159
Works Cited	165
Index	177

Figures

4.1 *Jerusalem*, copy E, obj. 54, c. 1821. Yale Center for British Art. The William Blake Archive. 124
4.2 *The Marriage of Heaven and Hell*, copy D, obj. 2, 1790. Lessing J. Rosenwald Collection, Library of Congress. Copyright © 2022 The William Blake Archive. 128
4.3 *The Marriage of Heaven and Hell*, copy D, obj. 9, 1790. Lessing J. Rosenwald Collection, Library of Congress. Copyright © 2022 The William Blake Archive. 130
4.4 *The Marriage of Heaven and Hell*, copy D, obj. 6, 1790. Lessing J. Rosenwald Collection, Library of Congress. Copyright © 2022 The William Blake Archive. 135
4.5 *The Marriage of Heaven and Hell*, copy D, obj. 27, 1790. Lessing J. Rosenwald Collection, Library of Congress. Copyright © 2022 The William Blake Archive. 136
4.6 *The Marriage of Heaven and Hell*, copy D, obj. 1, 1790. Lessing J. Rosenwald Collection, Library of Congress. Copyright © 2022 The William Blake Archive. 138
4.7 *The Marriage of Heaven and Hell*, copy D, obj. 3, 1790. Lessing J. Rosenwald Collection, Library of Congress. Copyright © 2022 The William Blake Archive. 140

4.8	*The Marriage of Heaven and Hell*, copy D, obj. 14, 1790. Lessing J. Rosenwald Collection, Library of Congress. Copyright © 2022 The William Blake Archive.	141
4.9	*Jerusalem*, copy E, obj. 2, c. 1821. Yale Center for British Art. The William Blake Archive.	145
4.10	*Jerusalem*, copy E, obj. 18, c. 1821. Yale Center for British Art. The William Blake Archive.	147
4.11	*Jerusalem*, copy E, obj. 99, c. 1821. Yale Center for British Art. The William Blake Archive.	151
4.12	*Jerusalem*, copy E, obj. 100, c. 1821. Yale Center for British Art. The William Blake Archive.	153

Acknowledgements

Thank you to my advisors, mentors, colleagues, editors, reviewers, confidants, friends, and family for the years of labor, support, and care you provided to help me realize this book. I am grateful to the Edinburgh Critical Studies in Romanticism series editors, Ian Duncan and Penny Fielding, for supporting, refining, and fostering this project. Thank you as well to my Edinburgh University Press editors—Susannah Butler, Fiona Conn, and Michelle Houston—for your help in the many stages of getting this manuscript into material form. Thank you to editor Rebecca Colesworthy at SUNY Press, for being the first to believe in this manuscript. The early reviews of the manuscript you provided were thorough and generous. Thank you to Liu Kuo-Sung for letting me use your incredible work, *The Sunrise of East*, as the cover to my book. It is the perfect distillation of the book's ideas.

So many thanks to my dissertation committee, Clare A. Simmons, Jake Risinger, and David G. Riede, for your generous guidance, feedback, and openness to the development of my dissertation and scholarly writing. You witnessed the beginning of this book and helped to nurture it into a worthy contribution to the fields of literary and cultural studies. To my other Ohio State mentors and friends—first and foremost, Pranav Jani, thank you for being the most courageous, illuminating, and benevolent mentor to me during a time of intense personal trauma and recovery. Your postcolonial and South Asian literature classes were the fulcrum of my academic career at OSU. Thank you to Jill Galvan, Robyn Warhol, Jian Neo

Chen, Amanpal Garcha, Beth Hewitt, Kathleen Griffin, and Mike Bierschenk for guiding me during the six years of a rigorous academic timeline that strengthened my ability to research, write, and address feedback for the rest of my career. To my undergraduate advisors, Philip Metres and John McBratney, thank you for allowing me to shine as an English major in both literature and creative writing. Your instruction and feedback planted the seeds of my earliest dreams of being an academic.

To my Boston University community—Carrie Preston, Marilyn Gaull, Justin Mann, Emily Hainze, Trent Masiki, Joe Rezek, John Bell, Travis Franks, Amy Fish, Takeo Rivera, and Chuck Rzepka—thank you for being there as I started my first position after my doctorate. My generous three-year postdoctoral fellowship at Kilachand Honors College enabled me to submit to book presses, fine-tune my dissertation into book form, and meet so many colleagues and researchers from around the country who I will be friends and collaborators with for life. These include Yoon Sun Lee, Renee Hudson, Sarah Zimmerman, Douglas Ishii, Theo Davis, Andrew Warren, and many more. Thank you in particular to Yoon Sun Lee for your careful feedback on Chapter 1 of this manuscript. You helped me transform it into the book's anchor.

To my University of Toledo colleagues, friends, and mentors—Ayendy Bonifacio, Joey Gamble, Andrew Mattison, Dustin Pearson, Kim Mack, Tina Fitzgerald, Ben Stroud, Parama Sarkar, Tyler Branson, Tim Geiger, An-Chung Cheng, Paul Hong, Ally Day, Natalie Bullock, Malaika Bell, Mel Gregory, and Charlene Gilbert—thank you for supporting me as I started my first tenure-track position. I am lucky to be surrounded by such a brilliant, generous, reliable, and lively group of colleagues. Thank you to the University of Toledo's Research Awards and Fellowship program for the generous fellowship which helped me research full-time, travel, and complete the final stages of this manuscript without teaching responsibilities.

Thank you, Abbey Skovran and Steph Sung, for being my best friends since early childhood. Your friendships have been remarkably unyielding and I am lucky to still have you in my life. Thank you to my friends from graduate school and beyond—Samantha Charlip, Sidney Jones, Torsa Ghosal, Pritha Prasad,

Debanuj DasGupta, J. Brendan Shaw, Colleen Morrissey, Zach Harvat, Colleen Kennedy, Raena Shirali, Vinusha Autar, and Matt Connolly. I am grateful for the community you provided and continue to provide.

To my dearest family— Mom and Dad, Jennifer, Christine, Esther, Victor, Jonah, Adeline, and Sophia—thank you for cheering me on throughout this journey of intellectual love and sacrifice. Without you all, this project would not exist. Thank you to Ana, José, Ramón, Jessica, Estarly, Isaura, Ángel, and Isabella. I am honored to be a part of your family, and I hope this book makes you proud.

Finally, thank you to my love and life partner, Ayendy Bonifacio. Meeting you in graduate school turned into the best adventure of my life. Your advice, belief, love, and support of this book and all of our life's journeys have been and continue to be limitless. 사랑해.

Introduction: Romanticism, Orientalism, Orientation

Orientation, n.
1. The relative position or direction of something; the bearing or lie of a thing.
2. The placing or arranging of something so as to face the east.
Oxford English Dictionary

It is time for us to consider the significance of "the orient" in orientation, or even "the oriental."
Sara Ahmed, *Queer Phenomenology*

The *Oxford English Dictionary*'s first definition of "orientation" reads "the relative position or direction of something" (*OED*). This definition is clear and reflective of current usage. However, the second definition of "orientation" reads, "the placing or arranging of something so as to face the east" (*OED*). What does it mean, then, to "face the east?" What is, who stands for, and where exactly is the east? To where does it lead? What happens when we redirect our lines of reading along new lines, borders, and orientations—those that fail to fit neatly into the cardinal directions of North, South, East, and West? In asking these questions, I seek a change in perspective—one that recovers our understanding of cultural appellations like the East and its historical counterpart, the "Orient." These words constitute fundamental parts of an ambiguous and persistent taxonomy of racial, ethnic, and gendered subjects and objects. This book, at its root, interrogates the creation of the "Orient" and its "Oriental" subjects during the Romantic period.

From Immanuel Kant's question, "What Does It Mean to Orient Oneself in Thought?" (1786) to the question of the exact locale of the "Orient" or "East" in Romantic literature, the interconnected logic of orientation and "Orient" has not been excavated in Romantic literary and cultural studies. How do geographical, continental, and hemispheric divisions buttress aesthetic investments in poetic forms and subjects? If hemispheric divisions make location, position, and subject possible, what happens when continental and hemispheric divisions mark certain subjects as perpetually other and distant? Sara Ahmed writes in *Queer Phenomenology*, "We might not be able to imagine the world without dividing the world into hemispheres, which are themselves created by the intersection of lines (the equator and the prime meridian), even when we know that there are other ways of inhabiting the world" (13).[1] These "other ways" outside of hemispheric divisions are the grounds for perceived otherness, distance, difference, inscrutability—traits that during the Romantic period became increasingly associated with the Orient, the East, and its racialized subjects. Ahmed points out that the question of Orientalism is also a question of orientation, arguing that "it is time for us to consider the significance of 'the orient' in orientation, or even 'the oriental': what relates to, or is characteristic of the Orient or East, including 'natives' or inhabitants of the East" (113). Map-making and geographical systems create and command the logic of directionality, thus making orientation itself an act of power in which the Orient is "made oriental" through its "submission" to the Occident (Ahmed 114). Ahmed concludes that "to become oriental is both to be given an orientation and to be shaped by the orientation" (114). I take up Ahmed's call to consider the significance of the "orient" in orientation through a focus on the Romantic period, a period when Orientalism had a "renaissance" and found its modern-day bearings.[2] I trace how "to become oriental" was essential to the rise of a Romantic poetics situated around white authors. This situatedness, as we know, became the overwhelming orientation of how Romantic poetry is commonly studied today.

Romanticism and the Poetics of Orientation confronts the racial and ethnic logics of the Oriental subject undergirding the development of Romantic poetics. It traces shifting poetic orientations—cultural, geographical, aesthetic, racial, and gendered—through Orientalist sites, subjects, and settings. I coin the term "poetics of orientation" to describe a poetics newly aware of cultural difference as a site of aesthetic contestation and ambiguity of representation. I focus on the contestation that occurs at the site of the lyric subject. By contestation, I am referring to the ways in which Romantic writers themselves transformed the notions of the subject while centering their own whiteness. This double move—transformation and centering of white subjects—consolidated a Romantic poetics founded on Orientalist ambivalence. A "poetics of orientation," rather than situating the lyric subject in assumed claims of whiteness, repositions the lyric subject within heterogeneous and shifting notions of self, place, race, and culture. This repositioning frames the lyric subject within discussions of Orientalism and racial formation, tracing the white supremacist logics that have for too long been dismissed as inessential or non-consequential to Romantic studies.

Thus, the construction of the modern lyric subject depends on the very creation and invention of the "Oriental" subject. This invention of the "Oriental" subject is a racialized subjectivity that depends on whiteness and white dominance to exist. As Ahmed notes in "A phenomenology of whiteness," whiteness has an "ongoing and unfinished history, which orientates bodies in specific directions" (150). Reified whiteness functions as the "background" to universal experience so that the "what" of the world becomes white. In essence, "whiteness becomes 'worldly'" (150). This worldliness, however, is predicated on the noticeability of non-white "others." As a creation of coloniality and empire, the "Oriental" subject is that racial and cultural wedge insulating whiteness from non-whiteness through the veil of cosmopolitan intrigue and worldliness.

Bringing together new formalism, anti-racist and anti-colonial critical thought, I thus retrace the Orientalism at the root of the white lyric subject, uncovering a lineage that has not been fully attended to in the history of the expressive lyric dating back to its Romantic inception.

As Kamran Javadizadeh argues, "Race has not, so far, been a central preoccupation of the 'new lyric studies'" in the wake of Virginia Jackson and the rise of historical poetics (476). In conversation with the work of Manu Chander, Patricia Matthew, Bakary Diaby, Marlon Ross, and others, this book interrogates the racialized and ethnic subjectivities at the core of the Romantic lyric subject. I analyze the contested space of lyric representation and how it yields to historical pressures, orienting around various figurations of Orientalism, non-whiteness, and ambiguous "otherness." By "otherness," I am referring to authors' representations of alterity, Easternness, and/or cultural difference in the formation of a generic "other."

This book contrasts with the historicizing thrust of the last few decades of scholarship on nineteenth-century European literatures of empire. I do this with intention: scholarship on Romantic aesthetics, genre, and form have been delinked from racial and ethnic questions. The formal developments of Romantic poetics have not been interrogated in and of themselves as Orientalist regimes of whiteness made "worldly." A focus on the aesthetic contours of Romanticism and Orientalism brings the contestation of the lyric subject to the fore of my argument and shows that Orientalism is not just colonialism or historical events. It is imbricated in the aesthetic genealogy of Romantic poetics and theory.

This aesthetic genealogy runs alongside the historical events of the period, including global revolutions, transatlantic slavery and abolition, British colonialism and empire, and the inception of a modern British subject of "the world." Literary and aesthetic production reflects these changes through hybridity and experimentation with old and new genres and forms. As a subgenre of poetry that rose to prominence during the period, anglophone Orientalist poetry shifted poetic theory and production toward transnational and comparative modes. This shift in orientation came to be alongside the rise of the Romantic imagination as central to poetic production. This imaginative turn found in the "Orient" a host of inspirations and influences, many of which have been left uncited and forgotten. Authors incorporated new subjects and representations from outside the British Isles and often relied on invention over authenticity. In effect, the British Romantics linked individual expression and imagination with universal, increasingly cosmopolitan ideals of person and place.

In Book Ten of *The Prelude*, William Wordsworth reflects on living in France during the revolution, calling himself a "patriot of the world" (242), and is eventually saddened by England joining the war against France's egalitarian factions. As a self-deemed "patriot of the world," Wordsworth conjures a Western cosmopolitanism that is still with us today. This being "of the world" is often expressed through racialized and gendered representations devoid of historical or cultural accuracy. It evokes Ahmed's phenomenology of whiteness made "worldly" (150). To be "of the world" in the Romantic period became an act of individual expression, imagination, and self-creation reifying whiteness as the implicit norm.

This book surveys the shifting orientations of subject and setting in the works of Sir William Jones, William Wordsworth, Samuel Taylor Coleridge, Percy Bysshe Shelley, George Gordon, Lord Byron, Felicia Hemans, Phillis Wheatley, and William Blake. The white authors in this study rely on an individual imagination that codifies Orientalism, but not only this. Orientalism was one of many racial and racist systems of the period working to consolidate whiteness as the dominant race. Atesede Makonnen points out that the first recorded usage of "white supremacy" occurred in the Romantic period.[3] The period birthed a model that subjugated not only the Oriental subject but the entire non-white world. These authors represent a gathering around and toward whiteness as the racial *sine qua non* of anglophone poetic subjects. "Towardness" is a directionality stemming from the space between subject/object or self/other and can be both a negation but also "form of extension" (Ahmed 115). This extension of white self and subject beyond Britain became a poetics of not only world-facing but also world-building an Orient during a period of political and cultural revolution and regeneration. The anglophone "world" as we imagine it today is a product of this Orientalist inheritance.

I use "Orientalism" as a literary concept—the pivot between imaginative idea and historical and political reality. I argue that "Orientalism" and its expressions of otherness transform common conceptions of British Romantic poetry, specifically the subject position of the poet and their role in artistic creation and expression. I follow the lineage of Edward Said's *Orientalism* (1979) and Lisa Lowe's de-essentializing of Orientalism in *Critical Terrains: French and British Orientalisms* (1991) and reroute more explicitly along the lines of race and gender. I show how Orientalism is one part of the global project of an anglophone poetic tradition rooted in gendered antiblackness and white supremacy, which I discuss in Chapter 3. Chapter 3 routes us away from the Orient, finding in Phillis Wheatley Peters an alternative poetic trajectory—one that offers a world apart from whiteness and its logics of racial control and objectification.

To be "of the world" and apart from the world—this gatekeeping persists in the way Romantic texts have been studied. Thus, this book responds to the growing body of scholarship resistant to normalized erasure of "bad" anglophone Orientalist texts, including Wael B. Hallaq's call to restate Orientalism. Hallaq argues in *Restating Orientalism* that Orientalism needs to be "restated" and qualified in terms of "the constitution of the modern self" (vii). Hallaq finds in the word "Orientalism" a "profound ambiguity" and asks, "Is Orientalism an academic scholarly field or is it an ideological construction?" (1). While Hallaq focuses on disciplinary trends, I join both sides of this debate and think in terms of scholarly field and ideological construction. By returning to the problem of Orientalism in Romantic texts, I build upon recent approaches to reading race in Romanticism—not through imperial or colonial thought structures but through anti-racist and anti-colonial methods like Kandice Chuh's "aesthetics of illiberal humanism" (xii). I trace the relationship between a generic Orientalism and more specific instances of Orientalist formation through racial, racist, and gendered hierarchies. In doing so, I interrogate the literary and cultural history of Orientalism and, in turn, Romantic entanglements with ethnic and racial logics of control, erasure, objectification, and aestheticization.

These entanglements abound particularly in second-generation Romantic authors' corpuses through their host of speakers, subjects, and settings. From Lord Byron's minimally read

Eastern Tales (1813–16) to Percy Bysshe Shelley's *The Revolt of Islam* (1818), there is a preponderance of Orientalist representations and constructions of the "Orient" or "East" that belie reality and facticity in favor of aesthetic experimentation. These representations also show the "prehistory of Orientalism" behind an English modern subjectivity. As Eugenia Zuroski notes, the formation of this modern subjectivity is a "paradoxical process: by refusing versions of the self that are 'strange,' it produces—and compulsively reproduces—estranged versions of itself" (217). This creation of self through the strangeness of the other produces the dialectic upon which the authors in this book find self-definition. For example, in the final canto of Byron's *Childe Harold's Pilgrimage* (1818), the initial setting of Venice is personified as a sensual woman figure with "spoils of nations, and the exhaustless East" (III, IV.2, 15–16).[4] Only a few years earlier in his Eastern Tale, *Lara* (1814), Byron writes of the eponymous, ethnically ambiguous hero lying on the ground about to die. Lara's faithful page, Kaled, cannot save him but listens to Lara's "dying tones" in "that other tongue, / To which some strange remembrance wildly clung" (2.444–5). Before dying, Lara's final gesture is to raise his hand and point "to the East."[5] Orientalist deployments like these occur throughout Romantic literature, and they bring the conditions of cultural imperialism, objectification, and British self-fashioning into view.

Keywords: Orientation, Orient, Orientalism

While it is easy to overlook the fact that before 1839 the word "orientation" did not exist in English, anglophone writers knew from long experience that there was a spatial and geographic side to individual subjectivity. By focusing on orientation in Romantic literature, I look particularly at how poets positioned themselves aesthetically and geopolitically in the changing terrain of anglophone culture right before "orientation" entered the lexicon. I use the term "orientation" as a mode of positioning self, subject, and object within and towards different, oftentimes competing, cultural and aesthetic norms. The first recorded use of the word "orientation" in 1839 comes from the Cambridge Camden Society's *A Few Hints on the Practical Study of Ecclesiological Antiquities*. This guidebook uses the word "orientation" in regards to "the deviation of a church from east, because it is supposed that the chancel points to that part of the horizon where the sun rises on the Feast of the Patron Saint" ("orientation, n."). In a later edition of this handbook, the aforementioned section reads, "Orientation. It is important to notice the deviation of the direction of a church from the True East" (*A Hand-book of English Ecclesiology*). Both uses of "orientation" share the description of spiritual iconography and secondly, the naming of the shared "deviation" in direction from the east/"True East." The relation between "orientation" and religious iconography is something I will return to in my final chapter on William Blake's prophetic books.

Later definitions of "orientation" include "the relative position or direction of something; the bearing or lie of a thing," "the action or process of ascertaining one's position relative to the points of the compass," and *"the action of taking up a particular position or bearing"* ("orientation, n." emphasis mine). I want to highlight this last usage, as it speaks to the way one's orientation can become a willful, intentional, embodied act. As an *action*, the orientation of a poet and their work—whether geographical, aesthetic, cultural, philosophical—takes on material impact and consequence. The action of taking up a position or space in the "West" in opposition to the "East" becomes a formative trope through which the authors in this study participate in the hardening logic of Orientalist control.

While "orientation" is a relatively new word, the "orient" as noun has been used since the Middle Ages. According to the *Oxford English Dictionary*, the first recorded use of the word "orient" dates back to 1375 in Chaucer's "Monk's Tale" ("orient, n. and adj."). Chaucer writes, "They conquered manye regnes grete In thorient" (3504), describing the "thorient" in terms of a generalized "Eastern" realm, which aligns with the word's historical usage to reference "countries lying immediately to the east of the Mediterranean or Southern Europe (i.e. east of the Roman Empire)" ("orient, n."). Today, however, the noun "orient" is "usually understood to mean East Asia, or occas. Europe or the Eastern hemisphere, as opposed to North America" ("orient, n."). Over time, the word "orient" has denoted and connoted various subjective things, including, "[t]hat part of the heavens in which the sun and other celestial objects rise," "The rising of the sun; daybreak, dawn," and "[t]he colour or special lustre of a pearl of the best quality" ("orient, n. and adj."). Given the different etymologies yet connotative linkage between "orientation" and "orient," there is clear hermeneutic potential in connecting the literary "Orient" to the concept of orientation. These definitions provide a way of reading the "orient" and Orientalism as creations of a history of directions, moves, and "acts"—acts that are human-made, relative, impermanent, and perhaps, reversible.

The first recorded usage of the word "Orientalism" is attributed to 1747 and Joseph Spence's third edition of "An essay on Pope's *Odyssey*: in which some particular beauties and blemishes of that work are consider'd." Spence writes, "This whole prophetical vision of the fall of the suitors ... gives us an higher Orientalism than we meet with in any other part of Homer's writings. You will pardon me a new word, where we have no old one to my purpose" ("orientalism, n."). The "purpose" of the word "Orientalism" was largely unmoored, culturally imprecise, and individualistic, until Edward Said's restatement of the term in *Orientalism*.

The rise of Orientalism during the Romantic period marks a pivotal moment in anglophone literature when poetry moves from aesthetic to political act. This shift moves the task of the poet beyond individual experience to collective representation of other peoples, places, and cultures. It raises the question of the ethics of representation in relation to the poet's expressive impetus.

As a negative or restrictive example, Orientalist representation reinforces stereotypes, propagates invention over scholarship, and stalls the progression of anglophone poetics into newer, more culturally diverse forms and genres. By negative and restrictive, I am referring to instances of cultural appropriation, erasure or elision, stereotypes, and erroneous or fictive cultural references. Emily Haddad writes about nineteenth-century

Orientalist poetry as the intersection of various "matrices" such as English and French poetics (2). She elucidates how nineteenth-century poetry uses Orientalist tropes to create "an alternative aesthetic space" and Orientalism functions "as a diffuse avant-garde, a matrix for the reexamination of both pre-existing conventions and contemporary expectations in poetry and poetics" (2). I argue that Romantic poets take old poetic forms and join them with new representations of the "Orient." The collision between old and new forms creates an aesthetic landscape that is only as "avant-garde" as its perceiver or poet imagines.

This new aesthetic matrix relies on a habitual return to the self over other as the prime agent of perception. As Maurice Merleau-Ponty asserts, "the word 'perception' indicates direction more than a primitive function" (12). This recurrent direction towards the self seeks a referent beyond etymological coherence, like the hypostatized "Orient," to situate its own sense of place. If perception's "essential function" is "to establish or to inaugurate knowledge, and we view perception through the lens of its results," what unifies the lens of this experiential "knowledge" (Merleau-Ponty 17)? How does perception steered toward the "Orient" transform the idea of space and world into a cultural, racial, ethnic amalgamation of motifs, symbols, imagery, and representations? Rita Felski points out that literary critique "is not just a matter of content ('knowing that' something is the case) but also a matter of style, method, and orientation ('knowing how' to read a text or pursue a line of reasoning)" (26). What happens when we read the literary archive of Romantic Orientalism through a critical mode of orientation and, as Chapters 3 and 4 will show, disorientation?

The Chapters

These chapters work from the concept of "orientation" as always situated differently in Romantic texts. The first chapter draws on the shared aesthetic project of Sir William Jones, William Wordsworth, Samuel Taylor Coleridge, and Percy

Bysshe Shelley. I explain the defining attributes of a poetics of orientation—individual subjectivity, the faculty of the imagination, cultural plurality, universalized experience, the aesthetic schema of poet as center, the lack of a coherent "other," and dislocated place and/or setting. I argue that Sir William Jones—a philologist and jurist who learned thirteen languages and founded the Asiatic Society of Bengal—advances a new account of the poet's task of creation and expression in his 1772 collection of essays and poems. In doing so, he also turns poetic production toward comparative practice. I trace how Jones's largely forgotten text lays the poetic groundwork for Percy Bysshe Shelley's Orientalist allegory of the French Revolution, *The Revolt of Islam* (1818). *The Revolt*'s egalitarian ethos both normalizes and decenters the British point of view. By representing the literary "Orient" as a space between self and the self's constructed other, Shelley's work signifies radical otherness through an aesthetics of shapes. In analyzing these works, I explain how Orientalism constitutes a fundamental part of the poetics of orientation—a poetics in which the subject finds one's bearings in an increasingly disorienting world of political upheaval, misrecognition, and geographical ambiguity. This poetics newly constructs the modern lyric subject and reinforces Western individualism and a white-male-dominant poetic tradition.

The second chapter explains how Byron's constructions of the lyric subject are forged directly by his early-career aesthetic and Orientalist inventions in his Eastern Tales. It links the rise of Orientalism and racialized representations to the development of the "cosmopolitan" Romantic subject and its "Oriental" counterpart. By "cosmopolitan," I am referring to the modern view of a common humanity across social and cultural borders in the long tradition of Immanuel Kant's writings in *Toward Perpetual Peace* and "Idea for Universal History with a Cosmopolitan Purpose." Understanding the limitations of postcolonial theory as a framework for understanding cosmopolitanism, I uncover the racial aesthetics of Byron's brand of cosmopolitanism in his Eastern Tales. Crafted in the immediate success of *Childe Harold's Pilgrimage*, Byron's Eastern Tales challenge any fixed notion of Byron's identifying traits of cosmopolitanism and evidence his creation of a textualized and simulated "East"— a space of disidentification and defamiliarization that creates a poetic subject incommensurate with commonplace notions of the lyric subject. This "East" is depicted in terms of Byron's competing personal, aesthetic, and cultural impulses. These impulses culminate in his fourth tale, *Lara*, and the myth of the fundamentally obscure cosmopolitan figure for which Byron's heroic subjectivity became known. Byron locates his poetry in a destabilized space that is also legible as a revised cosmopolitanism such that neither the "Orient" nor the "world" is imaginable without the other. In expanding the poet's subjectivity beyond clearly delineated cultural and geographical borders, these tales show Byron's own self-fashioning as a poetic figure through the logics of Orientalism.

Byron's transatlantic celebrity was fostered by the creation of a Byronic figure who influenced writers around the world. Matt Sandler writes of Black writers' engagement with Byron and the development of what he calls a Black Romantic revolution. Black writers from George Moses Horton, George Boyer Vashon, Frances Ellen Watkins Harper, and Albery Allson Whitman took up Byronic themes of liberation and situated them within anti-slavery discourse and Black self-emancipation. Much work has been and continues to be done by Black studies scholars including Saidiya Hartman, Christina Sharpe, Katherine McKittrick, and others to uncover the racial, racist, and antiblack logics undergirding anglophone literature. This work is essential to showing how the rise of the Oriental subject is not singular or alone as a racialized subject during the Romantic period.

Chapter 3 builds on the work of these scholars and focuses on the rise of the racialized poetess figure. As Tricia Lootens reminds us, "Who made the Poetess [and poet] white? No one, not ever" (7). I illustrate how the historic racialization of the poet and poetess as white diminishes the work of Phillis Wheatley Peters and other Black, Indigenous, and women-of-color writers during the Romantic period. In new readings of works by Wheatley and Felicia Hemans—the most widely read woman poet in the nineteenth century— this chapter asks how explicit engagement with women's poetry like Wheatley and Hemans can redraw the map and future orientations for later "poetess," non-white, and non-binary poet figures.

As Omar Miranda argues, Wheatley's poetry is an important precursor to the "global Romantic lyric" as we know it today (323), and I highlight Wheatley's importance to Romanticism. In turning to Wheatley's poetry, I open an alternative space of what Lisa Lowe and others would call a "*past conditional temporality* of the 'what could have been'" and alternative narratives of affirmation, recovery, and presence (*Intimacies* 40–1). Through this chapter's unexpected juxtaposition of Wheatley and Hemans, I disorient a neat chronology of Romantic women's writing and seek a rereading of the transatlantic poetess tradition through Wheatley's poetics. Her poems cross boundaries of race, gender, culture, time, and space, invite double meaning and paradox, upend expectations, mingle new forms and images, and forge a Black lyrical tradition that speaks back to histories of antiblackness and erasure.

If the authors in this study express the lyric subject through shifting notions of cultural and racial difference, what happens when "difference" is transplanted to visual forms? After explicating the "poetics of orientation," my final chapter turns to William Blake's visuality of images and text. In ending the book with William Blake's visuality of world-making and prophecy, I analyze Blake's mode of disorientation—his turning away from the fixed East through a queer orientation of shifting typographical, human, spiritual, and animal forms. I focus on Blake's multimodal use of image and text in his prophetic works, specifically *The Marriage of Heaven and Hell* and *Jerusalem: The Emanation of the Giant Albion*. While Jones, Coleridge, Shelley, Hemans, and many Orientalists face the "East" through imitation, repetition, and habituation, Blake builds a world of global coordinates that is comprehensive and includes the East as an ideal form. The four cardinal points Blake uses in his prophetic schema turn Romantic poetics away from Western individualism tied to colonial and imperial realities. This disorientation of poetic subject and setting dislodges any fixed understanding of Romanticism and moves this understanding beyond the space of the page and cardinal directions of East/West from which the Orient is commonly constructed.

I show how Blake's composite art—calligraphy, illustration, and innovative printing technique—comprises a plurality of referents and styles. These styles are segmented by his use of plates, a type of module that is moveable and changeable. This modular form proposes new forms of life beyond human, gender, and racial classification and rewrites the literary landscape of Romantic Orientalism through a phenomenological understanding of individual and embodied subjectivity. In doing so, this chapter moves beyond normative distinctions of text and image, problematizes binary gender categories and heteronormative representations (particularly via Blake's illustrations of non-gendered bodies), and reorients conceptions of the Romantic lyric subject toward questions of visuality, phenomenology, and alternative aesthetic horizons beyond the lyric poem.

As these chapters show, I have organized the book in resistance to a normative, linear, chronological approach to the period. This book works in the spirit of the Bigger 6 Collective and its insistence that "all have a right to claim Romanticism, to define as Romantic those texts that do not already fit existing models of Romanticism, to question the central place of European men in the study of Romanticism, and to propose models of the Romantic that reconfigure social positions along more equitable lines" (140). This reconfiguration builds on the collective work of "undisciplining" across field boundaries that Ronjaunee Chatterjee, Alicia Mireles Christoff, and Amy Wong call for in their special issue of *Victorian Studies*. The work of "undisciplining" can "yield opportunities for different aesthetics that will no longer uphold racial hierarchies" (380). Through this book's organization and unexpected trajectory, I hope to articulate the value in undisciplined reading—a type of disorientation that reads for an alternative past. Through this alternative past, this book begins to clear the ground for a different future.

Notes

1. Sara Ahmed, *Queer Phenomenology: Orientations, Objects, Others* (Durham, NC: Duke UP, 2006), 13.
2. I am referring to Raymond Schwab's *The Oriental Renaissance: Europe's Rediscovery of India and the East, 1680–1880* (New York: Columbia UP, 1984). Since Schwab, the rise of postcolonial theory and comparative studies via Edward Said's *Orientalism* (1979) has shown the centrality of Romanticism to forging Orientalism and Occidentalism as hemispheric nomenclature.
3. Makonnen writes, "The *OED* records the first usage of the phrase in 1824, in T. S. Winn's *Emancipation: Or Practical Advice to British Slave-holders: with Suggestions for the General Improvement of West India Affairs*. Winn writes of the enslaved in the West Indies, '[i]t may be too late by any means, however wisely and honestly attempted, to reduce them to order and obedience under White supremacy, or even among themselves.'" (19).
4. Lord Byron, *The Complete Poetical Works*, ed. Jerome McGann, 7 vols (Oxford: Clarendon Press, 1980–93), III, IV.2, lines 15–16. All quotations are from this edition, hereafter *BCPW*.
5. Byron, *BCPW*, III, II, line 467.

Chapter 1

Situating the "Orient" in British Romantic Poetry

The orient sun in shadow:—not a sound
Was heard
          Percy Bysshe Shelley, *The Revolt of Islam*

Their language is vitally metaphorical; that is, it marks the before unapprehended relations of things.
          Percy Bysshe Shelley, *A Defence of Poetry*

Literary representations of the East and other deployments of Orientalism signal an unprecedented shift in poetics and aesthetics during the Romantic period. This shift in orientation was in many ways a turn to the poetic self over the other. This turn to the self valorized the individual poet and the rhetoric of universal experience. It was in tension, however, with the rise of new literary forms, Orientalism, comparativism, and increasingly "global" frames of reference. Through these tensions, the Romantic period saw the rise of Western individualism and a white-male-dominant poetic tradition. This tradition forged a modern lyric subject reliant on and in contrast to the Oriental other. Through Orientalist difference, the Romantic poet became themself—a subject of world-facing, cosmopolitan, white associations. By foregrounding expression over imitation, newness over tradition, heterogeneity over uniformity, and hemispheres over national borders, British Romantic writers expressed and reimagined themselves, taking routes through a literary "Orient"—a fictive space of cultural, political, sexual, and religious differences postured as "Oriental" forms.

Situating the "Orient" in British Romantic Poetry 17

As translator, colonial judge, and poet, Sir William Jones occupies a broad, paradoxical framework of Orientalist interests and influence on the authors in this study. His public role as a judge and imperial representative in colonial India, and his eventual defense of the first "Governor-General of Bengal," Warren Hastings, situate Jones as an unlikely progenitor of Romantic expressive theory. Not only law, but Jones was also a polyglot and philologist dedicated to the study of twenty-eight different languages throughout his life. After he moved to India to serve as a judge, he founded the Asiatic Society of Bengal and started the journal *Asiatic Researches*, creating lasting scholarly interest in what he called "Indology" and non-Western social sciences. After his death, the five editions of his works published between 1799 and 1810 show his significance and popularity, but only recently has Jones's impact on the literature and literary history of this period been acknowledged.[1] Part of a larger shift in British engagement with Eastern cultures, Jones is a central figure in the changing relationship between British culture and "Eastern" poetry which began with his focus on Arabic and Persian poetry. As Tim Fulford and others note, Jones's theories were the "first comprehensive discussion of an eastern poetry as a tradition shaped by a particular culture and a specific environment" ("Plants, Pagodas and Penises" 189). Thus, Jones was also a cultural historian who transformed British reception of Eastern poetry, challenged Orientalist fantasy, all while creating the specific environment from which British poetry reimagined itself. Jones's 1772 collection of Orientalist miscellany, *Poems Consisting Chiefly of Translations from the Asiatick Languages. To which are added two essays; I. On the poetry of the eastern nations. II. On the arts, commonly called imitative* is both the founding of an Orientalism grounded in aesthetic appreciation for the "East" *and* a revival of anglophone lyric poetry. This latter contribution is what makes his theories so influential on the authors of this study. By foregrounding the lyric as a reputable form used by cultures around the world, Jones forged the grounds for a British lyric subject of global aims.

These global aims, however, quickly turned to Western individualism and white male dominance. By valorizing the lyric,

Jones's theories also formalize the literary practice of creating and writing from one's personal subjectivity as a site of intrinsic aesthetic value. This focus on the individual imagination and not cultural scholarship, particularly using "Eastern" representations, marks a pivotal moment in literary history when cultural fictions, errors, stereotypes, and generalizations were produced and reproduced to create and imagine an "Oriental" subject—a site of objectification, cultural erasure, and ambiguity of representation.

Jones, under the names of "agreeable fictions" and "translations," proposes from the "East" a reanimation of English poetry with new cultural images, allusions, and representations.[2] As Srinivas Aravamudan notes, the British Orient was a combination of "pseudoethnographies, sexual fantasies, and political utopias" that were "nine parts invented and one part referential" (4). This imaginary projection is the space for a growing tension between aesthetic center and periphery, new subjects and objects. The fulcrum of this tension is the poet and their changing role, reflecting an energetic, anxious, experimental looking towards the East about which James Watt, Saree Makdisi, Nigel Leask, Marilyn Butler, Humberto Garcia, Sara Suleri, and others have written. This looking towards the Orient as a literary phenomeon produces ambivalent gestures of artistic license, appropriation, and appreciation. These gestures propel an oriented and relational subjectivity as one common characteristic of a poetics of orientation. This poetics turns away from traditional and fixed conceptions of the lyric, ballad, prose, and poetry forms to elucidate the poet's task of expression within culturally heterogeneous repertoires, patterns, and structures.

Jones's description of "the finest parts of poetry" as "expressive of the passions" and "operat[ing] on our minds by sympathy" lends force and warrant to the eventual Orientalist sites, subjects, and settings that other Romantics co-opt and re-imagine in works of self-expression ("On the arts, commonly called imitative" 216). During the Romantic period, Orientalist poetry brought the possibility for writers and artists to redraw the settings, subjects, and aesthetic boundaries of individual human expression in overtly fictive ways. With my historical span and focus on British Romantic texts, I linger on this turn toward self-expression—writing from one's personal subjectivity—because it marks a pivotal moment in literary history when expression becomes vital to poetry's purpose. This expressive turn, however, occurs at the beginning of a changing world order of hardening Eurocentrism and comparative studies in tension with transatlantic independence struggles and the continued bifurcation of Eastern/Western geopolitical positions. What results, in many ways, is a reorientation of the geoaesthetic space of human subjects and their assumed perspectives. M. H. Abrams writes that "[a]n orientation in aesthetic theory is not an idea, or even a premise, but a habitual direction of reference" and that for the Romantics, the common reference point was the poet (100). Romantic Orientalist poetry helps us better trace contemporary Orientalisms back to a moment of paradox in literary studies—when anglophone literature moved to comparativism and when the individual subject was guaranteed the power of individual expression as aesthetic practice.

After the publication of Jones's 1772 *Poems,* more authors turned to Orientalism for inspiration, turning Orientalist poetry into a genre of its own. In this chapter, I will look at three examples, including Samuel Taylor Coleridge's "Kubla Khan," "Mahomet," and Percy Bysshe Shelley's genre-crossing *The Revolt of Islam*. These three works demonstrate the germinating of an "Oriental" subject created by white aesthetic regimes of coloniality, cosmopolitanism, and self-creation.[3] From what Watt calls Jones's "scholarly particularism" to Shelley's more universalized aesthetics (201), the Orient—sometimes Eastern Europe and increasingly eastward toward Asia as the period progresses—functions as a site and premise of literary exploration and appropriation for these writers. In different ways, Jones, Coleridge, and Shelley are invested in and enact a poetics of expression over imitation, imagination over tradition, and Orientalist modes in lieu of classical and Christian elements. They represent the shifting poetries that comprise a poetics of orientation that consists of the following attributes: relational subjectivity and intersubjectivity, the dominant literary imagination, plurality amidst universalism, the aesthetic centrality of the poet, the lack of a coherent "other," and dislocated place and setting.

Jones's Orientalist Poetics

The appended essays to Jones's *Poems, Consisting Chiefly of Translations from the Asiatick Languages* (1772) validate an expansion of the Eurocentric lyric form and insist upon a turn to expressive over imitative art. *Poems* does not consist "chiefly" of "Asiatick" translations, but rather, includes an uneven amalgam of bowdlerized, imitative, and adapted works from sources as varied as Petrarch, Joseph Addison, and the Turkish poet, Mesihi. Jones does write an Orientalist "lyric" called "A Hymn to Narayena" several years later in 1785, and its Pindaric ode form and representation of aspects of Hinduism reflect the cross-cultural impetus that fuels much of Jones's work. There are only two poems in Jones's 1772 collection that are translations, and they are translations from Persian and Turkish poetry. As a whole, *Poems* is comprised of Orientalist poems and miscellany, including erratic translations and creative pieces. The collection presages an impulse for a more global sense of British literature while claiming certain genres and cultures as exemplary or capable of literary "genius" (174).

The first appended essay in *Poems*, "On the Poetry of the Eastern Nations," is a series of observations on the poetry of "the manners of the *Arabs, Persians, Indians, and Turks*, the four principal nations, that profess the religion of Mahomet" (174). Jones examines these nations' poetry to argue for the value of including these cultural literatures in British curricula. He specifically praises the poetry of these "Eastern nations" and how these "poets of Asia have as much genius as ourselves; and, if it be shown not only that they have more leisure to improve it, but that they enjoy some peculiar advantages over us, the natural conclusion, I think, will be, that their productions must be excellent in their kind" (174). This valorization is also a means to strengthen the relevance of classical studies and its historical tradition, as Jones points out later—in effect predicting resistance to his introduction of Orientalist texts into Greek and Latin classical studies. By making a connection between these different schools of poetry, Jones not only brings multiple languages into the study of anglophone poetry, but he also poses Orientalist poetics as a legitimate topic of study.

Jones is careful, however, not to claim any of these "Eastern nations" as dominant or better than previous national traditions. In the ending paragraph to this essay, he writes:

> [I]n bestowing these praises on the writings of Asia, I may not be thought to derogate from the merit of the Greek and Latin poems, which have justly been admired in every age; yet I cannot but think that our European poetry has subsisted too long on the perpetual repetition of the same images, and incessant allusions to the same fables: and it has been my endeavour for several years to inculcate this truth. (198–9)

This problem of the impending exhaustion of "European" poetry's well of "images" and "fables" creates a new expressive task for the poet as well. Jones argues that the poet must seek new poetic images and finds in "the writings of Asia" a source to ameliorate the "perpetual repetition" of current anglophone poetry.

Jones's essay acts as a primer for what comes later in the volume, which includes a series of poems and purported translations. Zak Sitter tracks Jones's Orientalist mode through its "typographical and generic precedents, and the rhetoric through which Jones attempts to influence his volume's reception" ("William Jones" 386). In looking more closely at Jones's appended essays and not the poems themselves, I approach Jones's essays as contradictory theories that countervail the aesthetic mode of his poems which are imitative and derivative. Jones's call for creation over imitation is validated in the next essay, "On the arts, commonly called imitative." M. H. Abrams famously describes this essay as "the first explicit codification of an expressive theory of poetry" in British literature (88). In this essay, Jones defines poetry as "originally no more than a strong, and animated expression of the human passions, of *joy* and *grief*, *love* and *hate*, *admiration* and *anger*, sometimes pure and unmixed, sometimes variously modified and combined" (202–3). Jones continues:

> If the arguments, used in this essay, have any weight, it will appear, that the finest parts of poetry, musick, and painting, are expressive of the passions, and operate on our minds by sympathy; that the inferiour parts of them are descriptive of natural objects, and affect us chiefly by substitution; that the expressions of love, pity, desire, and the tender passions, as well as the descriptions of objects, that delight the senses, produce in the arts what we call the beautiful; but that hate, anger, fear, and the terrible passions, as well as objects, which are unpleasing to the senses, are productive of the sublime, when they are aptly expressed, or described. (216–17)

For Jones, poetry is "expressive of the passions" and "operate[s] on our minds by sympathy," rather than being a mimetic or imitative art. As a proponent of expressive poetry, Abrams writes that Jones "employs the lyric not only as the original poetic form, but as the prototype for poetry as a whole, and thereby expands what had occasionally been proposed as the differentia of one poetic species into the defining attribute of the genus" (87). Thus, this essay both reorients poetic theory toward expression and proposes the lyric as a paradigmatic expressive form.

The development and evolution of the lyric form since Jones's collection is a history of aestheticizing the lyric speaker and subject through dominant notions of whiteness and the racial and ethnic logics of white dominance. This returns us to Javadizadeh's important point that "Race has not, so far, been a central preoccupation of 'the new lyric studies" (476). By making more visible the Orientalist attachments undergirding the Romantic lyric subject, I open up the gaps that could yield different aesthetics and disrupt the perpetuation of white lyric subjects as the assumed center of not only Romantic but Western poetic tradition. The notion of a lyrical tradition that is supposedly universal is troubling given the history of non-white subjectivities as non-human or inferior to white subjects.

As Virginia Jackson has pointed out, the nineteenth-century definition of the lyric was particularly muddled and diffuse, and during the Romantic period there was not "not one kind of poem in the romantic period that could be definitively named the romantic lyric."⁴ Jonathan Culler has seen in the lyric a narrative, historical, and social efficacy. This efficacy can be a form of "social action" or world-making that contrasts with "reified common sense" (8–9).⁵ In response to the range of lyric theorizations today, I ground my conception within the Romantic period. Hegel's lectures on Aesthetics prescribe that "[t]he lyric poem should possess unity,— not the objective unity of the Epic, but the subjective one of the poet's soul, some attitude of it resolutely kept; otherwise the thoughts fall into a didactic level" (284). The emphasis on individual subjectivity or "personal consciousness" is something that Hegel sees potently in "the Oriental lyric [which] exhibits the personal consciousnesss absorbed in the contemplation of nature" (285). Hegel concludes that it "possesses a more objective quality than the Lyric of the Occident" (285). This objectivity remains ambiguous, as Hegel then describes the "Oriental lyric" as the expression of a "naïve expansion, where the imagination loses itself easily . . . because its object is the Infinite Being, which cannot be represented by images" (285–6). Without images, the "object" becomes metaphysical and Hegel describes "Oriental" lyric poetry as "a kind of hymnic elevation . . . by the liberty and wealth of expression" (286). The use of "hymnic" as a descriptive adjective here reinforces a spirituality or otherworldliness to "Oriental" lyric poetry that Hegel does not qualify or explain with clear elements or characteristics. A convenient binary for Hegel and many others in his time, the "Occident/Orient" distinction furthers the propulsion of Orientalist tropes and their association with lyric, expression, and imagination. Both Hegel and Jones prioritize the lyric in terms of its expressiveness, yet Jones goes a step further and produces Orientalist poetry. Jones's poetry, however, lacks the very expressive qualities he espouses.

"Solima, an *Arabian* eclogue" is the first poem in Jones's collection and immediately positions the Orientalized woman as a Muse-like figure in his anthology. The fact that this poem is called an eclogue, a classical short verse form, positions the work in terms of Western verse forms. The poem's verse form, when infused with the Orientalist subjectivity, setting, and tropes, seems to excuse itself of the responsibility for accurate cultural representation through the mode of "expression" instead of scholarship. As a result, the poem becomes an exercise in fancy and imitation that fails to live up to the expressive nature that Jones argues for in his essays and preface. The poem is one of three in the collection that combine various Orientalist motifs in Jones's own creative pastiche of purported translation and invention. Jones prefaces this "eclogue" by arguing that the poem "is not a regular translation from the *Arabick* language; but all the figures, sentiments, and descriptions in it, were really taken from the poets of *Arabia*" (3). The modern-day reader is left with the question of cultural appropriation: How does one *take* the "figures, sentiments, and descriptions" of poetry in another language and adapt them to one's own?

Jones's composition of "Solima" consists in selecting "those passages, which seemed most likely to run into our [British] measure" (3). Jones includes one passage from an unidentified "original" Arabic poem and translates it into English, hoping that including this will help the reader "form a tolerable judgment of the rest" (ii). In reality, as scholars such as Sitter have argued, "Solima" does not have any recorded provenance outside of Jones's collection. By framing this "eclogue" in terms of its emotional register as taken from an Arabic tradition, Jones avoids the task of verisimilitude and invents his own cultural imaginary. This imaginary is one that universalizes the goodness of "benevolence and hospitality" across Arabic and English cultures but also withholds a "regular translation." This editorial choice prioritizes the English language over Arabic in a pose of "*Arabian*" culture for poetic expression.

The poem describes a charitable host, "Fair Solima," through her embodiment of passive womanhood. The poem is written in heroic couplets, and celebrates Solima and her caravanserai, where she welcomes weary pilgrims with rest and repast, and listens to their sorrows:

> To Solima their sorrows they bewail,
> To Solima they pour their plaintive tale.
> She hears; and, radiant as the star of day,
> Through the thick forest gains her easy way. (57–60)

As not only a host but also a listener to others' tales, this scene recalls the host of the Tabard Inn in Chaucer's *Canterbury*

Tales. Jones introduces the storytelling aspect that the rest of his poems proffer. While inspired by Arabian fables, this poem reflects more notably, as Michael J. Franklin has argued, a certain "Popean artificiality" and rhyme scheme (80). It is devoted to celebrating Solima's healing powers, such as when she "cheers [the] gloom" of a "trembling pilgrim" or "with a smile the healing balm bestows" (69, 75, 65). Solima's hospitality is a type of feminine alignment, but also newly Orientalist. "Oriental" men, as we will see, are yoked with feeling and/or effeminacy in ways that make Orientalist literature a site of experimentation with gender norms. This poem, like the rest of the collection, is neither an original work of creative inspiration nor faithful translation, but rather, an assortment of cultural imagery and scenes without clear citation or precedent. The figure of Solima represents one racialized and gendered "Oriental" subject of enduring creative consequence. She is part of an imagined archive of "Oriental" womanhood, paradoxically signaled by her very absence in dialogue—subjected and spoken for, a muse for Jones's imaginative projection.

Jones's essays and poems reflect the mutually determining relationship between the discourses of poetry and Orientalism during a large-scale reorganization of the terms of aesthetic and literary value. Jones himself is aware of the limitations of his project. For example, before delving into what he calls the "miscellany" of his collection, he writes in the preface:

> THE reader will probably expect, that ... I should give some account of the pieces contained in it; and should prove the authenticity of those *Eastern* originals, from which I profess to have translated them: indeed ... that I should have wished, for my own sake, to clear my publication from the slightest suspicion of imposture. (vi)

By anticipating the criticism of his work's "imposture," Jones shows he is aware of the inaccuracy of his method. Later in the preface, he argues, instead, for the "novelty" of his collection, basing this novelty on the fact that they are adaptations and translations, "which have never appeared in any language of Europe" (vi). Furthermore, because these poems are touted as "translations," Jones suggests their comparability to classical works that have been translated. He writes that "[t]he heroick poem of *Ferdusi* might be versified as easily as the *Iliad*, and I see no reason why the delivery of *Persia by Cyrus* should not be a subject as interesting to us, as *the anger of Achilles*, or *the wandering of Ulysses*" (vii). By comparing the works of "Asiatick" artists to works of Greek mythology, Jones invokes both comparative literary studies and the foothold of "Eastern" literature as a topic and field worthy of study. He argues, however, that these "Eastern" traditions are ones "which future scholars might explain, and future poets might imitate" (199).

Jones's placement of his collection within the discourse of classical education legitimizes the value of his own poetry while also modeling cultural imitation and appropriation ("*Arabia* and *Persia* in an *English* dress") for the benefit of the "learned." This ideological dialectic of aesthetic appreciation and appropriation is the contradiction upon which Romantic writers continually visualize and express their imaginative works of self-projection and world-building.[6]

The New Orientalist Lyric

Samuel Taylor Coleridge, Lord Byron, Percy Bysshe and Mary Shelley, Robert Southey, and many other writers and thinkers of the day were all familiar with and drew from Jones's work.[7] Coleridge read Jones, offered him criticism, and adopted Persian references in Jones's style. Byron wrote his own "oriental tale" *The Giaour* after reading Jones's translations. As we will see, Percy Bysshe Shelley echoes Jones's call for new poetries in *Defence of Poetry* and invents an Orientalist imaginary of generalized "shapes" in *The Revolt of Islam*.

After Jones's centering of lyric poetry, Wordsworth and Coleridge sought to redefine theories of poetry in *Lyrical Ballads* and *Biographia Literaria*.[8] In the 1800 Preface to *Lyrical Ballads*, Wordsworth writes of the "purpose" of poetry and how the poems in his collection veer away from "popular Poetry" of the day. He writes, "[I]t is proper that I should mention one other circumstance which distinguishes these Poems from the popular Poetry of the day; it is this, that the feeling therein developed gives importance to the action and situation, and not the action and situation to the feeling" (para. 7). For Wordsworth, "feeling" is the forerunner of an action/situation's significance and/or importance. It is not an action or situation that foregrounds the importance of "feeling." This shift in orientation—"feeling" as antecedent to action—reorients the root of poetic creation and reminds us of Jones's definition of poetry as an "animated expression of the human passions." Wordsworth's claim for "feeling" activating or making possible the importance of "action and situation" has not been interrogated as a poetic impetus in Orientalist poems such as Coleridge's "Kubla Khan." Wordsworth's shift in the orientation of creative expression—feeling first, action next—modifies the conception of the lyric form. This affective focus is seen in Hemans's poems, which I will discuss in Chapter 3.

While for Wordsworth the focus may be between feeling and action, Coleridge's theories of imagination and fancy become faculties behind the production of poetry and his idea of the poetic genius. Coleridge writes of the imagination as "the living Power and prime Agent of all human Perception, and as a repetition in the finite mind of the eternal act of creation in the infinite I Am" (*BL* 313). Possessing a supernatural or divine faculty, Coleridge's ideal poet, "brings the whole soul of man into activity ... diffus[ing] a tone and spirit of unity" (402). This drive for unity is a twofold mode of perception. Coleridge writes earlier in *BL*:

> There are evidently two powers at work, which relatively to each other are active and passive; and this is not possible without an intermediate faculty, which is at once both active and passive. In philosophical language, we must denominate this intermediate faculty in all its degrees and determinations, the imagination. But in common language, and especially on the subject of poetry, we appropriate the name to a superior degree of the faculty, joined to a superior voluntary control over it. (222)

As both an active and passive faculty, the imagination is inherently contradictory, and this contradiction generates its production.[9]

Both active and passive, Coleridge then writes of the imagination "either as primary, or secondary" with the primary imagination being "the living power and prime agent of all human perception" and the secondary imagination being "an echo of the former ... yet still as identical with the primary in the kind of its agency, and differing only in degree, and in the mode of its operation" (396). For Coleridge, the imagination's power is one of creative perception and transformative duality. Coleridge's secondary imagination "dissolves, diffuses, dissipates, in order to recreate; or where this process is rendered impossible, yet still, at all events, it struggles to idealize and to unify" (396). This struggle projects an ideal that cannot be realized.

Often associated or synonymized with imagination, Coleridge's "Fancy" is different from the primary and secondary imagination. It is "a mode of Memory emancipated from the order of time and space; while it is blended with, and modified by that empirical phenomenon of the will, which we express by the word choice" (313). Fancy, for Coleridge, is altered by empirical choice and not a divine faculty like the primary imagination. Coleridge's definition of fancy places the onus on an empiricism freed from time and space, rooting the empiricism in memory, not first-hand observation. This contradiction positions fancy as a fundamental mode of Orientalist invention over first-hand experience. The mere imagining or memory of a thing constitutes the work of fancy. Fancy, often relegated to a position of inferior or disposable importance in terms of Romantic "genius," is an essential mode of the Orientalist genre. It is through fancy and imagination, not visionary genius, that deployments of otherness and representations of the imagined "East" populate the works of Samuel Taylor Coleridge, Percy Bysshe Shelley, Felicia Hemans, Lord Byron, and William Blake.

Along the lines of Hegel's lyric "unity," Coleridge describes poetry as a type of art in which "the principle of unity must always be present, so that in the midst of the multeity the cetripetal [sic] force be never suspended, nor the sense be fatigued by the predominance of the centrifugal force. This unity in multeity I have elsewhere stated as the principle of beauty" (para. 17). The "unity in multeity" reflects a plurality of differences that propagate totalizing images of beauty that are momentary, in flux, and provisional. In the preface to Coleridge's "Kubla Khan" he compares a poet's vision to "the images on the surface of a stream into which a stone has been cast," where "a thousand circlets spread / And each misshape the other," dissipating continuously in order to make way for other unities that "[c]ome trembling back, unite, and now once more / The pool becomes a mirror" (353). This totalizing impulse to unify the "multeity" also reflects traces of Jones's Hindu hymns and Charles Wilkins's translation of *The Bhagvat-Geeta*. Deirdre Coleman notes that Coleridge's images of unity "resemble] the Hindu visions of oneness" that both Jones and Wilkins describe (54).

This dynamic between centripetal and centrifugal forces of relation—center and periphery—drives Romantic poetry toward new forms of expression that steer poetic form and content beyond nation-based alliances while continually shifting the bearings of literary representation. This literary *terra incognita* continues its problematic hold on the global imagination through the continued dismissal or disregard for the lesser-known, Orientalist works of these well-known Romantic authors. Left understudied and in the margins of the literary canon, works like Byron's Eastern Tales, Blake's *Jerusalem*, and Shelley's *The Revolt of Islam* mark a pivotal shift in the Romantic period toward comparativism and Orientalism. By returning to the well-known "Kubla Khan," I propose the birth of a new Orientalist lyric form. Omar Miranda describes "Kubla Khan" as a "global lyric" seeking out "the foreign, the other, and performative interaction" in comparison with Wordsworth's "Tintern Abbey" which turns to the local and the personal (322–3).[10] If "Kubla Khan" is "an emblem and product of its globalizing times," what do we make of the rise of Orientalism concomitant with what Leask describes as the poem's "worldliness" centered within a British anglophone poetic tradition?

In terms of the poem's Orientalist genre, its belated publication reflects the steady rise in popularity and prominence of Orientalism as a field of study in the Western world from the late seventeenth to the late nineteenth centuries. Written in 1797, it was not published until 1816, after the publication of Southey's *Thalaba* and *The Curse of Kehama*, as well as other popular Orientalist works by Lord Byron, Thomas Moore, and Leigh Hunt. Although titled a "fragment," critics have tried to read "Kubla Khan" as a complete work reflective of Coleridge's poetic drive for unity. While Raymond Schwab links the concept of the poem's unity to religious comparativism between Eastern and Western religions, this argument has been supplanted by analyses of Coleridge's formalist, not religious, conceptions of unity. For Seamus Perry, "Kubla Khan" is an "irresolved" poem, one that tests Coleridge's "notions of unity and wholeness" (132). This irresolution, I argue, reinforces a tension between Coleridge's theories of imagination and fancy. In this "vision" and "fragment," imagination and fancy work to create a a cultural imaginary that serves as a symbol for poetic production unbounded by cultural boundaries.

Coleridge writes in a 1797 letter to Thomas Poole of his childhood reading and subsequent theories of unity and division:

> For from my early reading of Faery Tales, & Genii &c &c— my mind had been habituated *to the Vast*—& I never regarded *my senses* in any way as the criteria of my belief. I regulated all my creeds by my conceptions not by my *sight*—even at that age. Should children be permitted to read Romances, & Relations of Giants & Magicians, & Genii?—I know all that has been said against it; but I have formed my faith in the affirmative.—I know no other way of giving the mind a love of "the Great", & "'the Whole".—Those who have been led to the same truths step by step thro' the constant testimony of their senses, seem to me to want a sense which I possess—They contemplate nothing but *parts*—and all *parts* are necessarily little—and the Universe to them is but a mass of *little things*. (354)

For Coleridge, unity and the imagination function together as a heightened perception of the "*Vast.*" Coleridge notes his childhood readings on "Genii[s]" and "Faery Tales" as formative parts of his imagination and learning. He argues for his "faith in the affirmative" of allowing children to read these supernatural tales to influence their sensory engagement with the world beyond the empirical or physical. Rather, Coleridge aligns "'the Great'" and "'the Whole'" in all their vastness with his own imaginative mode of perception that encompasses universal visions and is not "marked by a microscopic acuteness" (354). What's more, this vision is stoked by an "Oriental" tale, most likely *Arabian Nights*, with which Coleridge was not only familiar but also of which he was fond.[11] In another 1797 letter to Poole, Coleridge writes:

> At six years old I remember to have read Belisarius, Robinson Crusoe, & Philip Quarll—and then I found the Arabian Nights' entertainments—one tale of which (the tale of a man who was compelled to seek for a pure virgin) made so deep an impression on me (I had read it in the evening while my mother was mending stockings) that I was haunted by spectres, whenever I was in the dark— (499–500)

Coleridge's "haunted" childhood imagination turns later into a vast, integrated, sometimes dark vision that he finds imperative to his "esemplastic" power. And it is through this imaginative vista of perception that the mind can gain a "love" of grand unity and not get lost in the particulars of everyday sensory evidence and individual logic. Although it is a purported "fragment," Coleridge's "Kubla Khan" endorses the imagination as something that can still be totalizing or unifying in practice.

When writing "Kubla Khan," Coleridge had a longer history of reading from which to derive inspiration.[12] Elinor Shaffer has analyzed "Kubla Khan" within its aesthetic context, in its intimate relations with artistic creation, and not simply to offer superficial and perfunctory "background history" (2).[13] She notes how in "Kubla Khan," Coleridge is "able to use the syncretist technique of 'piecing out' from a diversity of culturally uprooted mythologies" (142). Like Byron and others, Coleridge finds a source of mythological inspiration and potential in diverse traditions, most clearly the Judaic and Islamic traditions. The purportedly sublime inspiration to which Coleridge attributes the poem's creation is shown by Shaffer and many others to be implicit more than aesthetically or formally evidenced. Coleridge's poem, I conclude, models itself as a process of becoming and unbecoming more than a work of unity. This process is an interplay of unity and disunity that maps itself onto Orientalist divisions of East and West that are encoded within the geoaesthetic imaginary of the poem.

Coleridge's poem expresses his faculties of memory and association over first-hand experience so that his Orientalism is not materially based in historical time and space or real peoples and cultures. As both an Orientalist poem and a fragment, "Kubla Khan" reflects Coleridge's exercise of fancy in terms of historical and geographical allusions. These allusions are not purely invented but rather, reconfigured and incorrectly represented. If fancy is "associative," it can be marked, I argue, as more Orientalist than imagination in its non-creative tendency. Fancy's mode of creative assemblage by volition, not vision or invention, aligns Coleridge with Jones's method of pastiche and invention over authenticity. Fancy's ability to reconfigure and not reflect reality ultimately gives way, through the poem's eventual turn, to the overflowing "sacred river" Alph and the figure of the Poet-prophet. Both representations—the river and the Poet-prophet figure—express the power of the primary imagination and its ability to create anew and shatter pre-existing worlds or historical settings (3). The river and Poet-prophet, as we will see, represent the primary imagination's power to create an overflowing "vision," a vision that is temporary and "float[s] midway on the waves" (38, 32). This temporary vision appears in the geoaesthetic space of the poem and does not exist outside of this poetic space as anything other than fiction.

Before the poem begins, the well-known preface reiterates that the upcoming poem is a "fragment" from something conjured during sleep; thereafter, Coleridge was interrupted by the famous person from Porlock.[14] Coleridge nests a poem within this preface to illustrate his loss of the initial lines and images of the poem he once held before the interruption. Coleridge writes how, "with the exception of some eight or ten scattered lines and images, all the rest [of the poem] had passed away like the images on the surface of a stream into which a stone has been cast, but, alas! without the after restoration of the latter!" (353). He then cites an excerpt from another poem, writing of how "a thousand circlets spread" after the stillness is broken but then, "[c]ome trembling back, unite, and now once more / The pool becomes a mirror" (353). This idea of a fragmentation giving way to a unity, a crystallization of moving fragments into a clear, still image applies to the content and themes of the upcoming "Kubla Khan" as well. Not only does the preface augur the poem's series of attempted unities of vision, but it also shows the fragility and provisional nature of such unities, how when "a stone has been cast . . . [t]hen all the charm / Is broken" (353). The provisional nature of any image or motif achieved in the poem is an important and defining characteristic of Coleridge's writing process.

David Hogsette has argued for the preface's assertion of poetic and imaginative failure, "offer[ing] its readers a series of false poetic figures, ultimately demonstrating that the ideal (pro)creative and redemptive imagination lies beyond the grasp of the mortal poet, remaining an external and unobtainable other" (para. 3). Other scholars, including Tim Fulford and Peter J. Kitson, have argued for the Romantic poetic project as a "quest" that "ultimately leads, not unidirectionally out into the blank plains, dense forests, or nebulous skies of a beckoning or unknown land, but back into the tangled self" (167). This return to self is not an optimistic voyage, however. David G. Riede writes about the poem's "melancholy nature" as "seen in the dialogic structure of the preface and the two distinctly different sections of the poem as representative of the dialogue of the mind with itself, of a multitudinous and possibly melancholy consciousness" (*Allegories* 36). This dialogic imagination, if ultimately failing in its quest, still finds expression in fancy and its associative properties. Coleridge situates this imaginative process in psychological terms and qualifies the setting of the poem as a mental unity and disunity envisioned rather than realized.

The poem begins:

In Xanadu did Kubla Khan
A stately pleasure dome decree:
Where Alph, the sacred river, ran
Through caverns measureless to man
Down to a sunless sea. (1–5)

In this imagined geography, Xanadu refers to thirteenth-century Mongol emperor Kublai Khan's summer palace in Shangdu (the capital of Khan's Yuan dynasty in China). This imagined setting, however, contains a fictitious river, "Alph," that could reference the Greek river Alpheus of mythology. Historically Greece has been paradoxically encoded as both "oriental" and "classical" in cultural mythologies, and more presently, it is associated with the rise of the Occident and Philhellenism. Coleridge states in the poem's preface that he was influenced by Samuel Purchas's *Pilgrimage*, an early modern work studying the world's religions and people, including those of Asia, through an Anglican perspective. John Livingston Lowes writes that, in addition to Purchas, Coleridge had read William Bartram, James Bruce, and Thomas Maurice prior to composing "Kubla Khan" (383). All were eminent travel writers who wrote at least in part about Asia during the eighteenth and nineteenth centuries. Thus, Coleridge was exposed to multiple sources of Orientalist place names, and this exposure fueled Coleridge's imaginary setting in historically and culturally incoherent place names and references. The depiction of the mystical poet at the end of the poem recalls a broad swath of cultural influences; the poet is a being akin to both the Greek god Dionysus and the Hindu god Vishnu. This closing image of the bard-like or prophet figure subsumes the imagery and supernatural impulses within the figure's ambiguous trance-like state.

Largely mapped out in the envisioning speaker's mind, the poem's allusions and tropes exist in an Orientalist psychological space that the perceiver has grafted onto the "Xanadu" landscape. And this displacement of psyche onto setting serves to aesthetically contain the eruptive imagination within the poem's lines. Within this setting, the poem experiments with a range of different unities or closures, such as the attempted unity of the first thirty-six lines, and then the last eighteen lines. Through its meter and rhyme, there is a patterning that adds not only melody and rhythm but an attempt at unity or coherence-making.

The speaker ends the poem wishing he could revive the "symphony and song" of an "Abyssinian maid" so that

I would build that dome in air,
That sunny dome! those caves of ice!
And all who heard should see them there,
And all should cry, Beware! Beware!
His flashing eyes, his floating hair! (39–50)

As opposed to the pleasure-dome grounded in Kubla's palatial landscape, the speaker dreams of building the dome mid-air through a mystical act of spiritual thrall. John Drew writes, "One constant in Coleridge's philosophy is his concern to establish that increasingly meditative states … are the most reliable condition within which knowledge may be apprehended. Thought is considered the most effective form of action, potential the most powerful expression of actuality" (47). As the completion of the poem lies in the future, the poem can be read as a totality deferred, about the open-ended potential of the human imagination to unify and create new images.

A lesser-known Orientalist work by Coleridge is his fourteen-line poem "Mahomet" (1799), which is a proposed "fragment" initially meant as a collaboration between Coleridge and Robert Southey. Southey proposed that they co-write a hexameter epic on the prophet Muhammad, and Coleridge readily agreed. After starting the poem together, Coleridge pledged to continue working on it during September and October of that same year (1799), but the work was never finished. The "complete" poem was published in Coleridge's 1834 *Poetical Works*, and the version I am using is the expanded version (in accordance with the manuscript) from Coleridge's *Collected Works*. Humberto Garcia has argued that the poem "casts the [Muslim] Prophet as a Protestant revolutionary" and reads the poem in terms of its "sympathetic literary and cultural representations of the Islamic republic" (2, xi).[15] As a "Song" addressed to the speaker's "soul," I want to focus on the poem's interiority and opening up of a subjectivity that is both imitative and othered. Coleridge writes about the "Soul-withering" effects of the "flight and return of Mahomet" to the speaker's soul (1, 4, 1). The poem uses water imagery akin to the imagery of "Kubla Khan." The revolutionary "Mahomet" "who scattered abroad both evil and blessing" is a figure of contraries (2). Coleridge limits this poem's focus to Mahomet's story alone, not an amalgam of various cultural topoi and allusions, with one geographical reference being to the yearly Islamic pilgrimage to Mecca at poem's end:

> ... – the people with mad shouts
> Thundering now, and now with saddest ululation
> Flew, as over the channel of rock-stone the ruinous river
> Shatters its waters abreast, and in mazy uproar bewildered,
> Rushes dividuous all—all rushing impetuous onward. (10–14)

The "ruinous river" shattering its "waters abreast" reminds us of the river Alph in "Kubla Khan," the river as a fount of creative imagination and prophecy. However, the river here is a metaphor for those who have come to Mecca to both shout and ululate at the "fane of the idol," Mahomet (9). Coleridge aligns imagination and "uproar" with religious devotion in a syncretism of natural and religious imagery, while objectifying the individual human and their role in the pilgrimage. By poem's end, the "ululation" that spawns the flight of these "people" has led to a "dividuous" rush "onward" (10, 14). This onward move is a break away from the repetitive ululation of the "naked and prostrate ... people" and an action of forward momentum that ends the poem in a universal rush by the "dividuous all" (14). This paradoxical phrase reflects the tension between unity and fragmentation that characterizes Coleridge's poetics. As the dynamism propelling the poetic imagination and its expression is located in religious fervor and displaced cultural settings, the scale of the individual perspective is expanded beyond the provincial. The scale expands to a more global or distant experience obscuring cultural difference. In addition, the union of "all" is "dividuous," and this divisiveness reflects a plurality of voices who do not cohere into individualized figures.

Garcia argues that for Coleridge, "Mahomet replaces Napoleon as the new republican prophet" and gestures toward a Christian "egalitarian vision—the Second Coming—while also returning to the sublime tyranny and Oriental despotism of earlier centuries" (2). Whether replacements, symbols, or ornamental images, racialized subjects populate changing notions of the poetic subject, as "Mahomet" shows us. "Mahomet" is one example of a long history of Orientalist representations that cohere around imaginary distinctions between the West and Orient. As Ahmed notes "Objects become objects only as an effect of the repetition of this tending 'toward' them, which produces the subject as that which the world is 'around.'" (*Queer Phenomenology* 120). The formation of a poetic subject around traits of individualism, expression, and imagination is made possible through this tending toward an imagined "other" who is neither discrete nor autonomous. This habituation orients the world of an Orientalist aesthetic regime dominated by white subjects.

Shelley's Disorienting Shapes

The poet's expressive task routed through the Orient—many young writers, including Percy Bysshe Shelley, use this route for differing purposes. Whereas Coleridge uses Orientalist imagery as a metaphor for creative genius and heightened states, Shelley focuses on a universalized Orientalism that often serves as a metaphor for political revolution and regeneration. Like Coleridge's "Mahomet," Shelley proposes an egalitarian political vision through the traversal of symbolically obscure subjects and regions in the *Revolt of Islam*.

Jones's influence on Shelley is a bit less explicit, but there are multiple records of Shelley reading Jones. Meena Alexander writes at length about Shelley's history of reading prior to and after writing *A Defence of Poetry*, including his readings of India and Sir William Jones. As Nigel Leask and James Watt note, Shelley often obscures detail and generalizes the East/Orient as a universalist metaphor for political despotism and/or pathologies of empire. In *A Defence of Poetry*, Shelley writes, "Poetry enlarges the circumference of the imagination by replenishing if with thought of ever new delight, which have the power of attracting and assimilating to their own nature all other thoughts, and which form new intervals and interstices whose void for ever craves fresh food" (517). This craving for "fresh food" is the impetus for experimental, cross-genre works like *The Revolt of Islam*, which represents an unbounded poetic universe of disorienting shapes and figures.

The Revolt offers a rather autonomous example of Shelley's aesthetics, specifically in its epic verse form in contradistinction to its Orientalist subject matter.[16] Anahid Nersessian, Andrew Warren, and Gerard Cohen-Vrignaud have written on *The Revolt of Islam*'s troubling of an Orientalist East/West binary. Tightly structured into twelve cantos with Spenserian stanzas throughout, *The Revolt*'s metrical form belies its radical themes and motifs. These include shifting conceptions of gender identity and expression, revolutionary politics, and non-normative families. These representations question what it means to be part of a collective and individual identity category. As twinned revolutionaries, protagonists Laon and Cythna make themselves martyrs in service of their "Muslim" faith, embodying a precarious intersubjectivity that comprises the central plot. In 1817, Shelley writes to William Godwin on the process behind writing the work:

> I felt the precariousness of my life, and I engaged in this task, resolved to leave some record of myself. Much of what the volume contains was written with the same feeling, as real, though not so prophetic, as the communications of a dying man. I never presumed indeed to consider it anything approaching to faultless; but when I consider contemporary productions of the same apparent pretensions, I own I was filled with confidence. (*Letters* I, 577)

Shelley shares that the impetus for this work includes autobiographical "pretensions," not a scholarly or historical endeavor, political tract, or "Oriental" tale. Shelley's sense of "precariousness" and looming death motivate him to write a work on political and religious "revolt" that reflects Shelley's "series of thoughts which filled my mind with unbounded & sustained enthusiasm . . . and "a genuine picture of my own mind" (*Letters*, 11 December 1817).

Shelley's impetus is rooted in a vulnerability to death and bodily harm that invokes concepts of bodily injury and precarity.[17] Judith Butler writes about precarity as the condition of living a precarious existence through intersectional frameworks of sex, gender, race, ethnicity, ability, and class. Precarity,

Butler asserts, can be a "resource for politics" in that "our very survival can be determined by those we do not know and over whom there is no final control ... and politics must consider what forms of social and political organization seek best to sustain precarious lives across the globe" (*Undoing Gender* 23). Asking what forms of the social and political can help sustain marginalized lives, Butler's turn to politics understands that politics can both enable and restrict these very lives. Shelley turns to themes of revolutionary politics in response to his own mortality and "precariousness." His social and political forms are often obscure, unidentifiable, commonly represented through the idiomatic figure of "shapes." These "shapes" of life disorient any clear moral or political impulse to the work.

Protagonists Laon and Cythna anchor the multi-genre work, but are represented ambiguously in that they mirror each other and lack heteronormative description, sometimes described with similar physical traits. Their lack of fixed representation raises the question of language's limits as a discourse of subject-formation. They are adopted siblings who grow up together, fall in love, and are separated by the political revolution of an unnamed "golden city." Thus, they have a range of kinships through familial, romantic, and political affiliations. As Laon's "second self," Cythna is both shadow and mirror to Laon's soul (II.24). Both Laon and Cythna, upon reaching adulthood, eventually embark on parallel journeys of political rebellion, with their juxtaposed narratives seeping into and out of each other without clear diegetic distinction throughout the remaining cantos.

Part of its Orientalist staging, the setting poses a conundrum of time and space. In an earlier letter to his publisher, Shelley explains the setting of the poem:

The scene is supposed to be laid in Constantinople and modern Greece, but without much attempt at minute delineation of Mahometan manners. It is, in fact, a tale illustrative of such a revolution as might be supposed to take place in an European nation, acted upon by the opinions of what has been called (erroneously, as I think) the modern philosophy, and contending with ancient notions and the supposed advantage derived from them to those who support them. It is a Revolution of this kind that is the *beau idéal*, as it were, of the French Revolution, but produced by the influence of individual genius and out of general knowledge. (*Letters* I, 563–4)

The poem's setting is clearly intended but not executed in terms of verisimilitude, because of the tale's supposed availability "to take place in an [*sic*] European nation" and its pursuit of the "the *beau idéal*."[18] In addition, the setting's lack of "minute delineation" amplifies the disorienting, nature of its geopolitical imaginary, of which "shape" becomes a consistent idiomatic reference. Shelley gestures towards a "European" setting in *The Revolt*, but it is never made clear and exists allegorically within the time-space conundrum of the work.[19]

I anchor my reading in Shelley's aesthetically autonomous usage of "shapes" throughout the *Revolt*. Through his metonymic usage of shapes, Shelley avoids and/or refuses to clearly or singularly depict any one character in the work. *The Revolt* and its myriad "shapes" thwart the straightforward binaries of East/West and self/other, giving way to a more radical sense of disorientation. This disorientation, rather than completely delinking the East/West or self/other binary, paradoxically endorses a new post-human universalism in the face of British geopolitical expansion and expanding notions of the British subject and its "Oriental" other. Shelley's language of shapes in *The Revolt* makes him less of an Arnoldian "ineffectual angel" and more of a queer visionary in terms of genre and literary representation (Arnold, para. 27). Andrew Warren argues that *The Revolt*'s "quasi-Oriental" staging engages "Regency England's political imaginary, shot through as it is with the discourse of the solipsistic Oriental Despot" (186). Warren concludes from this staging that the East/West Orientalist binary can be undone, prompting a confrontation with Regency England as well as European ideology on "the level of the political imaginary" (191). The political imaginary for Shelley, however, being dislocated from any one time and place, furthers Shelley's expressive turn toward Orientalist ambiguity. I contend, accordingly, that the East/West binary is not undone so much as reoriented toward a broader, universalizing paradigm via Shelley's use of shapes. This paradigm implies an individual unsurety and fluidity that enable Shelley to represent "life" as including all living things, mortal and supernatural, living and dead. *The Revolt*'s "[o]ne shape of many names" enables Shelley to metonymize the idea of life as sweepingly universal and disrupt the aesthetic regimes of gendered and racialized taxonomies and hierarchies (I. 27).

Shelley avoids clearly describing and depicting any one character in the work, most notably Laon and Cythna. This avoidance is staked on Shelley's prefatory claims for the work as "an experiment on the temper of the public mind." He writes:

> I have sought to enlist the harmony of metrical language, the ethereal combinations of the fancy, the rapid and subtle transitions of human passion, all those elements which essentially compose a poem, in the cause of a liberal and comprehensive morality; and in the view of kindling ... those doctrines of liberty and justice, that faith and hope in something good, which neither violence, nor misrepresentation, nor prejudice, can ever totally extinguish among mankind. (*The Complete Poetry* 113)

It is "metrical language" along with "combinations of the fancy and "human passion," not history or verisimilitude, that Shelley will use for this "experiment." While Shelley echoes Jones's own expressive intention, they differ in their pursuits, with Shelley finding purpose in a more "comprehensive" and moralistic impetus. Shelley, by noting his poem's ethical underpinning—"liberal," "liberty," "justice," "good"—positions his intention in contrast to the despotism of the work's villain, the Sultan tyrant referred to as "Othman."

The Revolt may express the "*beau ideal*" of the French Revolution without imitating its action. However, at its core, Shelley reminds us, is "a story of human passion in its most universal character" (Preface 113). This "story" represents

> no attempt to recommend the motives which I would substitute for those at present governing mankind, by methodical and systematic argument. I would only awaken the *feelings*, so that the reader should see the beauty of true virtue, and be incited to those inquiries which have led to my moral and political creed, and that of some of the sublimest intellects in the world. (*The Complete Poetry* 113, emphasis mine)

As in Wordsworth's Preface to *Lyrical Ballads*, Shelley is motivated by prioritizing feeling over action or situation. Returning to Wordsworth's Preface to *LB*, he writes that in his poems "feeling therein developed gives importance to the action and situation, and not the action and situation to the feeling" (para. 7). Like Jones's assertion "that the finest parts of poetry, musick, and painting, are expressive of the passions," Shelley also reinforces the *Revolt* as an expressive piece. By inciting his "moral and political creed" alongside "some of the sublimest intellects in the world" Shelley proposes an aesthetic ideal that is explicitly political.

After the preface and an affectionate dedication "To Mary [Shelley]," the reader is vaulted into the geopolitical imaginary of *The Revolt*'s narrative. Shelley writes:

> WHEN the last hope of trampled France had failed
> Like a brief dream of unremaining glory,
> From visions of despair I rose, and scaled
> The peak of an aerial promontory (I.1–4)

By alluding to the suppression of the revolutionary spirit, Shelley immediately sets the theme of revolution. Not only this, but the speaker's cinematic vantage point is one of all-encompassing sublimity, a perspective echoing Shelley's ideal poet in *A Defence*, who "participates in the eternal, the infinite, and the one; as far as relates to his conceptions, time and place and number are not" (513). The speaker, atop a promontory, sees the earth below him "shaken" and torn asunder, in a war of nature's forces. We are introduced to "a speck, a cloud, a shape" appearing mid-air before the speaker "like a great ship in the sun's sinking sphere" (I.178–9). This "shape" is then described as "a winged Form" and finally manifests into "[a]n Eagle and a Serpent wreathed in fight" (I.186, 193). This aerial progression from "shape" to "form" to living animals embodies Shelley's poetics of imaginative expression. More indirectly, however, it also reflects his Orientalist proclivities, for this "monstrous sight!" establishes the dual idealism of self/other and East/West that undergirds the work.[20]

Donna Richardson argues that the opening snake and eagle symbolize intertwined moral categories and not absolute distinctions or polarizations. Accordingly, Shelley writes that the two animals are "Twin Genii, equal Gods—when life and thought / Sprang forth, they burst the womb of inessential Nought" (I.25). Neither are equivalent to absolute good or evil, but together, they are necessary parts of human experience. As aesthetic archetypes—the snake of circuitous, labyrinthine movement and the eagle of sweeping, overarching prospect—both signify forces of change that characterize the geoaesthetic time-space compression of the work.[21] This compression of setting occurs in abstract references to landscape such as, "Hark! 't is the rushing of a wind that sweeps / Earth and the ocean. See! the lightnings yawn, / Deluging Heaven with fire" (I.3). The setting seems a limitless yet confined space wherein time becomes mutable to the point of inconsequence. Fittingly, Shelley argues in the *Defence* that "The grammatical forms which express the moods of time, and the difference of persons, and the distinction of place, are convertible with respect to the highest poetry without injuring it as poetry" (513). While poetry can be considered as a static ideal "object," it can be read as an aesthetic mode of time–space compression that does not cohere into a fixed referent. Benedict Anderson's concept of the "meanwhile" is part of his configuration of the "imagined community" and provides an alternative temporality for *The Revolt of Islam*.[22] Influenced by Walter Benjamin, Anderson calls the "meanwhile" a kind of "'homogeneous, empty time,' in which simultaneity is, as it were, transverse, cross-time, marked not by prefiguring and fulfilment, but by temporal coincidence" (24). This is to say, the "imagined community" creates and recreates the space and policies that govern and shape individual partakers of this "meanwhile." If we consider Anderson's "meanwhile" and the abstract sovereign states of *The Revolt of Islam*'s setting, the geography of Shelley's "golden city" could also function as a type of coincidental transnational force.

The lack of clear delineation of setting and time period, as well as the shared initial "shape" between Snake and Eagle, introduce Shelley's "shape" as fundamental signifier for his various forms of life in this *"beau ideal"* of a revolution. It is important to note the proleptic function of this Snake/Eagle scene for the upcoming story of Laon and Cythna. As Deborah A. Gutschera notes, it re-enacts Shelley's intentions in the Preface and Dedication, as well functions as a primer for what is to come. After the battle between the Snake and Eagle, the speaker sees,

> a Woman, beautiful as morning...
> It seemed that this fair Shape had looked upon
> That unimaginable fight, and now
> That her sweet eyes were weary of the sun
> As brightly it illustrated her woe
> For in the tears, which silently to flow
> Paused not, its lustre hung (I.16–17)

This woman is described as a "fair Shape," the first time that shape is used as a proper noun in the work, making this woman an autonomous representation. The woman is also able to communicate with the Snake "in language whose strange melody / Might not belong to earth" (I.289–90). She eventually returns the speaker's gaze and they silently greet each other, embarking on a suddenly appearing "boat of rare device, which had no sail" (I.325).[23] While sailing together for an unknown destination, she recounts her past history to the speaker, detailing her orphaned upbringing and political quest to the present moment of seeming world upheaval. The woman grew up alone in "a deep mountain glen" except for when "[a] dying poet gave me books, and blessed / With wild but holy talk the sweet unrest / In which I watched him as he died away" (I.36, 37). Exposed to the written word of poetry as her only source of human communication, she internalizes, as cipher, the intersubjective dynamics between her solitary physical existence and the roaring, tempestuous, and "unimaginable fight" around her. She has no clear sense of time and place as she tells her story to the speaker, speaking of the "Morning Star" that "from its beams deep love my spirit drank, / And to my brain the boundless world now shrank / Into one thought—one image—yes, for ever!" (I.485, 490–2). Rather than mentioning places, years, or seasons which would accurately give us a sense of place and setting, all are one in her mind which is an ambiguous site of expression.

In addition to this woman as "Shape," Shelley repeatedly uses the word "shape" to describe both living things and human emotions in the work. When recounting her childhood to the speaker, this unnamed woman dreams of an unidentified "shape of speechless beauty" who is later identified as a "winged youth" who kisses her and asks her "How wilt thou prove thy worth?" to the "Spirit" who "loves thee, mortal maiden" (I.497, 500, 506, 505). She is led by this Spirit's "tongue" to an unnamed city of "holy warfare" to fight for "liberty and truth," again foreshadowing Laon and Cythna's story (I. 515, 519). Once the woman and the speaker reach the Temple of the Senate in this kingdom, they see a throne surrounded by unidentified "assembled shapes—with clinging charm / Sinking upon their hearts and mine" (I.497, 637–8). The lack of clear representations and body/spirit distinctions in this world evoke Shelley's poetic faculty of approximation, described in the *Defence* as part of the coloring and composing power of the imagination, of observing "an order which approximates more or less closely to that from which highest delight results" (512). If the ideal of beauty can only be approximated and never reached by humans, then a "shape" of something is the only fundamental unit of measurement for this type of approximation. It should be noted that Shelley's "shape" is distinct from "form" in that form can denote rigid structure and boundary, whereas shape denotes curvature, movement, and non-straight lines. Thus, Shelley's shapes are more specific than "forms." They are dynamic configurations of multiple meanings, orienting and disorienting the world around them. Earlier in the canto, Shelley calls "the Spirit of Evil, / One Power of many shapes which none may know, / One Shape of many names" (I.27). These "shapes" also have many unknown names and reflect the multitudinous variety of Shelley's representations.

After this opening frame narrative which is never fully closed, Laon's coming-of-age story begins in Cantos II–V. Cythna's parallel story appears shortly after in Cantos VII–IX. The interchangeability, at times doubling, of Laon and Cythna deconstructs traditional distinctions of body/soul, human/spirit, and gender categories and expression. Laon's and Cythna's stories are notoriously hard to follow, as Byron also noted, writing in an 1818 letter to John Murray that "nobody would have thought of reading [the work], and few who read can understand—I for one" (*BLJ* 83). As it unfolds, it becomes "a series of nesting-doll narratives," with the initial frame narrative of the unnamed speaker and beautiful woman completely superseded by the story of Laon and Cythna until the twelfth canto (Nersessian 91). The difference between the first canto as frame narrative for Laon's and Cythna's stories has been carefully analyzed by Frederick L. Jones.

In the fifth canto when the revolution is under way and Laon and Cythna are both fighting, separately but equally, for the revolution's success, Shelley writes of the revolting "Federation" of "millions" (including a "hundred nations") that comes together under the cause of Liberty and Equality (V.2072, 2074, 2210). Tellingly, "Equality" is the "Eldest of things" and 'Wisdom and Love are but the slaves of thee" (V.2212–13). As the eldest and master of "Wisdom and Love" in this revolution, "Equality" aligns not only with Shelley's *Defence* but also his leveling of difference through "shapes." Laon's "mien" is called "[t]he likeness of a shape for which was braided / The brightest woof of genius" and Cythna "a shape of brightness" (IV.1677-8, II.865). The "Equality" of the shapes in Shelley's world situates Shelley's expressive poetics within an egalitarian impulse that levels his aesthetic representations beyond hierarchical or categorical distinctions of class or rank.

Until one realizes the unfixity of body/soul and gender distinction in the protagonists Laon and Cythna, it is easy to overlook the significance of shapehood as a structuring motif. Within the narrative of Laon and Cythna, the themes of political revolution and optimistic populism become more pronounced, as critics such as Gerard Cohen-Vrignaud have noted: "Laon and Cythna proleptically enact a democratic theory of peaceful political change not yet possible in the Ottoman Empire. Through words alone, Shelley's two prophets remake Turkish subjects into rights-bearing citizens" (77). Thus, as "rights-bearing citizens," Cohen-Vrignaud argues they do not represent an "imperial-liberal urge to set the Other free" but an "attempt to replicate the populist politics of Byron's Eastern poetry" (79,

76).²⁴ Through this populism, he sees in *The Revolt* a unifying theme of "liberal universalism via Orientalism" (78). In order to make more specific his argument for a "liberal universalism," I analyze Laon and Cythna through their representations as "shapes" of life. As shapes, they represent the body politics and "the people," but also all forms of living matter.

During the narrative's rising action in cantos three to seven, Cythna and Laon think each other lost. Cythna, disguised as "Laone," attends a festival drawing those "which from their isles / And continents, and winds, and oceans deep, / All *shapes* might throng to share, that fly, or walk or creep" (V.2305-7, emphasis mine). Rather than denoting a human/spirit distinction, Shelley again uses the word "shape" to reference but not clearly name the figures in this scene. Later, the abstract emotion "hate" is described as a "*shapeless* fiendly thing / Of many names, all evil, some divine, / Whom self-contempt arms with a mortal sting" (VIII.3379-81). The alignment of hate, an abstract emotion of ethical dubiety, with a lack of shape, in effect aligns shape with love and Shelley's conception of beauty. Eventually, when Laon and Cythna do physically reunite in the seventh canto, Cythna recounts her story to Laon. Cythna, having been previously seized by the troops of the Sultan tyrant "Othman" for his harem, has now escaped captivity. Laon has spent seven years recovering from "sufferings" and "madness" due, in part, to Cythna's capture by the Sultan (VII.2839). Finally reunited, they vow to assist in the golden city's Revolution as the "chosen slaves" of virtue, hope, and love, a strange and compelling formulation that sustains the precarity of Laon and Cythna's intersubjectivity (IX.3668).

As the revolution is underway, a famine and unknown pestilence strike the city, causing crops and animals to suffer, leading some to sell human flesh (X.3956). Different religious leaders come together and arise, including:

Oromaze, Joshua, and Mahomet
Moses, and Buddh, Zerdusht, and Brahm, and Foh,
A tumult of strange names, which never met
Before, as watchwords of a single woe,
Arose (X.4063-7)

This "single woe" causes an unnamed "priest" to call for "Atheists" Laon and "Laone" to be burned on the pyre, so that "with this sacrifice the withering ire / Of God may be appeased" (X.4075, 4137–8). As both rebels and slaves embodying Shelley's anti-clerical sentiment, the paradox of Laon and Cythna/Laone's precarity propels the poem to its climax. Laon and Cythna's revolt against Othman fails, and they are burnt together at the war-torn city's pyre.

After mortal death, Laon and Cythna are transmogrified into spirits of the afterlife in the final canto. Here, Laon asks:

> And is this death? The pyre has disappeared,
> The Pestilence, the Tyrant, and the throng;
> The flames grow silent, slowly there is heard
> The music of a breath-suspending song. (XII.4594–7)

This paradisiacal afterlife is filled with Orientalist "incense-bearing forests and vast caves / Of marble radiance to that mighty fountain," as well as "a chasm of hills" and a "river deep," reminding one of the River Alph setting in Coleridge's "Kubla Khan" (XII.4613–20). While acclimating to their surroundings, Laon and Cythna are joined by a third, triangulating figure:

> As we sate gazing in a trance of wonder,
> A boat approached, borne by the musical air
> Along the waves which sung and sparkled under
> Its rapid keel. A wingèd Shape sate there,
> A child with silver-shining wings, so fair
> That, as her bark did through the waters glide,
> The shadow of the lingering waves did wear
> Light, as from starry beams; (XII.4621–8, emphasis mine)

Laon and Cythna join this "Shape" turned "child," and the three of them set sail for their ultimate haven, the "Temple of the Spirit" (XII.4815). Earlier, the same unnamed "Shape of light" sits next to the tyrant as he watches Laon and Cythna burn, and the shape is described as "[a] child most beautiful" (XII.4466). This shape is presumably Cythna's child, born during Cythna's captivity, and the child crosses into the afterlife as a genderless "shape." As the work began, we see another boat appear, this time sailing into the land of "the Spirit," where the intertwined narratives of Laon and Cythna end. The boat sails "as on a line suspended / Between two heavens, that windless waveless lake" which is surrounded by "snow-bright mountains rear[ing] / Their peaks aloft" (XII.4805–9, 4811–12). Thus, as in "Mont Blanc," silence is treasured as a quality of the sublime. Here, in "this glorious earth around, / The charmed boat approached, and there its haven found" (XII.4817–18). Laon, Cythna, and the child are enveloped by this paradise of "motionless resting" and silence. And the price for this passage is their liminal shapehood, a type of subjectivity without clear bounds or signifying features.

"Shape" expresses a paradoxical figuration of life that reflects not only the work's themes of disillusionment with the failed revolution or populist reform. It is an unfixed embodiment of corporeal, racial, and gendered ambiguity. The ambiguity of this language of shapes is a defining feature of the work. Indeed, the word "shape," singular and plural, is used forty-four times in the work, referring to emotions, humans, spirits, unnamed creatures and animals, forces of good and evil, and celestial bodies. In contrast, the word "form(s)" is used only nineteen times in the work. Shape implies form, body, but also angle, pitch, slant, curve—words denoting orientation and findings one's bearings. As Ahmed notes:

> Bodies as well as objects take shape through being oriented toward each other, as an orientation that may be experienced as the cohabitation or sharing of space. Bodies are hence *shaped* by contact with objects and others, with "what" is near enough to be reached. They may even *take shape* through such contact or take the shape of that contact. ("Orientations" 552, emphasis mine)

Bodies take shape and are shaped through orientations that are habital, proximal, and mutable. Through these orientations, Shelley's shapes gather and coalesce around and along the "complicating lines" of race, ethnicity, gender, and sexuality, constructing an idiom of subjects beyond the limits of human taxonomy (I.14). The essence of a shape is curvature, a type of towardness. As previously noted, towardness can be both a negation but also a "form of extension" (Ahmed, *Queer Phenomenology* 115). The extension of the poetic subject toward the subject's constructed other becomes a world of shapes in *The Revolt of Islam*.

Shapes recur in Shelley's final and unfinished *The Triumph of Life*. The speaker asks of a chariot carrying an unknown "Shape,"

> "And what is this?
> Whose shape is that within the car? & why" —
> I would have added —"is all here amiss?"
> But a voice answered . . . "Life" . . . (*The Triumph of Life*, ll. 87, 177–80)

For Shelley, Shape can represent an abstract "Life". A shape's capaciousness and evocation of curvature or movement propagates a sensorium of unfixed attractions, allusions, and influences that have no clear blueprint. Shelley's shapehood can be a space of disorientation and defamiliarization that counters what M. H. Abrams calls the "habitual direction of reference [for romantic writers and critics] . . . to the poet" as unifying center (100). In contrast, Shelley's shapes delink life from the Anthropocene, ushering in new and unfixed forms of existence to bear life with otherwise.

The idea of bearing life through the revolutionary and inscrutable space of the Orient shows the ethical paradox in Shelley's project. Returning to *The Revolt*, the "liberal" impulse evoked in Shelley's preface manifests into an allegory of valor and persistence without clear justice at work's end. Rather than resulting in a clear sense of Shelley's moral vision or call for sociopolitical reform, the work deploys figurative language and images in furtherance of an egalitarian ethos that decenters a singularly British point of view. But in doing so, it must confront the politics and ethics of Orientalist representations. Shelley uses "orient" in one singular instance at work's beginning:

> When, gathering fast, around, above and under,
> Long trains of tremulous mist began to creep,
> Until their complicating lines did steep
> The orient sun in shadow:—not a sound
> Was heard. (I.12–16)

This "orient sun in shadow" is silent and surrounded by the "gathering fast" of "long trains" and "complicating lines"

(I. 12–16). Eclipsed, shadowed, complicated, steeped, and silent—these words signify the Orient as a geoaesthetic space of seeming everywhere and nowhere—"above and under"— a floating signifier that reinforces an aesthetic mode of cultural ambiguity. This mode normalizes the convenient invocation of the Orient without the expectation of material histories, scholarship, or verisimilitude.

In the "golden city" of an "Orient" dislocated from place, setting, and era, Shelley thus deploys the figurative language of shapes, demands metonymy and metaphor over clarity of individual subjects, and participates in the racial and ethnic logics underpinning the white aesthetic regimes of Romantic poetry. Within these regimes, Shelley's image of the "orient sun in shadow" shows the centrality of the speaker or poet figure in visualizing and constructing the Orient. This image is one of many in the works of Jones, Coleridge, Shelley, and a host of other Romantic writers—images that are repeated, recycled, and adapted throughout the period for different effects. What they all share is the construction of an "Orient" that cannot be found or reached, for it is a fiction of the poetic imagination.

Conclusion

In analyzing these works, I begin to trace an alternative aesthetic Romantic genealogy through the poetics of orientation. This poetics exposes the Orientalist attachments undergirding the ascendancy of a modern lyric subject rooted in Romantic self-expression. This self-reflexivity operates through a host of orientations toward the Orient or "East." Thus, Orientalism constitutes a fundamental part of the poetics of orientation—a poetics in which the subject finds one's bearings in an increasingly disorienting world of political upheaval, misrecognition, and cultural and geographical ambiguity.

I now return to the fundamentals of this poetics of orientation: relational subjectivities, particularly as evidenced in Shelley's works, the dominance of the Romantic imagination, dislocated place/setting, plurality amidst universalism, the aesthetic centrality of the poet, and the lack of a coherent "other."

Poetics is a type of perception and, as Pierre Bourdieu states, "aesthetic perception is necessarily historical, inasmuch as it is differential, relational, attentive to the deviations (*écarts*) which make styles" (4). Bourdieu notes that aesthetic perception and taste are based on a cultural logic and an "economy of cultural goods" that produce a type of "historical culture" attentive to distinctions more than similarities (4–5). The distinctive "styles" of Orientalist structures and motifs are always in relation to something such as the actual poet, speaker, or subject of the text. These Orientalist deployments are not rigid or homogeneous. They are self-reflexive, ornamental, fetishistic, antagonistic, sympathetic, and culturally disparate to the point of confounding or disorienting the aggregate whole of the poet's vision. This disaggregation is the grounds from which a poetic regime of white subjects propagates in opposition to the figurative and increasingly obscure Oriental subject.

Notes

1. For more on Jones's influence, see James Watt, *British Orientalisms*, 147.
2. *Discourse*, 3. Edward Said writes, "The difference between representations of the Orient before the last third of the eighteenth century and those after it (that is, those belonging to what I call modern Orientalism) is that the range of representation expanded enormously in the later period. [...] When around the turn of the eighteenth century the Orient definitively revealed the age of its languages—thus outdating Hebrew's divine pedigree—it was a group of Europeans who made the discovery, passed it on to other scholars, and preserved the discovery in the new science of Indo-European philology. A new powerful science for viewing the linguistic Orient was born, and with it, as Foucault has shown in *The Order of Things*, a whole web of related scientific interests" (*Orientalism* 22).
3. For more on aesthetic regimes of whiteness, see David Lloyd's *Under Representation: The Racial Regime of Aesthetics*.
4. "Lyric," in *The Princeton Encyclopedia of Poetry and Poetics*.
5. Jonathan Culler sees in the lyric form an unpredictability that makes it always contingent to its historical time and place. He continues, with this comes its function in society and its "historical efficacy ... A socially oriented critic can treat the work as its

recurrent coming into being in a social space, which is itself in part the effect of that work and always to be constructed by a reading of one's own relation to it" (301).
6. More well known for his lexicography, Samuel Johnson writes at length about the "dangerous prevalence of the imagination" in his 1759 apologue, *The History of Rasselas, Prince of Abyssinia*. Johnson's work presages the Orientalist poetry in the latter part of the century, but *Rasselas* imagines the cultures of Africa, including modern-day Ethiopia, and the work is deemed a "philosophical romance," rather than an expressive lyric or tale.
7. James Watt gives a thorough analysis of Jones's influence on Romantic writers including William Blake, Percy Bysshe Shelley, Robert Southey, Thomas Moore, and more in Chapter 4 of *British Orientalisms* (1759–1835).
8. Hereafter *LB* and *BL*.
9. Seamus Perry writes in *Coleridge and the Uses of Division* (1999) that Coleridge poses two types of genius—commanding and conciliatory. These types align with the active/passive duality Coleridge references.
10. Omar Miranda discusses the resonances between "Kubla Khan" and William Jones's "Hymn to Surya" in *Hindoo Hymns* in "The Global Romantic Lyric," *Wordsworth Circle* (Spring 2021).
11. Paulo Lemos Horta has written a monograph, *Marvellous Thieves: Secret Authors of the Arabian Nights* (2017) examining "three of the most influential European translators of the story collection . . . [Antoine] Galland, Edward William Lane, and Richard Francis Burton" (2–3). Horta explores how these translations in English and French "still retain their power to define these tales in the Western imagination, and [how] each has played an important role in analyses of Orientalism as a framework for understanding the Middle East" (3).
12. As both a fragment and a complete poem, "Kubla Khan" has generated readings in tension with each other. Agneta Lindgren identifies five major approaches to the poem that twentieth-century criticism seemed to orient around, including reading it as a description of the poetic process, its usefulness in exemplifying Coleridge's prose-writing, its "Freudian-psychoanalytical-biographical lines of thought," its "biblical imagery," and its "sources, references and allusions" (178–9). These approaches are useful delineations because it is hard to find consensus amongst the diverse arguments that this poem has spawned.
13. For Shaffer, "there is no separation between 'background' and literary analysis; the separation, so familiar to us as to seem natural and unavoidable, is the result of arbitrary and conventional and therefore ill-considered selection of subject-matter. It

is the result of an inadequate methodology of literary criticism" (4). Shaffer chooses "Kubla Khan" for her new methodology because it is "poetry often claimed to be 'pure poetry', poetry of extreme lyricism, emerging unwilled from a consciousness loosed from considerations of rational order" (5). She then wants to bring it "into relation with Biblical criticism, a body of highly technical information and intricate, specialized, restricted practice," to write criticism that recognizes the importance of "the common experience of the Bible that was altered in the period" (5–6). This is to say, Shaffer finds it vital to have "precise knowledge of the critical texts [such as the Bible] and their diffusion" because a "historical analysis of the roots of modern Biblical criticism" is a "critique of all 'positive' claims for the objectivity of the interpretation of texts, Biblical or poetic" (5–10). She traces Coleridge's first intellectual influences to Anglicanism, then to the Enlightenment tradition à la Voltaire, and finally to Unitarianism (9).
14. Cf. The Crewe manuscript for Coleridge's differing commentary on poem's inception.
15. Garcia constructs a revisionist argument that "decolonizes the historical imagination by approaching early modern Afro-Eurasia as an integrated whole, complicating nationalist and imperialist histories of eighteenth-century Britain" (4).
16. *The Revolt of Islam* is Shelley's longest work, as well as one of his least studied and anthologized.
17. For more on precarity, see Judith Butler's *Precarious Life*.
18. For a detailed analysis of Shelley's "idea of Europe" in relation to the work's Orientalism, see Paul Stock, "The Shelleys and the Idea of 'Europe,'" *European Romantic Review* 19, no. 4 (2008): 335–49.
19. Vasant Kaiwar notes how, "to an extent, Orientalism is misrepresentation if the agenda of such a form of thought is taken literally to be about the realities of places in the 'East' (or whatever gets drawn into this geographic commonsense) and their social, political and cultural developments over time" (xii).
20. Cf. Teddi Lynn Chichester, "Shelley's Imaginative Transsexualism in *Laon and Cythna*." Adela Pinch, Karen Swann, and many others have written on Shelley's preponderance of shape idioms, with no clear consensus on his defining attributes of shape other than its association with light. Pinch specifically correlates Shelley's "shapes" with objects of love for Victorian readers, arguing that these readers "focused on the relation of shape to light, and the relation of abstraction to affection. Victorian readers were as fascinated and perplexed by the 'shape all light' in *The Triumph of Life* (a poem they

loved, often going into ecstasies over Shelley's use of *terza rima*) as have been contemporary critics, but they also honed in on the presence of shapes of light throughout his poetry" (para. 123). Adela Pinch, "'A Shape All Light,' in *Taking Liberties with the Author: Selected Essays from the English Institute*," ed. Meredith L. McGill (Cambridge, MA: English Institute, 2013), Karen Swann, 'Shelley's Pod People,' Romantic Praxis Series: *Romanticism and the Insistence of the Aesthetic* (2005). <https://www.rc.umd.edu/praxis/aesthetic/swann/swann.html>.

21. Time-space compression refers to a phenomenon traced, according to David Harvey, to the Enlightenment era when the geographical concept of space is made abstract, into a concept, and from this conceptualization comes its linkage with conceptual time. Thus, with the rise of the modern post-medieval period comes a common affinity to conceptualize time and space in a twinned formation so that the way the world is represented in literature is fundamentally changed (240). With this compression comes a mythologization of conventional real time and space and the imagination as a renewed heuristic for cultural production.
22. Anderson writes of the concept of the "nation" as an "imagined political community—and imagined as both inherently limited and sovereign" (49). This is because a nation and, in effect, nationalisms, are constituted by both geographical and political borders. Within this "imagined community," the "meanwhile" makes it possible to "'think' the nation" into existence (49).
23. Cf. Coleridge's "Kubla Khan."
24. Cf. Nigel Leask and Humberto Garcia's arguments on *The Revolt of Islam*.

Chapter 2

Byron's Cosmopolitan "East"

> And once as Kaled's answering accents ceas'd,
> Rose Lara's hand, and pointed to the *East*
>
> Byron, *Lara*

In this chapter I focus on Byron's Eastern Tales, published in the period between the second and third cantos of *Childe Harold's Pilgrimage*. I explain how Byron's constructions of the lyric subject are forged directly by his early-career aesthetic and Orientalist inventions in his Eastern Tales. These racialized constructions provoke the development of Byron's "cosmopolitan" Romantic subject and its "Oriental" counterpart, a counterpart that serves to reinforce Byron's increasingly deracinated cosmopolitanism. I will show how this cosmopolitanism depends on a textualized and simulated "East"—a space of disidentification and defamiliarization that gestures back to Byron himself as an Orientalized figure. As a result, the Byronic subject ultimately inhabits a racially and ethnically flattened space such that neither the "Orient" nor the "world" is imaginable without the other.

Sir William Jones's description of "the finest parts of poetry" as "expressive of the passions" and "operat[ing] on our minds by sympathy" lends force and warrant to the eventual Orientalist sites, subjects, and settings that Byron deploys and re-imagines in the Eastern Tales ("On the arts, commonly called imitative" 216). Jones's description of the poets of the "Eastern nations" as "excel[ing] the inhabitants of our colder regions in the liveliness of their fancy, and the richness of their invention"

(77), points to the "East" as a site of not only aesthetic novelty but an entrenchment of colonial, imperial, and racial logic. This logic makes the aesthetic act of turning to the "East" an appropriation of the "fancy" and "invention" of the East. The geographic "East" is discarded for an ornamental space of projection, one that writers like Byron capitalize upon to propel his early celebrity, or as Lady Byron called it, "Byromania."[1]

While cantos I and II of the *Pilgrimage* inaugurated Byron's celebrity, it was the Eastern Tales that followed—*The Giaour* (1813), *The Bride of Abydos* (1813), *The Corsair* (1814), and *Lara* (1814)—that garnered him popular literary acclaim and readership.[2] Multiple editions and reprints of these four tales turned Byron into not only a literary brand name but also a celebrated Orientalist. Byron may have famously parodied himself in *Beppo* (1817)—writing "How quickly would I print (the world delighting) /A Grecian, Syrian, or Assyrian tale; / And sell you, mix'd with western sentimentalism, / Some samples of the finest Orientalism!" (4: 405–8)—but this ironic distance was produced in part by the unprecedented sales of the Eastern Tales.[3]

Prior to the tales, *Childe Harold's Pilgrimage* proposes Byron's poetic subjectivity as a type of cosmopolitan ideal.[4] The *Le Cosmopolite* epigraph to *Childe Harold's Pilgrimage* compares the "universe" to a "sort of book whose first page one has read when one has seen only one's own country."[5] This cosmopolitan "universe" heralds the search for new settings and cultures found in Byron's Eastern Tales.[6] The *Pilgrimage*'s culturally heterogeneous settings serve as a palimpsest for the Eastern Tales to come. Its repertoire of imaginative geography centers the Western European continental experience as a type of assumed, presumably white perspective.[7] In the final two cantos of the *Pilgrimage* the influence of William Wordsworth and Percy Bysshe Shelley become apparent, until the final stanzas when Italy becomes the meeting point between East and West. For example, the final canto of the *Pilgrimage* begins with the initial setting of Venice personified as a seductive woman figure with "spoils of nations, and the exhaustless East / Pour[ing] in her lap all gems in sparkling showers" (4.2.15–16). Venice is positioned in contradistinction to the far "East," yet a cultural association is apparent. This type of cultural comparison fuels much of Byron's work after the *Pilgrimage*, as I show in the Eastern Tales.

For Byron, Orientalist trends came at a specifically opportune time in his career.[8] While working on *The Giaour*, the first of his Eastern Tales, he wrote a letter to Thomas Moore instructing him to "stick to the East," for "the public are Orientalizing" (3: 101).[9] Byron followed his own advice, publishing *The Bride of Abydos*, *The Corsair*, and *Lara* over the course of the next year. The Eastern Tales show a charged apposition between Orientalism and worldliness—a burgeoning cosmopolitanism—that marks Byron's character representations. In using "cosmopolitanism," I am referring to both the modern view of a common humanity and the long tradition of Immanuel Kant's writings in *Toward Perpetual Peace*, "Idea for Universal History with a Cosmopolitan Purpose," and the *Critique of Judgment*.[10] Kant's model of cosmopolitanism also sets the terms of aesthetic taste-making and disagreement over what constitutes universal forms of literary production.[11] As Manu Chander asserts, however, Kant's model of cosmopolitanism argues for "ideals of global participation" only to a point (*Brown Romantics* 9). For Byron, like his peers, this point is the marginalization, oftentimes exclusion, of women and people of color from the same legislative and representational rights as their white male counterparts.

By the time he composes his fourth Eastern Tale, *Lara*, Byron has created an ambiguously "other" persona that is predicated on a cosmopolitan subjectivity delinked from time and space. At the end of the tale, Lara is mortally wounded, and his last living gesture is to point "to the *East*" (*CPW* 2: 467, emphasis mine). After the predominantly European settings of the *Pilgrimage*, Lara's gesture confirms Byron's creation of an imagined and textualized "East"—a space of disidentification and obscurity that disrupts the white male singularity of the poetic subject. This dying gesture culminates Byron's provocation of settings in "the East" and raises a host of questions for Byron's poetics, including the role of early nineteenth-century discourses of Westernization, the link between poetic subjectivity and place, and geographical and ethnic significations as verse tale motifs.[12]

In effect, these tales represent how Byron's cosmopolitanism is forged directly by his creation of an imagined "East." To create and populate this "East," Byron moves the hero archetype of the *Pilgrimage* into an invented poetic space without clear signifiers of cultural representation. As a series, the Eastern Tales forge a poetic space peripheral to Westernized and British poetics, reinforcing the "Oriental" subject as a figure in the poetics of orientation.

Byron's Emergent Orientalism: A Revised Cosmopolitanism

If, as Kant defines it, cosmopolitanism is "the matrix within which all original capacities of the human race may develop" (cited in Brown and Held 51), what happens when this "human race" is presumed to have a European center and Eastern periphery, as Byron's Eastern Tales propose?[13] Gerard Cohen-Vrignaud identifies a Romantic-era "radical Orientalism" "that is invested in giving a "contrarian" voice to marginalized or non-conforming Britons (8). Saree Makdisi recognizes an imperial aspect of Byron's cosmopolitanism in terms of a bourgeois "self who can come and go unfettered and feel, or claim to feel, at home anywhere" (*Making England Western* 152). Building on these claims for the contrarian and imperial effects of Byron's Orientalism, I argue that these tales popularize and normalize Orientalist modes of irony and imitation. Byron's white male poetic subject ironizes and imitates through and against an imagined racial "other," an other silenced and confined to the textual "East" of Byron's creation.

These four Eastern Tales share literary devices and motifs that inform a larger paradigm shift in British cultural representations. These devices and motifs include the universalized "Oriental" subject, non-British hero/anti-hero archetypes, inconsistent geographical settings, cultural generalizations, and sexual objectification.[14] These choices reflect the larger developing genre of Orientalist poetics discussed by Emily Haddad, Mohammed Sharafuddin, Saree Makdisi, and others. In addition, they demonstrate how Byron invests in and enacts a poetics aware of cultural difference as a site of aesthetic ambiguity and experimentation. Byron's poetics, like Coleridge, Percy Bysshe Shelley, Felicia Hemans, and Sir William Jones, is rooted in an oriented or relational subjectivity. This orientation reinforces the turn toward expressivism during the Romantic era. This expressive turn calls for a shift in the speaker's cultural and historical perspective in Byron's Eastern Tales. As an aestheticization of not only Byron's persona but also continental histories and conflicts, Byron's Eastern Tales broaden the hero persona to cosmopolitan and global spaces. The Romantic period's turn to imagination and expression affords the formative topoi from which Byron is able not only to gain celebrity status in Britain, Europe, and the Americas but also to market his vision without the expectation of verisimilitude or realistic representations. Without this expectation, Byron creates new poetic spaces and subjects lacking clear geographical or cultural boundaries.

These lacks and gaps create a diffuse problem of representation across all the works in this book. For Byron, the problem is rooted in his construction of a fundamentally obscure poetic figure for which Byron himself becomes known. Emily Haddad argues for the aesthetic link between nineteenth-century poetry and Orientalism, noting that "[n]ineteenth-century aesthetics constitutes the Islamic Orient in particular as a fundamentally amimetic site" (3). This amimesis results in literary characters and settings that lack a basis in empirical or first-hand experience. Given Byron's own travels, an experiential writing of the "East" could have been expected—the type of literature based on an increasingly direct knowledge of the "East" through travel, ethnographic reports, and studies. However, Byron's "literary orientalism," as Stephen Cheeke notes, "relied upon just such firsthand knowledge, but it was a knowledge that was carefully prepared for the reading public's consumption" (13). Byron's ironic and imitative Orientalism furthers the demands of a readership increasingly receptive to Orientalist productions. The tales were produced and reproduced at a rate of consumption for the "reading public," and their defining features are not empirical, but aesthetic. For Byron, what exact Orientalist line to take, and from what sources, remained an open question complicated by the runaway sales of each Eastern installment.

Byron relies less on ornamental settings, lurid plot development, or supernatural imagery than contemporary works like William Beckford's *Vathek* or Southey's *Curse of Kehama*.[15] In terms of genre, his tales also shift in verse form and meter, reshaping the romance form and Spenserian stanzas of *Childe Harold's Pilgrimage* into octosyllabic and heroic couplets as well as complete versus fragment forms. Byron pays close attention to character development and poetic voice, as well as the representations of disillusioned and anxious subjectivities. Oftentimes, these representations are deployed along the lines of sex and gender, whereas other times, Byron renders his characters interchangeable without clear individuation.[16] These choices reflect a long line of anglophone writers writing during an era of British Orientalism's popular rise. In turn, the tales' marketability and popular success legitimate the practice of ambiguous cultural representation as part of Romantic poetics.[17]

With their distant settings oriented toward "the East," the tales experiment with drawing and creating literary worlds along hemispheric and/or geographical lines. Scholars including Cheeke, Katarina Gephardt, Saree Makdisi, Diego Saglia, Andrew Warren, and others, have written on Byron's geographical and cultural poetics.[18] As Makdisi argues, "the space that would eventually come to be established as the Occident had to be Occidentalized—that England, among other sites, had to be made Western" (*Making England Western* xiii). This Westernization occurred, in literature, via poetic form and content shifts such as Byron's choice of traditional and newer verse forms, cultural stereotypes, and generalizations coded as "Eastern" or "Oriental" expression.

Byron's turn to the "East" after the *Pilgrimage* also reflects an important juncture of Byron coming to terms with his new literary celebrity, what Jerome McGann calls Byron's "careerist calculation" (*Byron and Romanticism* 37). In addition to being careerist opportunities and "Orientalist" miscellany, the tales reflect Byron's self-reflexive anxieties in contributing to an anglophone poetic tradition that he wants to opt in and out of freely. This notion of choice, choosing to participate or not in traditional forms, also registers Byron's shift in literary aesthetics to less familiar and newer forms of cultural production and commodification. The tales, in effect, reinforce a defamiliarized poetic perspective oriented towards newly foreign subjects and content. The commodification of "Byron" as a poetic brand happened throughout Byron's career, but after the runaway success of the *Pilgrimage*, the subsequent moment of aesthetic invention, the Tales, have been overlooked by critics largely, I would argue, due to their difficulty to read and situate in Byron's larger oeuvre.

While *Childe Harold's Pilgrimage* ends with Harold's point of view fully discarded for Byron's own, the Eastern Tales shift the characters and settings to far-flung settings that never are reintegrated fully into Byron's position as poet. These representations mark a clear shift in Byron's aesthetics, propelling his poetic form and content towards less mimetic modes.[19] This shift yields Byron the opportunity to create and self-create, to avoid the expectation of realistic representations, and to aestheticize his own poetic subjectivity.[20]

Byron's Early Tales: *The Giaour* and *The Bride of Abydos*

The first of these tales to be published, *The Giaour: A Fragment of a Turkish Tale*, announced Byron's claiming of the "East" as a part of the cosmopolitan realm ushered in by the *Pilgrimage*. Byron writes in the Advertisement, "The tale which these disjointed fragments present, is founded upon circumstances now less common in the East than formerly" (*CPW* 3: 39).[21] The tale resists a coherent reading via its "fragment" form and usage of multiple narrators, including that of the eponymous Giaour.[22] Contemporary reviews of the poem picked up on these questions of form, genre, and fragmentation, but they did not attend to the heterogeneity of the geographical and ethnic significations.[23] To do so was to overlook the potent forces of literary world-making and, "empire building" at play within each new "fragment" added to the "snake of a poem" (*BLJ* 3: 100).[24] Marilyn Butler notes that critics should take the tales' "geographical significations" at "face value" since for Byron and his contemporary "materialist poets . . . the place of a poem's setting means what it says, and the time is always in some sense the present" (78). If she is correct, one must attend to the work's geographies and inconsistent cultural significations. This attention offers a key to understanding not only Byron's creation of a textualized East, but also an acknowledgment of the messiness of racial and racist logics embedded in Byron's early-career Orientalism.

The tale's "present" place and time involve the "Giaour," a Christian-born Venetian and infidel who fights against the Turkish emir Hassan for the love of a young Circassian woman, Leila.[25] Eventually Leila is drowned by Hassan upon his discovery of her affair with the Giaour.[26] Byron's footnotes contextualize the romance narrative, enacting what Ruth Knezevich calls a type of "textual imperialism" in that the footnotes "take a colonial stance *vis-à-vis* the simulated Eastern content and context of the verse narrative, even while the work as a whole (the poem plus its notes) remains markedly anti-colonial in tone" (37).[27] Rather than a colonial/anti-colonial binary, it is important to note the emergent aesthetic of Orientalism and cosmopolitanism that fuse through Byron's choices.[28]

The opening speaker laments Greece's lost classicism, under Turkish rule at the time, in a continuation of the themes of antiquity from the *Pilgrimage*. Continuing to aestheticize the "East," Byron describes Port Leone's shore as awash in "the lovely light / That best becomes an Eastern night" (177–9). Amid this scene, an anonymous Turkish fisherman arrives at Port Leone and sees the Giaour, riding by with "Christian crest and haughty mien" (256). These lines immediately position the identifiable heroism away from the Venetian Giaour, and the reader is transported to Byron's "boundless East" (452). This space, as Byron describes, is one of the "Edens of the eastern wave" (15)—water imagery that invokes Leila's story of drowning.[29]

After the Giaour has ridden by on a steed, Byron introduces Leila for the first time, yet she is neither named nor given dialogue.[30] Leila's layered identity as Turkish woman, Muslim, slave, and sexualized object is obfuscated by her lack of dialogue and point of view throughout the work.

Furthermore, her symbolism of ideal womanhood reinforces normative conceptions of gender and heteronormative relationships. Thus, she occupies the space of Spivak's subaltern, "caught between tradition and modernization" (102). This liminality, as Shahidha Bari notes, makes Leila "the void around which the entire narrative is generated" (710). The speaker ponders if Leila is a "soulless toy for tyrant's lust?" and then describes her "fair cheek's unfading hue" as well as "[h]er hair in hyacinthine flow" and how "midst her handmaids in the hall / She stood superior to them all" (490–9). Leila's "fair" Circassian skin and "superior" status constitute her racialized whiteness, yet she remains otherwise unrepresented in terms of physical description, race, and ethnicity. Leila's representation reinforces the disjointed nature of the work and opens a gendered space of imagined alterity and opacity for Byron's audience.

Leila's opacity of representation is not singular. Byron represents the Giaour and Hassan sparingly in terms of physical description, often likening them in terms of appearance.[31] Once the battle between Hassan and the Giaour commences, Byron brings in Turkish references to weaponry like "arquebuss," "ataghan," "pasha," "Tartar," and "Chiaus" (522, 530, 549, 571)—verbiage that adds a type of Orientalist "firsthand knowledge" to the imaginative setting. Said argues that "standardization and cultural stereotyping have intensified the hold of the nineteenth-century academic and imaginative demonology of 'the mysterious Orient'" (*Orientalism* 26). Said distinguishes between "academic," "scholarly," and "imaginative" Orientalisms, yet Byron's unsystematic practice of cultural references creates an Eastern orientation without clear center or periphery. Comparing Shelley's *The Revolt of Islam* to Byron's Eastern Tales shows the distinctions between Shelley's and Byron's representations. For example, while Shelley focuses on abstract "shapes" as forms of human and non-human life, Byron turns to human subjects and a host of ethnographic footnotes and references. These differences show the heterogeneity in Orientalist literary devices and tropes and how the individual imagination drives Orientalism, not a codified sense of Orientalist genres or styles.

Nowhere does Byron more conspicuously veer away from a clear Orientalist logic than in this climactic battle between Hassan and the Giaour. Rather than deploying a binary framing of self/other or East/West, the speaker extols sympathy on Hassan while rebuking the Giaour. The Giaour is condemned by the speaker for being "array'd in Arnaut garb, / Apostate from his own vile faith, / [that] shall not save him from the death" (615–17). The reference to the Giaour's cultural appropriation and apostasy interrogates the heroism of both the Giaour and Hassan, culminating in their mirroring at battle scene's end. The Giaour bends over "Fall'n Hassan," "that foe with brow / As dark as his that bled below—" (669, 673–4). This mirroring compresses Byron's hero trope into the intersubjective perspective of the Giaour and Hassan. The Giaour speaks for the first time in the next passage, responding, "Yes, Leila sleeps beneath the wave, / But his [Hassan] shall be a redder grave . . . He call'd the Prophet, but his power / Was vain against the vengeful Giaour" (675–80). The Giaour's illeism reflects not only narcissism but the artifice of his representation, further evidenced by the convenient end-rhyme. This illeism implies external observation, the constructedness of the Orientalist imaginary, and Byron's experimentation with new ways of describing the world through his simulated "East."

After the battle scene, the disjointedness of the work is increasingly apparent in the continuous shifting of narrative perspectives. Byron turns to the perspective of an unnamed Turkish person who reflects on the contrasting fates of the Giaour and Hassan. Next, he reverts to the initial fisherman who saw the Giaour chasing Hassan by horse (723–86).[32] This fisherman converses with a monk in the abbey where the Giaour has become a religious recluse and "lone Caloyer" (787). The Giaour has become a fallen hero, unable to live in society, who steadfastly "broods within his cell alone, / His faith and race alike unknown" (806–7). The tale's anonymous speaker, in a tone of imperial anxiety, ponders, "Yet seems he not of Othman race, But only Christian in his face" (810–11). The Giaour has acquired a religious and racial obscurity that does not fit within the purview of the racialized identities hitherto scaffolded by Byron in the work.

Instead, the Giaour becomes a spectral presence and persistently "mutters" in his cell of Leila, raving of his past to the empty cell walls (822). As a haunted figure, the Giaour internalizes the violence and murders of Leila and Hassan. He seeks relief in "hate":

> If solitude succeeds to grief,
> Release from pain is slight relief;
> . . . .
> The heart once left thus desolate
> Must fly at last for ease—to hate. (937–40)

Following this internal meditation, the Giaour, in a dramatic monologue expressed to the abbot, confesses his responsibility for Leila's death. Contrasting with the abbot's "generous tear," the Giaour's "glazing eye" evokes the prophet-seer figure in Coleridge's *The Rime of the Ancient Mariner* and Beckford's eponymous character in *Vathek* (1323). The Giaour's "glazing eye" registers a type of paralysis or self-reflexive condemnation. Rather than responding or absolving him of sin, the abbot remains silent. Like the silence of Leila and Hassan's mother, the silence of the abbot reifies the Giaour's solipsism.[33]

This moment of confession is the resolution for the narrative, but the "tale" ends, in the words of the Giaour, "broken" (1333). In the final footnote to the poem, Byron tries to explain the scholarly and historical credibility of the work. This footnote reveals not only Byron's ironic self-fashioning of his cultural repertoire, but his awareness of the work's questionable "correctness" and "originality." Byron writes:

> The circumstance to which the above story relates was not very uncommon in Turkey . . . The story in the text . . . I heard it by accident recited by one of the coffee-house story-tellers who abound in the Levant, and sing or recite their narratives . . . and I regret that my memory has retained so few fragments of the original . . . For the contents of some of the notes I am indebted partly to D'Herbelot, and partly to that most Eastern, and, as Mr. Weber justly entitles it, "sublime tale," [Beckford's] the "Caliph Vathek." . . . for correctness of costume, beauty of description, and power of imagination, it far surpasses all European imitations; and bears such marks of originality, that those who have visited the East will find some difficulty in believing it to be more than a translation. (*CPW* 3: 422–3)[34]

The prolepsis of this footnote recalls the preface, where Byron stakes a claim for the intended authenticity of his tale. As one of many "European imitations" that still "bears such marks of originality," Byron writes *The Giaour* in the service of "originality" more than "correctness of costume" or credibility. By work's end, Byron's perspective overshadows the characters and setting of the Giaour, Hassan, and Leila.

Just eight months after the initial publication of *The Giaour*, *The Bride of Abydos* was published in December 1813.[35] In a letter to Thomas Moore a month earlier, Byron apologizes for his lack of correspondence and shares with Moore that he will be sending along another work soon, *The Bride of Abydos*, which was written "for the sake of the *employment*" (*BLJ* 3: 184).[36] Seeking Moore's approval and feedback on his next Eastern work shows Byron's more apprehensive and calculated approach than in *The Giaour*, which Byron's publisher John Murray published "at his own risk" (*BLJ* 3: 59). Byron also asserts that *The Bride* is "another Turkish story" but "*not* a Fragment" (*BLJ* 3: 184, emphasis mine). In indicating that the tale is not a fragment like *The Giaour*, Byron's shift in genre and desire for coherence are apparent. Byron is careful to note that *The Bride* "does not trench upon your [Moore's] kingdom in the least, and, if it did, you would soon reduce me to my proper boundaries" (*BLJ* 3: 184). In "kingdom" Byron is referring to Moore's Orientalist romance, *Lalla Rookh*, which Moore conceived of writing a year earlier.

Byron's more measured approach to this tale can be seen in his series of correspondence with his publisher, John Murray.[37] In addition to his correspondence with Moore and other friends, Byron sends over thirty letters of correction and revision to Murray in the month leading up to the 2 December publication of the *Bride*. At the beginning of November of that year, Byron writes to Murray, "Pray attend to the *corrections* they are slight but *important* and remember the *Bride*" (*BLJ* 3: 156). On 13 November, after a series of corrections and edits, Byron specifically asks Murray to revise lines 1073–4—a speech by Zuleika, the work's heroine:

(the only one of *hers* [speech] in that Canto)—
it is now thus—
   "And curse—if I could curse—the day"
it must be
   "And mourn—I dare not curse—the day" (*BLJ* 3: 163)³⁸

This change in Zuleika's dialogue from "curse" to "mourn" and "could curse" to "dare not curse" tempers her ire and reinforces a passive characterization and idealized "purity" (*BLJ* 3: 199).³⁹ While in *The Giaour* Leila remains silent within the text, Zuleika's dialogue and actions in the *Bride* play a role in the plot's resolution. The resolution of the *Bride* offers narrative closure in contrast to the disjointedness and "fragment" form of *The Giaour*.⁴⁰

As the tales progress, what forms and motifs Byron chooses to continue upon or adapt remain erratic. While Byron turns from fragment to complete "story" in the *Bride*, he maintains varying tetrameter and octosyllabic couplets, continuing with *The Giaour*'s meter. The *Bride*'s epigraph from Robert Burns's Scots song "Ae Fond Kiss" and a dedication to Lord Holland (the third) contrast with the tale's opening landscape. Byron begins the work with an idyllic scene of culturally diffuse images, writing of "cypress and myrtle," "cedar and vine," and "gardens of Gúl" where "the flowers ever blossom, the beams ever shine" (1–13).⁴¹ This imagery heralds the Pasha Giaffir's introduction in the next stanza.

Viewed through the omniscient narrator's point of view, Giaffir is placed as object among the Orientalist accoutrements and characters that surround him. Byron writes:

Old Giaffir sate in his Divan,
Deep thought was in his aged eye;
And though the face of Mussulman
Not oft betrays to standers by
The mind within, well skill'd to hide
All but unconquerable pride,
His pensive cheek and pondering brow
Did more than he was wont avow. (1. 24–31)

At first wordless, Giaffir is depicted as sitting in a "Divan," with single "aged eye" and "the face of Mussulman" with a

"Nubian" servant at his behest (1.35). These signifiers create a character of ornamentation who is objectified through association with "Oriental" objects. Unlike the obscurely drawn "shapes" that populate Shelley's *The Revolt of Islam*, Byron attempts to give inchoate human form to his Eastern characters but ultimately fails, reinforcing an "East of things" (Saglia, "Words and Things" 169).

In the next canto, the "Turkish" setting is reinvoked through an imagined setting of the Dardanelles strait/the "Helle" (2.1). In a moment of shock and awe, Byron describes Selim's impassioned reveal to Zuleika. Selim throws off his "robe of pride" and "high-crown'd turban" in a Byronic flourish, and confesses to Zuleika,

> I said I was not what I seemed –
> And now thou see'st my words were true;
> I have a tale thou hast not dreamed,
> If sooth—its truth must others rue. (2.151–4)

After his circuitous invocation, Selim confesses, "Zuleika! I am not thy brother!" (2.163–4). Having learned of his true identity from Giaffir's servant, Haroun, Selim's mistreatment by Giaffir now makes sense to him.[42] Zuleika responds, "God! Am I left alone on earth?— / To mourn—I dare not curse—the day / That saw my solitary birth!" (2.166–8). Here, her revised speech reads differently from Byron's edited line in his letter to Murray: "And curse—if I could curse—the day" (*BLJ* 3: 163). This change from "curse" to "mourn" hedges Zuleika's agency. In the narrative's next scene, Zuleika is described as "mute and motionless," standing paralyzed as "statue of distress," and dying of sorrow (2. 491–2). The tale's narrative closure and Zuleika's diminished agency through Byron's line edit reinforce Zuleika's own objectification into silent and dying "statue."

With line edits and a turning away from fragment form, Byron's more calculated approach to the *Bride* does not result in what he deems a success. Byron, on completing the work, deems *The Bride of Abydos* "horrible enough," and, in effect, a poetic disappointment (*BLJ* 3: 160). Byron attempts to set and reset the terms of his developing poetics through new and unfinished aesthetic spaces and subjects. In doing so, he creates new literary worlds but also tests the limits of his own literariness and literary taste. His growingly obscure cosmopolitan realm offers a number of cultural representations that trouble the boundaries between himself and the imagined "others" who seem both part of and apart from a Byronic self-posturing. Rather than reinforcing the imagined "East" and its attendant cultural heterogeneity as a trope par excellence, Byron's next two Eastern Tales, *The Corsair* and *Lara*, often default, instead, to self-reflexive representations of Byron's own deracinated lyric subject.[43]

Conrad and Lara: The Shifting Coordinates of Byron's Cosmopolitan "East"

After selling out of 10,000 copies on its first day of sale, the next of the Eastern Tales, *The Corsair* (1814) is another boon for Byron's career. Byron's name, by this point, is culturally codified and commodified in Britain with a host of assumptions. This height of "Byromania" occurs during a related moment of escalation—popularized representations of the cultural "other," oftentimes the "Oriental" subject.[44] As part of this escalation, Byron's poetic subjectivity and the forging of his textual "East" yoke into a shared project of Orientalist invention rooted in his own self-selecting choices and interests.

In terms of *The Corsair*'s inception, Byron's personal anxieties are explicit. For example, Byron's prefatory letter to Thomas Moore at the beginning of *The Corsair* deems the tale "the last production with which I shall trespass on public patience, and your indulgence, for some years; and I own that I feel anxious to avail myself of this latest and only opportunity" (*CPW* 3: 148). Byron then raises the notion of national identity and his and Moore's shared poetic alliance. He asserts that:

> While *Ireland* ranks you [Moore] amongst the foremost of her patriots—while you stand alone the first of her bards in her estimation, and *Britain* repeats and ratifies the decree—permit one, whose only regret, since our first acquaintance, has been the years he had lost before it commenced, to add the humble, but sincere suffrage of friendship, to the voice of more than one *nation*. (*CPW* 3: 148, emphasis mine)

This "suffrage" is formed in part, through their shared projection and appropriation of "the East" (*CPW* 3: 150). Referring to *Lalla Rookh*, Byron flatters Moore's current "composition of a poem whose scene will be laid in the East" and notes how in *The Corsair*, Byron will use "the good old and now neglected heroic couplet" (3: 150). In terms of aesthetic invention, Byron is thinking not only in terms of setting, but also form and verse. Tellingly, Byron shifts from octosyllabic couplets in *The Bride of Abydos* to classical form and meter–narrative epic and heroic couplets—in both of his next two tales, *The Corsair* and *Lara*.[45] This return to classical forms signals Byron's continued experimentation with culturally heterogeneous forms of prosody. Byron's impulses to both control and co-opt the aesthetic potential of a textualized East seek a cosmopolitan, world-facing poetic subject without attending to the ethnic and racial entanglements of such a project.

What becomes apparent in both *The Corsair* and *Lara*, I argue, is not only Byron's ironic and imitative Orientalism but his poetry as a self-projection. Byron ends the dedication of *Corsair* by both defending and criticizing his previous cast of heroes, deeming the Giaour immoral, Childe Harold "a very repulsive personage," and the upcoming corsair a possible "gloomy vanity of 'drawing from self'" (*CPW* 3: 150). This "drawing" reflects Byron's self-fashioning and growing disenchantment with his personal and public identity. Although by 1813 Byron has risen to a celebrity level of literary success via the *Pilgrimage* and *The Giaour*, Byron generally does not think he is writing satisfactory poetry and finds deficiency in poetry's "scale of intellect."[46] A month before *The Bride of Abydos* is published, Byron writes in a November 1813 letter to Lady Byron:

> I by no means rank poetry or poets high in the scale of intellect . . . I prefer the talents of *action*—of war—or the Senate—of even of Science—to all the speculations of those mere dreamers of another existence . . . and spectators of this. — —Apathy—disgust—& perhaps incapacity have rendered me now a mere spectator—. (*BLJ* 3: 179)

As "a mere spectator" of "the talents of *action*," Byron finds his own limitations and the limits of poetry as an intellectual and public project. With these final two tales, the representations and characters register this sense of "[a]pathy," "disgust," and "incapacity." Indeed, Byron's Eastern tales are viewed not only by the public, but perhaps, most intensely, by Byron himself. As spectator and creator, Byron expresses his personal reactions against provincial ties and his self-fashioning within an increasingly transnational poetic space. This space valorizes expression and associates the popular with foreign places and past times—a poetic enterprise that belies not only poetry's "scale of intellect" but also the scale of the individual poetic subject (*BLJ* 3: 179).[47]

These personal impulses undergird Byron's production of *The Corsair* and *Lara* much differently than in the previous two tales. Byron's "Oriental" subject is expanded to a scale of unclear borders, sometimes a mirror and sometimes an antithesis to British subjectivity. Perhaps this disenchantment with poetry's "scale" is why Conrad in *The Corsair* has no clear nationality or religion—an "outsider" in his illegibility as a recognized subject of any nation state. Conrad is an isolated man who, like Selim in *The Bride*, is a contested hero. While the stereotype posed by the tale is initially clear—a battle between the Western liberal and "Oriental" despot—Conrad's haunted conscience and perpetual bafflement with his own heroism thwart the straightforwardness of this stereotype.[48] Byron describes Conrad as "that man of loneliness and mystery" and "Stranger!" (1.173, 243). Conrad is described physically as having "swarthy cheek with sallower hue" and, like the Giaour, is masculine, heroic, with ineffable features and "mien" (1.207). Byron writes, "His features' deepening lines and varying hue / At times attracted, yet perplexed the view, / As if within that murkiness of mind / Worked feelings fearful, and yet undefined" (1.209–12). In effect, the consistent motif in Conrad's representation is his guilty conscience rather than his physical—racial, ethnic, gendered—appearance. Recursively thwarted by his conscience and "undefined" feelings, Conrad often seems to mirror Byron's personal anxieties and the semi-autobiographical posturing of *Childe Harold's Pilgrimage*. This mirroring is an example of Byron's projection of his poetic "mien" onto multiple personae of illegible provenance, creed, sexual orientation, race/ethnicity, and national ties.[49]

The Corsair's main characters—Conrad, Seyd, and Gulnare—populate an imagined universe left open to Byron's experimentation with poetic form and content, yet this universe is also less explicitly "Eastern" and Orientalist than in the previous tales. Byron refers to the "East" once in the work, when Gulnare urges Conrad to assassinate Seyd: "Oh! Could'st thou prove my truth, thou would'st not start, / Nor fear the fire that lights an Eastern heart" (3.352–3). This "Eastern" stereotype blunts Gulnare's personhood and agency. It also marks a shift from Byron's previous representations of women, including Leila and Zuleika. Gulnare is given the role of hero and assassin, and Conrad is accessory to Gulnare's heroic act of killing their "oppressor" Seyd (3.357). By raising a woman, Gulnare, to the status of Byronic victor when she assassinates Seyd, Byron recasts female heroism as central to the question of political borders and their allegiances.[50]

Instead of resolution for Gulnare or Conrad, the tale ends with the Corsair's disappearance and "death yet dubious" (3.694). This unclear fate of Conrad sets the scene for Byron's fourth tale, *Lara*, where the character of Conrad is supplanted for a tormented and obscure protagonist in Lara.[51] While Byron notes in *Lara*'s "Advertisement" that it might be seen as a "sequel" to *The Corsair* (*CPW* 3: 214), the narratives do not cohere into a unified storyline. In addition, the setting of *Lara* moves beyond any notion of preconceived "East" and to an imagined world of persistently obscure time and setting without clear geographical or ethnic signifiers. In *Lara*, Byron hardens a Westernized cosmopolitan myth of the poetic subject delinked from clear historical or cultural context.[52] This delinking culminates in a deracinated cosmopolitan subject who is free to roam and wander beyond geographical, national, and aesthetic borders. This freedom, however, is an imitation. Byron mimics the idea of a "world citizen" in *Lara* through Orientalist repetition and othering that is, in fact, habituated and reiterative.

Unlike the previous heroes, Lara is "home" and no longer voyaging across the imaginary "Orient." The protagonist has no travelogue or narrative of past experience for the reader to envisage. What the reader is given is Lara's *immediate* provincial past. Byron wrote to publisher John Murray on 24 July 1814 that Lara's "name only is Spanish—the country is not Spain but the Moon" (*BLJ* 4: 146).[53] This equivocation manifests in an array of characters and representations of ambiguous or unknown gender, religion, and ethnicity affiliations. The obscure Lara exists amidst this array of characters within a dislocated setting and era, uprooted from a familial, national, and racial identity.

Rather than starting with a clear Eastern setting or invoking classical antiquity as in the prior tales, *Lara* begins by describing the eponymous protagonist's inherited property. Byron describes a provincial scene with serfs as "gay retainers" "[w]ith tongues all loudness, and with eyes all mirth" (1.1–10).[54] In this environment, Lara is described as "self-exiled chieftain" and "Lord of himself;—that heritage of woe" (1.4, 14). This ambiguous "heritage of woe" reflects a world-weariness and resistant heroism lacking racial or ethnic signification. Thus, in addition to a deracinated cosmopolitan subject, the tale shows Lara's overexpansion of poetic subjectivity to the point of isolation and solipsism.

This overexpansion contrasts with the minuteness of individual experience when placed in the imagined Orient—a type of Eastern "sublime" upon which Byron capitalizes his cosmopolitan myth. In Book II of the *Critique of Judgment*, Kant writes:

> The sublime is that in comparison with which everything else is small. [...] because there is in our imagination a striving toward infinite progress and in our reason a claim for absolute totality, regarded as a real idea, therefore this very *inadequateness* for that idea in our faculty for estimating the magnitude of things of sense excites in us the feeling of a supersensible faculty. (87–9, emphasis mine)

This "inadequateness" is seen in Byron's distant and obscure narrative trajectory in *Lara*. In turn, the Eastern sublime confronts the limits of representation and representational techniques.[55] In *Lara*, Byron reinforces this sublime distance through commonplace hero tropes that deflect the details of Lara's personal history. Although Lara is home, no longer voyaging across the imaginary "Orient," he remains obscure. Essentially, Byron's Oriental subject is brought within and contained—an act of control and the subsuming of difference under Byron's cosmopolitanism. This act of containment separates a British identity from an Eastern "non-identity" in *Lara*, giving Byron the license for obscurity and a non-representational setting coded as "sublime."

In one scene, Lara walks through his halls alone at night, a phantom figure who does not interact with his environment. Lara's terrifying "aspect" emanates "a vital scorn of all: / As if the worst had fall'n which could befall / He stood a stranger in this breathing world" (1.313–15). As stranger and "thing of dark imaginings" whose "madness was not of the head, but heart," Lara's representation displaces anxieties of alterity onto the rhetoric of "madness" and Lara's "mental net" (1.317, 358, 381). Lara's identity depends on his obscurity and unknown past.

By tale's end, Lara has been mortally wounded and his faithful page, the gender-fluid Kaled, cares mutely for Lara's limp body. In this death scene, Lara's "dying tones are in that other tongue, / To which some strange remembrance wildly clung" (2.444–5). This "strange remembrance" seems known only to Kaled, who is not given dialogue throughout the scene. Byron continues:

> And once as Kaled's answering accents ceas'd,
> Rose Lara's hand, and pointed to the *East*:
> Whether (as then the breaking sun from high
> Rolled back the clouds) the morrow caught his eye,
> Or that 'twas chance, or some remembered scene
> That raised his arm to point where such had been (2.444, 466–71, emphasis mine)

Lara's gesturing towards the "East" marks a direction for his "mental net" of subjectivity. In response to Lara's gesture, Kaled "[s]carce ... seem'd to know, but turned away" (2.472–3). Kaled's turning away links impenetrability to the "East." This impenetrability challenges the ability of Byron's poetic subjects to freely traverse into the East, keeping it a space of obscurity unknown to all but Byron himself.

Evoking the shapes of Shelley's *Revolt of Islam*, Byron describes Kaled as talking "all idly unto shapes of air" in response to Lara's death, and her grief is compared to that of a "tigress in her whelpless ire" (2.607–9). Kaled's zoomorphic representation exacerbates her objectification and lack of humanity. Diego Saglia calls Kaled "the most conspicuous signifier of otherness and textual marker of dislocation" in *Lara* (401).[56] Throughout the work, Kaled remains ambiguously signified in terms of race, ethnicity, and gender. In the first canto, Kaled is praised for a hand "so femininely white it might bespeak / Another sex, when match'd with that smooth cheek" (1.576–9). In the second canto, Byron writes of Kaled as "that dark page / Who nothing fears, nor feels, nor heeds, nor sees" (2.427–8). Both "femininely white" and "dark page," Kaled's racial and gender switches never cohere into legibility. She occupies "a position without identity" akin to Spivak's subaltern (476). This position lacks agency, as seen in Kaled's "mute attention" and how "that stripling [Kaled] word or sign obey" (1.555, 511). What could have been a moment of sublime confession for Kaled at tale's end becomes an unexpected and wordless gender reveal to Lara's limp, dying body: "the sex confest; / And life return'd, and Kaled felt no shame— / What now to her was Womanhood or Fame?" (2.517–19). Kaled's description from wordless "stripling" to implied "Womanhood or Fame" is a scene of bewildered spectacle left ambiguous. This ambiguity of Kaled's gender reinforces her inscrutability and heightens the symbolism of Lara's gesturing to the "East."[57] Lara's gestural "East" serves as the defining motif through which Byron expresses Lara's geographical past and his connection to a distant and displaced "Orient."

Lara's death and Kaled's lingering presence at work's end reinforce Byron's Eastern sublime, a moment of obscure transcultural affiliation that positions Lara and Kaled in contradistinction to Lara's feudal staff. Byron writes that the "menials felt their usual awe alone, / But more for him [Lara] than them that fear was grown; [. . .] For them, at least, his soul compassions knew" (2.174–83). While Lara has "compassion" for his patrimonial staff, it is not a reciprocal relationship of mutual understanding. Lara trusts Kaled, his page from the

"East," more than his estate's vassals and serfs, via a shared sense of alterity. This alterity, however, is set in a bookended medieval dystopia, showing Byron's turn away from Orientalist practice. This turn can be seen in the lack of cultural allusions, footnotes, and Orientalist staging in *Lara* compared to his previous tales. Through Lara's return home and the transposed "Eastern" setting located in a feudal past, Byron defamiliarizes a Byronic poetic subjectivity into a category of its own alterity. This alterity is an imitative otherness, one also linked to Byron's own self-posturing of himself in these tales.[58]

"And Kaled—Lara—Ezzelin, are gone!": Concluding the Tales

As Edward Said has argued, at most "the 'real' Orient provoked a writer to his vision; it very rarely guided it" (*Orientalism* 22). We are reminded of Aravamudan's claim that the Orient is "nine parts invented and one part referential" (4). The fictiveness of the "Orient" provokes Byron's racially and ethnically disparate motifs and tropes—in sum, his Orientalist poetics. In this poetics, a seemingly unremarkable gesture such as Lara's dying gesture to the "East" takes on geopolitical import: Lara comes home to the "West" and Byron flattens the Westernized white male subject into a persona devoid of national, ethnic, or cultural ties. To do this, Byron depends on Kaled's inscrutable Eastern association, an East against which Lara's Westernization is constituted. Lara, like Byron, is of "no Country," but still ends up in the West—a West reliant on Byron's forging of a mutable, objectified Oriental other as the figure against which Lara is heightened into mythic heroism (*BLJ* 9: 156).[59]

This West is also an orientation toward whiteness. The global coordinates of East and West are racialized and gendered. As Ahmed notes in "A phenomenology of whiteness," "whiteness is an orientation that puts certain things within reach" (154). These things include "styles, capacities, aspirations, techniques, habits" so that race becomes a question of "what is within reach." Through this model of orientation, whiteness becomes "what is 'here,' as a point from which the world unfolds"

(154). The idea of "what is within reach" is seen in Lara's dying gesture to the "East," an East that is "there" and not "here." Over "there," this East is impenetrable, habituated into an unreachable counterpoint to white Western dominance.

In creating a textualized "East," Byron hazards an identity beyond the limits of one's nationality or place of origin—one that extends the poetic subject to unclear cultural and geographical signifiers. This extension and expansion of poetic identity represents the spirit of an era in which shifting global and cosmopolitan relations unsettle the limits and boundaries of poetic form and content. In addition, these tales starkly reveal the racial and gender politics of Byron's Orient and the power dynamics upon which Romantic subjectivity seeks aesthetic license. Reading these tales through a poetics of orientation provides an opportunity to interrogate Byron's shifting impulses and how these very impulses gave way to his later cultural and ethnic repertoires of global popularity, most notably *Don Juan*.

Like the other authors in this book, Byron's Eastern Tales show the contested space of lyric representation— how it yields to historical pressures and orients around various figurations of Orientalism to different effects. Byron's Orientalism is ironic, self-referential, imitative. It popularizes the self-conscious portrait of Byron as an Orientalist aesthete, reinforcing the centrality of the poet's gaze. This centrality, when read through the poetics of orientation, exposes the Orientalist attachments undergirding the ascendancy the white lyric subject rooted in the West. This lyric subject became Western and white, in part, through the racial, ethnic, and gendered logics of Orientalism. As I will discuss in my next chapter, the Oriental subject was forming alongside other racial and gender subjectivities during the Romantic period, including the Black woman poet or "poetess."

Notes

1. Ghislaine McDayter traces the rise of Byron's celebrity in *Byromania and the Birth of Celebrity Culture*.

2. After *Lara*, John Murray anonymously published two more of Byron's verse tales, *The Siege of Corinth* and *Parisina*. They appeared in the same volume in February 1816, two months before Byron left England.
3. For the texts/citations of Byron, I use *Lord Byron: The Complete Poetical Works*, ed. Jerome McGann, hereafter *CPW*.
4. As Nicholas Mason argues, tracing the marketing practices of *Childe Harold's Pilgrimage* recasts the material factors of "advertising and literature, the commodities industry and the culture industry" within a specific moment of literary history: Byron's popular rise (439). For more on Byron's rise to fame in the context of product branding and commodified aesthetics.
5. Translated from French, the epigraph from Fougeret de Monbron's *Le Cosmopolite* reads, "The universe is a sort of book, whose first page one has read when one has seen only one's own country. I have leafed through a great many that I have found equally bad. This inquiry has not been at all unfruitful. I hated my country. All the oddities of the different people among whom I have lived have reconciled me to it. Should I gain no other benefit from my travels than this, I will have regretted neither the pains nor the fatigues" (*CPW* 2: 3). For more on the epigraph, see Frederick Garber, *Self, Text, and Romantic Irony: The Example of Byron* and Joanna Wilkes, *Lord Byron and Madame de Staël: Born for Opposition*.
6. See also Naji B. Ouejian, "Orientalism: The Romantics' Added Dimension; Or, Edward Said Refuted."
7. By "imaginative geography" I am referring to Edward Said's discussion of the "universal practice of designating in one's mind a familiar space which is 'ours' and an unfamiliar space beyond 'ours' which is 'theirs' is a way of making geographical distinctions that can be entirely arbitrary" (*Orientalism* 54).
8. As Jerome Christensen has argued, Byron's literary and celebrity development consisted of the decades-long "collaborative invention of a gifted poet, a canny publisher, eager reviewers, and rapt readers" (xx).
9. Letter to Thomas Moore of 28 August 1813, in Lord Byron, *Byron's Letters and Journals*. Subsequent references to this edition will be cited as *BLJ*. While Moore's own deployments of Orientalism in works like *Lalla Rookh* are anchored in allegories of Irish nationalism, Byron, in addition to nationalist commentary, seeks expressions of anxious otherness, that is, alterity, in the literary and geographically unmoored "Orient" he creates.
10. All citations from Kant's political writings are taken from the second edition of Kant's *Political Writings*, ed. H. Reiss. I am thinking of Kant's argument for peaceful world interaction in

Toward Perpetual Peace including republicanism as the state norm, a worldwide "federation of free states," and "world citizenship" as defined by "conditions of universal hospitality" (99–106). See also Adriana Craciun, "Citizens of the World: Émigrés, Romantic Cosmopolitanism, and Charlotte Smith."

11. Kant deems taste a type of aesthetic judgment, See Immanuel Kant, *Critique of Judgment.*
12. After *Lara*, Byron's two remaining Eastern tales, *The Siege of Corinth* and *Parisina*, were published anonymously in the same volume in February 1816, just before his wife left him and after the Battle of Waterloo, both which would rupture his own poetic historiography. Also, in terms of historical narratives, they lack "Eastern" or "Turkish" perspective in that they lack Turkish characters, take place in classically imagined Greece and Italy, and presage Byron's philhellenic impulse. For more on Byron's Arabic-Islamic sources, see Samar Attar's *Borrowed Imagination* (2014).
13. In the third article of *Toward Perpetual Peace* Kant argues that "all men are entitled to present themselves in the society of others by virtue of their communal possession of the earth's surface ... Since the earth is a globe, they cannot disperse over an infinite area, but must necessarily tolerate one's company" (106).
14. Emily Haddad writes at length on the bridge between nineteenth-century poetry and Orientalism in *Orientalist Poetics: The Islamic Middle East in Nineteenth-Century English and French Poetry.*
15. *Vathek* inspired a host of other Orientalist enterprises, including the Middle Eastern setting of Southey's *Thalaba the Destroyer* (1801), Thomas Moore's *Lalla-Rookh* (1817), and John Keats's underworld setting in *Endymion* (1818), as well as Edgar Allan Poe's "Tamerlane" and "Landor's Cottage."
16. Scholars including Makdisi and Cohen-Vrignaud locate desire as integral to the character representations in the tales. In terms of Byron's representations of gender, his women characters are described inconsistently, disparately, and diffusely, as Shahidha Bari notes. See also, Caroline Franklin, "Some samples of the finest Orientalism: Byronic Philhellenism and proto-Zionism at the time of the Congress of Vienna," in *Romanticism and Colonialism: Writing and Empire 1780–1830*, ed. Fulford and Kitson, 229.
17. In terms of ethnic representation, *The Giaour*'s heroine, Leila, is Circassian. In *The Bride*, Zuleika is Turkish, along with the other protagonists, Selim and Giaffir. In *The Corsair*, the Aegean pirate hero, Conrad, is joined by a new heroine,

Gulnare. Described as "The Haram queen—but still the slave of Seyd," Gulnare assassinates the Turkish pasha Seyd after joining forces with Conrad (*CPW* 3: 2.224). In the *Corsair*'s supposed "sequel," *Lara*, Gulnare has been transplanted by Lara's faithful page, Kaled, who has ambiguous gender, ethnicity, and religious signification and is given no dialogue in the work.

18. See Stephen Cheeke, *Byron and Place: History, Translation, Nostalgia* (Basingstoke: Palgrave Macmillan, 2003); Katarina Gephardt, "The Occidentalist Costume: Lord Byron and Travelers' Perspectives on Eastern Europe"; Saree Makdisi, *Making England Western: Occidentalism, Race, and Imperial Culture* (Chicago and London: U of Chicago P, 2014); Diego Saglia, "Locating Byron: Languages, Voices, and Displaced Utterances"; and Andrew Warren, *The Orient and the Young Romantics*.

19. By the *Pilgrimage*'s final canto, published in April 1818, Harold's point of view has been discarded, and Byron writes in a letter to John Hobhouse that he [has or had] "become weary of drawing a line which every one seemed not to perceive: like the Chinese in Goldsmith's 'Citizen of the World', whom nobody would believe to be a Chinese, it was in vain that I asserted, and imagined, that I had drawn a distinction between the author and the pilgrim; and the very anxiety to preserve this difference, and disappointment at finding it unavailing, so far crushed my efforts in the composition, that I determined to abandon it altogether" (*CPW* 2: 122).

20. Edward Said's assessment of these types of "pilgrimage" literatures in *Orientalism* is fundamental to Orientalist poetics. Said writes of the Romantic pilgrimage, "From one end of the nineteenth century to the other—after Napoleon, that is—the Orient was a place of pilgrimage, and every major work belonging to a genuine if not always to an academic Orientalism took its form, style, and intention from the idea of pilgrimage there. In this idea as in so many of the other forms of Oriental writing we have been discussing, the Romantic notion of restorative reconstruction ([M.H. Abrams'] natural supernaturalism) is the principal source" (168).

21. The work's epigraph and prefatory "Advertisement" introduce the tale within a traditionary non-Eastern frame. The epigraph comes from Thomas Moore's *Irish Melodies* and the "Advertisement" famously invokes the tomb of ancient Athenian democrat, Themistocles, asking "When shall such hero live again?" (6).

22. Written in late 1812, *The Giaour* is not only fragmented but also filled with plot holes and disordered chronology, partially due to

Byron continually adding lines of different lengths to the work from an initial 344 to a final 1,334 lines by the seventh edition (*BLJ* 3: 100). In terms of verse, the tale is written predominantly in tetrameter verse and rhyming couplets. In addition to being inspired by Samuel Rogers's fragment, *Voyage of Columbus*, *The Giaour*'s genre can classified as "scholarly annotated poetry" and frame narrative poem.

23. For example, *The British Review* called *The Giaour* a "poetical anatomy" with a "mincing, comminuting, and subdividing method" (136, 134). *The British Review* 5 (October 1813).
24. Toni Morrison writes, "Canon building is empire building. Canon defense is national defense. Canon debate, whatever the terrain, nature, and range (of criticism, of history, of the history of knowledge, of the definition of language, the universality of aesthetic principles, the sociology of art, the humanistic imagination), is the clash of cultures. And all of the interests are vested" (132).
25. "Giaour" is used today as a derogatory term (Turkish: Gâvur), similar to the Arabic word "Kafir," both terms meaning a non-believer.
26. Byron cites William Beckford's villain in *Vathek* as a source for his "Giaour" (*CPW* 3: 415). Beckford's influence includes Byron's usage of the word "giaour." Byron began *The Giaour* in September 1812, the month he wrote the "Addition to the Preface" for the fourth edition of the *Pilgrimage*. See Lord Byron, *CPW* 2: 269; 3: 413.
27. See also Eric Meyer, "'I Know Thee not, I Loathe Thy Race.'"
28. *The Giaour*'s versification and footnote choices articulate what Alex Watson in *Romantic Marginality* calls "a new structure of national and global power [. . .] demonstrating the complex and important role of the margins of Romantic-period imaginative literature in the formulation of modern geopolitical identities" (5–11).
29. In terms of ethnographic influence, Byron's work invokes the Turkish oral tradition, as Leila's story of drowning at the hands of Hassan is a common folk tale derived from the drowning of several women by Ottoman Albanian ruler, Ali Pasha Tepelena, whom Byron famously met in 1809.
30. Via Hassan's implied point of view, Byron writes of Hassan's drowning of Leila, how he "watch'd as it [her bundled body] sank" into the "tide" where "all its hidden secrets sleep, / Known but to Genii of the deep" (376, 383, 384–5). This scene is a dialogue between another anonymous fisherman and Hassan/"Emir" (1.357).
31. The Giaour is described as having "dark hair" and "pale brow" (894–5), but he lacks the racialized whiteness of Leila.

32. Matthew J. A. Green writes that "[w]ith its provisions of fragmentary narratives focalized through multiple perspectives, *The Giaour* serves to demonstrate not only the power of the frame but also the [its] flexibility, [its ability] able to entertain radically opposed framing procedures without suspending ethical judgments" (30).
33. Like Leila, Hassan's mother is left without dialogue in the work, completely silent in the passage where she is told by an anonymous Tartar messenger of her son, Hassan's, murder at the hands of the Giaour (*CPW* 3: 689–722).
34. Cf. Byron's revised yet unpublished footnote referring to Lord Sligo (*CPW* 3: 423–4).
35 After the success of *The Giaour*, Byron wrote *The Bride* either in a purported four nights or one week alongside his editing and finishing of *The Giaour* (*BLJ* 3: 156).
36. The sentence continues, "—to wring my thoughts from reality, and take refuge in 'imaginings,' however 'horrible'"(*BLJ* 3: 184). It is also telling that Byron seeks validation from Moore, an Irish national poet who is unaffiliated with the Lake School.
37. Cf. Daniel P. Watkins's *Social Relations in Byron's Eastern Tales*. Leslie A. Marchand has noted that Byron's calculations and edits have also been attributed to the veiled expression of his love for his half-sister Augusta. *BLJ* (3: 199).
38. Later in the letter, Byron also asks that "in the last M.S. lines sent—instead of 'living heart' correct to 'quivering heart' it is in line 9th of the M.S. passage" (3: 163).
39. Byron writes to his friend Dr. Clark on his intention in writing *The Bride of Abydos*: "I also wished to try my hand on a female character in Zuleika—& have endeavoured as far as ye. grossness of our masculine ideas will allow—to preserve her *purity* without impairing the ardour of the attachment" (*BLJ* 3: 199, emphasis mine).
40. Byron's relationship with his half-sister, Augusta, influenced the creation of this work.
41. *CPW* (3: 1.1–13). All *Bride* quotations hereafter will be cited with canto and line number. "Gúl" is the Persian word for "rose."
42. Selim's father is Abdallah, Giaffir's brother, who Giaffir murdered. Selim does not understand exactly what "strife to rancour grew" in this Cain and Abel parable that Byron recreates between Giaffir and Abdallah (2.213).
43. This self-reflexive subjectivity mirrors the Byronic hero found at the end of *Childe Harold's Pilgrimage*. As Byron notes in *The Corsair*'s opening letter to Thomas Moore, "May I add a few

words on a subject on which all men are supposed to be fluent, and none agreeable?—Self" (*CPW* 3: 149).
44. Byron's "Oriental" subject exists, as Andrew Warren notes, within "a kind of Freudian Other Scene where memory and narcissistic projection are woven into narrative" (96).
45. Although heroic couplets often stress a line's final syllable, Byron varies his metrical foot, using unstressed rhymes as well as using heroic couplets for Gulnare's lines, leveling the gender dynamics of his verse.
46. Byron enjoyed their popular reception, but he considered the Eastern Tales largely inferior works. He called *Lara* "too little narrative—and too metaphysical" (*BLJ* 4: 295).
47. Part of the tales' difficulty lies in their stereotypes of the "East" and the rise of Orientalism simultaneously with comparative studies in the wake of Sir William Jones's foundational work. In Chapter 1 of this book, I discuss the intertwined genealogies of comparative studies and the lyric form in Romantic-era poetry.
48. Sharafuddin explains that Conrad "triumphs over him [Seyd] by assassination. Admittedly, he does not strike the blow, but he benefits from it, and he is responsible for it in that it was his action which puts Gulnare, the assassin, on his side. The fact that this action was an act of liberal generosity (protectiveness towards women) only serves to entangle the web of good and evil more thoroughly" (259).
49. Conrad's attraction to Gonsalvo is also a moment of queer evocation that shows Byron's use of Orientalism to experiment with gender and sexuality (1.153).
50. Felicia Hemans, who I discuss in Chapter 3, uses Byronic hero tropes in her poems with women speakers and characters. This scene is also notable for Conrad's passive response to Gulnare's power, as well as the relationship between Conrad and the young sailor, Gonsalvo.
51. *Lara* was anonymously published in 1814, between the publication of the second and third cantos of *Childe Harold's Pilgrimage*.
52. Thomas Peacock's *Essay on Fashionable Literature* (1818), which Byron's tales presage, can help us rethink the relationship between high Romanticism and Orientalism by virtue of Byron's heroic ideal. Paul Hamilton argues that "ascriptions of inferiority to the genre of popular Romanticism just beg the critical question for Peacock. Yet Peacock only highlights the political fear of the higher class of radicals that enfranchisement doesn't merely add to the numbers of the cultured classes, but rather takes them down. The new solidarity removes the very possibil-

ity of that finely tuned, imaginatively sympathetic gesture which had agitated in its radical cause" (227).
53. As noted by critics including Diego Saglia, the work's setting may evoke Spain, but it is never stated in the work. See Saglia (400–1).
54. *CPW* 3. All *Lara* quotations hereafter will be cited with canto and line number.
55. As Ian Balfour and others argue, conceptualizations of the sublime are rooted in "the poststructuralist critique of representation generally" (4). Cf. Harold Needler's "'She Walks in Beauty' and the Theory of the Sublime."
56. This is also a dislocation from the text of *Lara* itself. As Byron reminds us, Kaled is meant to stand in for his earlier character of Gulnare in *The Corsair*.
57. Kaled's marginalization is addressed in the work's closing lines. Kaled, in "quiet grief" over Lara's death and unable to leave Lara's mortal remains, "lies by him she lov'd; / Her tale untold— her truth too dearly prov'd" (2.626–7). The "untold" nature of Kaled's story is not singular, however, as Lara's life story is also left ambiguous.
58. After *Lara*, John Murray anonymously published two more of Byron's verse tales, *The Siege of Corinth* and *Parisina*. They appeared in the same volume in February 1816, two months before Byron left England.
59. Byron's letter to Count Alfred d'Orsay of 22 April 1823 (*BLJ* 9: 156).

Chapter 3

The Racialized Poetess

> THE poet asks, and Phillis can't refuse
> Phillis Wheatley Peters, "An Answer to the Rebus"

Along with male writers like Byron and Shelley, Romantic women writers including Felicia Hemans, Mary Shelley, Letitia Elizabeth Landon, Maria Edgeworth, Charlotte Dacre, Ann Radcliffe, and many others faced the consolidation of British national identity and the emergence of British imperialism as propellants for their writing. The white-male dominant literary tradition they entered was undergoing political, cultural, and aesthetic changes while they situated themselves and their positionalities in shifting notions and expectations of women authors. They grappled with increasingly global frameworks for literary production and placed themselves and their works within new Orientalist frameworks.

Women writers of the Romantic era tend to fall into several genres with Orientalist affinities, including the novel, the romance, and lyric poetry. Across these genres, prominent Orientalist tropes include fantasy, escapism, cross-cultural identification or sympathy, and later in the period, fear and antipathy. For many writers, Orientalist settings and representations became veiled projections of contemporaneous military and political struggles of the growing British Empire. For example, Felicia Hemans, the most widely read woman poet of the nineteenth century, was fascinated from a young age by stories of the Peninsular War. Hemans's upbringing in a military family propelled her to write *Tales and Historic Scenes*

(1819) and *Records of Woman* (1828), both of which represent women speakers through culturally diffuse and oftentimes Orientalist settings. Hemans's imagined global settings raise the question of a writer's responsibility or role in cultural production. Specifically, the ethics of representation in relation to the writer's identity—who/what they can or should represent in writing—is significant in reading Hemans's poems about women speakers from around the world. These questions feed into the larger examination of literary invention versus factuality in Orientalism and racial representation.

As a celebrated "poetess" figure of transatlantic celebrity, Felicia Hemans is known for creating imagined communities of women-centered poems, but the ethnic and racial logics of her global imagination have not been fully excavated.[1] In her poems about women, Hemans's imagination consolidates a white British woman's gender and racial identity in contrast to the racialized other. This consolidation has critical erasures, most glaringly Black women, and forges in Hemans's poetry an imperial, white standard against which other works by women have been measured and studied. How do we respond to this erasure? This chapter starts by offering new readings of Hemans's poems to uncover the historic racialization of the poet/poetess as white. This racialization is fueled by gendered Orientalism and antiblack logics rooted in the language of affections. As Tricia Lootens reminds us, "Who made the Poetess [and poet] white? No one, not ever" (7). To highlight Lootens's important provocation and question the implicit whiteness of the poet, the second part of this chapter discusses the poems of Phillis Wheatley Peters and centers her poetics.[2]

Through this chapter's juxtaposition of Wheatley and Hemans, I first disrupt the lack of attention to race in discussions of Hemans's poetry. From there I trace Hemans's ways of imagining global solidarity in contradiction with her consolidation of a particular kind of white femininity that appropriates and effaces forms of racialized suffering. In contrast, I show how Wheatley's Black poetic imagination counters Hemans's reproduction of whiteness, Orientalism, and the antiblack logics of the Romantic lyric tradition. In doing so, I advance what we can carry forth from poets like Wheatley and what we want to stop reproducing through a white-centered account of Romantic women's writing.[3]

Moving from Hemans to Wheatley, I disorient a neat chronology of women's writing in this chapter and seek an alternative genealogy of aesthetics in Romantic poetics. As Lisa Lowe writes, "the *past conditional temporality* of the 'what could have been'" opens up a space of a

> different kind of thinking, a space of productive attention to the scene of loss, a thinking with twofold attention that seeks to encompass at once the positive objects and methods of history and social science, and also the matters absent, entangled, and left unavailable by its methods. (*Intimacies* 40–1)

For Wheatley's poetics, this alternative space of seeing and thinking heralds a counter-narrative of aesthetic thought that resists the white-male dominant tradition she enters. Wheatley was a transatlantic celebrity and recognized "Poetess" figure before Hemans, and her poetics reorients this book's gaze. Orientation is both a looking forward and a looking back and, as Ahmed notes, orientation means a shift in "world facing; that is, a way of gathering things around so they 'face' a certain direction" (*Queer Phenomenology* 118). In gathering around Wheatley's works, I show how Wheatley's poetics illustrates an alternative route of Romanticism outside the frame of white supremacist logic.

Wheatley is commonly studied from the vantage point of an American literary tradition, but her first and only poetry collection, *Poems on Various Subjects*, was published in London in 1773. Reprinted throughout the nineteenth century, the collection was an undeniable transatlantic success, and its historic frontispiece of Wheatley is one of the first known frontispieces of an American woman writer.[4] To this point, Wheatley has been commonly read through early American, circum-, or transatlantic studies, but her relevance to Romanticism and other contemporaneous movements has been understudied. While critics like Nandini Bhattacharya, Christina Sharpe, Vincent Carretta, and Megan Walsh have done important work in reading Wheatley's literary aesthetics, few have claimed her importance and correspondence to Romantic poetics and theory.[5] At a time in literary studies when disciplinary divides are being challenged, examining the significance of Wheatley's poetics to Romanticism can also uncover the racial logics undergirding what we consider both aesthetically and methodologically important.

Sara Ahmed's queer phenomenology offers a route to map the entanglement between race, gender, poetics, and power in this chapter. Ahmed discusses a mixed or queer orientation of phenomenology, one that refuses the world's "inheritance of whiteness, refusing even the desire to follow that line" (*Queer Phenomenology* 155). This refusal creates new lines away from whiteness—lines that collectively intersect, merge, and create new spaces while expanding the ones we occupy. A new route requires a political energy that might disorient a world oriented around whiteness and reorient our own relation to this whiteness. In reorienting, the poetics of orientation seeks to include and amplify Black women—an integral part of the range of racialized others who are positioned, like the Oriental subject, in variously conflictual and antagonistic relations to the white male lyric subject of Romanticism.

Situating the Racialized "Poetess"

The figure of the "poetess" expands this book's readings of the rise of the Romantic lyric subject—a lyric subject rooted in Western imperialism and the rise of whiteness contrasted with racialized others. Both Wheatley and Hemans are part of a transatlantic poetess tradition during a period of national identity building and the politicization of the poetess figure itself.[6] As Tricia Lootens argues, Hemans's reputation as exemplary "Poetess" did not reach an apex until the second-wave feminism of 1975 and the publication of Cora Kaplan's *Salt and Bitter and Good: Three Centuries of English and American Women Poets*. Kaplan calls Hemans's poetic feelings that of "the most genteel English wife" (93). As a white British woman without much travel experience, Hemans orients herself in what Lootens calls "the poet's imagined transnational, multiracial, interfaith community of female suffering" (66). This community is hegemonic in that the European white woman speaks and writes on behalf of non-white women. Hemans, while writing about women and critical of patriarchal nationalism, positions her whiteness against an extensive and obscure backdrop of global, Orientalist representations. Hemans's proto-white feminism demonstrates the problem with imaginative representations existing apart from actual encounter and bilateral understanding. As a white woman poet, she stands in stark contrast to Wheatley's writing that takes up Romantic modes of lyric subjectivity and transcendence to imagine emancipation and counter white supremacist logic.

Bakary Diaby, reminding scholars of the marginalization of Black women in Romantic studies, urges, "Don't forget the women," and calls for "examining the period's aestheticization of women of color, across a variety of cultural productions and from a host of different authors" (252). Diaby's call is not a metaphor and seeks an active interrogation of the gendered and racial logics undergirding what we study and consider worth studying. I trace Wheatley's importance to Romanticism to create an aperture through which to see an alternative, Black-created field of poetics. Wheatley's difference from the poetry of Hemans and other celebrated "poetess" figures should not be marked as a negation or exclusion from Romantic poetics but an opportunity to read new formations of poetic subjectivities and representations.

In turning away from Hemans and toward Wheatley, I push back against what Christina Sharpe calls "the singularity of antiblackness" through which slavery and Black life are remembered and recorded in the "fictions of the archive" (106, 13). Sharpe writes that in the United States,

> slavery is imagined as a singular event even as it changed over time and even as its duration expands into supposed emancipation and beyond. But slavery was not singular; it was, rather, a singularity[.] ... Emancipation did not make Black life free; it continues to hold us in that singularity. (106)

The singularities of slavery and antiblackness constitute a density of space and time that forge the space from which Wheatley must counter-visualize new forms and temporalities against the white gaze. This counter-visualizing deconstructs the foundations of white poetic regimes of Black erasure. It also decenters a white womanhood founded on the preservation of patriarchal nationalism. In this countering, self-preservation of Wheatley's own subjectivity is not antithetical to resistance or activism. Rather, it is a determined act of willful imagining that places Black women's voices into culturally recognized positions of visibility and representation.

Spivak warns against "global laundry lists with 'woman' as a pious item." Representation has not "withered away" but needs to be rebuilt from the perspective of the marginalized and silenced (104). This reconstruction from a grassroots Marxist formation builds solidarity across different races, genders, sexualities, and classes. And within this new formation, marginalized subjects, such as Black women, Indigenous women, and women of color, can act in solidarity based on a shared common interest that is useful for a coalition of women beyond individual categories of race, ethnicity, sexuality, class, and nationality. Chandra Mohanty decenters Western feminism and uses a feminist praxis that is anti-racist and decolonial. This praxis avoids vague notions of sisterhood or collectivity based on assumed shared experiences or "complete identification with the other" (3). It avoids a white Western reductionist model of "woman" or "solidarity" and finds purpose in coalition building and a politics of difference. Difference is key, so I take a feminist route that maintains singularity while finding common ground—what could still connect disparate writers like Wheatley and Hemans.

Hemans's Affective Poetics

To trace the racialization of Hemans's poetess figure, I turn to representative poems from two of Hemans's most popular poetry collections, *Records of Woman (1828)* and *Songs of the Affections* (1830). Both collections describe a range of protagonists in varying private and public roles of individual heroism, rebellion, and resistance.[7] I argue that Hemans builds affinity between these protagonists through their consolidation of a universal white womanhood. Hemans's "The Indian City" is an Orientalist poem about motherhood, warfare, and the intersecting identity and gender roles of the protagonist, Maimuna. Her later poem, "Woman on the Field of Battle," is a symbolic poem that ponders an anonymous dead woman as an ideal model of battlefield prowess. "Woman on the Field of Battle" shows Hemans distancing her poetry from clear national and racial borders and invoking "affection" as a binding force of women's subjectivity.

By "affection" I am using the definition offered by the *Oxford English Dictionary*, as "senses relating to the mind" ("affection, n."). I illustrate how Hemans's poetics, in contrast to Wheatley's, legitimize white women's feelings ("affections") through her ultimate valorization of "affection's might" ("Woman on the Field of Battle"). This valorization excludes Black women and racializes affect/senses as white. It excludes those who are dispossessed of individual ownership and rights, such as Wheatley, who are writing poetry not for the engenderment of feelings alone but for the purpose of actual emancipation. In "Affective Economies," Ahmed asks, "How do emotions work to align some subjects with some others and against other others? How do emotions move between bodies?" (117). Hemans's tropes of emotions and affect use a coded language that aligns her speakers with British white imperialism. These poems work in concrete ways to shape not only the body of the speaker, but the "body" of the nation state. This collective body is shaped by Hemans's imagining of the shared suffering, loss, and death of women across nations and ages. Fostering fellow feeling and identification, Hemans participates in both imagining global solidarity in her poems about women while centering a white British women's gender and racial subjectivity in contrast to the racialized other.

In *Records of Woman* (1828), Hemans combines the stories of women from around the world and legitimizes them as "*Records*." Hemans creates affective and nationalist ties between their struggles. Her imagining of a sisterhood becomes a force of universalized "womanhood" that continues throughout her later works, such as *Songs of the Affections* (1830). *Records* features nineteen poems with women protagonists from history and contemporary life, including Joan of Arc, Lady Arabella Stuart, Italian sculptress Properzia Rossi, an unnamed Native American woman, and Indian war leader, Maimuna. Of the three victorious heroines in *Records of Woman*, Maimuna in "The Indian City" is the only woman of color. The other two victors are Joan of Arc and the Queen of Prussia. By including a Muslim Indian woman in her group of victors, Hemans seems to want to diversity the nationalist typology of her heroic women protagonists, but for what purpose? These *Records* make no mention of transatlantic slavery and exclude Black women (free or enslaved) from representation. This erasure contributes to the antiblackness of the Poetess tradition. It shows how Hemans's poetry is part of a larger project of racial erasure and control.

Like her contemporaries, Hemans's Orientalism in poems like "The Indian City," "The Wife of Asdrubal" (1819), "Moorish Bridal Song" (1825), and "Indian Woman's Death Song" (1828) is inflected with dualisms like East/West, ancient/present, commonplace/exotic. Sara Ahmed writes of the futurity of Orientalism that results from its orientation of "towardness," how "direct[ing] one's gaze and attention toward the other, as an object of desire, is not indifferent, neutral, or casual: we can redescribe 'towardness' as energetic. In being directed toward others, one acts, or is committed to specific actions, which point toward the future" (*Queer Phenomenology* 120). This future orientation is what Benedict Anderson would call homogeneous, empty time— that which deconstructs the "imaginary distinctions between the West and Orient, but would also shape how bodies cohere, by facing the same direction" (*Queer Phenomenology* 120). Ahmed's phenomenology of Orientalism produces a subjectivity that is interpellated by repeatedly being perceived by those "around" it.

The question of the Orientalized female subject in Hemans's poetry has been raised by scholars such as Susan Wolfson and Amy L. Gates and is interrogated comprehensively by Sharifah A. Osman. Osman asserts that "If woman's empire is her home, then Hemans's critique of the domestic ideal through the tragic lives of her Byronic mothers and sisters demonstrates the physical and emotional toll that a nation with imperialistic ambitions like Britain exacts on its devoted citizens" (para. 41). This pairing, however, does not hold in "The Indian City"; the patriotism and nationalism of Maimuna is one that, in addition to a sorority of domestic affections, is borne out of individualized precarity and necessity.

"The Indian City" is divided into three parts and written in third-person narration with rhythmic couplets; it describes the ruin of an unnamed Indian city as the result of a grieving mother, Maimuna. As a devout Muslim, Maimuna incites religious war between Muslims and Hindus to avenge her innocent son's death. She becomes a beacon of proud rebellion for the Muslim forces. While carrying her dead son through the Indian city, she vows not to weep until "'yon city, in ruins rent, / Be piled for its victim's monument'" (135–6). Once the war is underway, however, Maimuna does not enjoy the fruits of revenge but rather, feels "[v]ain, bitter glory!—the gift of grief" and "[s]ickening she [turns] from her sad renown, / As a king in death might reject his crown" (179, 185–6). Ultimately, her Muslim side is victorious and destroys the city, but Maimuna, now a "martyr," dies with a "broken heart" and wishes to be buried with her dead son (213, 214). The poem ends with a solemn description of the now seemingly abandoned city and a declaration that "This was the work of one deep heart wrung!" (228). The narrative here is one of trauma, grief, and revenge, ultimately ending in Maimuna's sacrifice.

Both Wolfson and Osman articulate the Orientalist representation of Maimuna, yet they overlook the physical setting, i.e. "wild vine," and its Orientalist description in the poem. While Wolfson juxtaposes Hemans and Percy Bysshe Shelley via themes of revolutionary violence, she focalizes the question of displacement through historical events and genres, not the Orientalist setting. She states that these displacements "dramatize tyranny in figures of ... female revenge, often in spectacular transgression of 'feminine' character" (115). Maimuna is one of these figures, but in addition to transgressing traditional ideals of femininity, she does so amidst a lush and exotic landscape that affords the British reader a safe distance or remove from the catastrophic trauma of the poem's narrative.[8]

The first part of the poem is where we see this Orientalist physical description most clearly. Hemans's begins this part with the focus on the unnamed Indian city suffused with verdant greenery and sunlight:

> ROYAL in splendour went down the day
> On the plain where an Indian city lay,
> With its crown of domes o'er the forest high,
> Red as if fused in the burning sky (1–4)

This suffusion of light is dotted with the "plantain [that] glitter'd with leaves of gold, / As a tree midst the genii-gardens old . . . And the stems of the cocoas were shafts of fire" (9–12). Here, the Orientalist setting is also supernatural ("genii-gardens"). Hemans paints a "royal" scene for the reader in which the "gleam" of a "white pagoda" shines (13), and through this "scene of beauty" wanders "a noble Moslem boy," Maimuna's son (27–8). The boy relishes his view of "the stately city . . . Like a pageant of clouds in its red repose," wandering "in breathless joy" until eventually, he trespasses on Hindu "holy ground" (29–30, 36). This act of religious defiance ushers the reader into the second part of the poem, which deals with the aftermath of the boy's trespassing on Hindu "holy ground" (36), for which he is mortally punished. He returns to his mother with "a gash on his bosom" (72), dying in her arms of mortal "wounds from the children of Brahma born" (80).[9] Maimuna witnesses her son's last breaths: "One moment—the soul from the [son's] face had pass'd! / Are there no words for that common wo?" (96–7). Instead of instantly reacting, Maimuna is motionless, "bow'd down mutely o'er her dead" (109). Once she sees "no reply" in her son's "half-shut eye" and knows he is surely dead (118, 117), she shrieks in agony. Suddenly enraged, she rises up and seek revenge for her son's death:

> And what deep change, what work of power,
> Was wrought on her secret soul that hour?
> How rose the lonely one?—She rose
> Like a prophetess from dark repose!
> And proudly flung from her face the veil,
> And shook the hair from her forehead pale (121–6)

In a moment directly linked to prophecy, Maimuna defiantly throws off her Muslim veil, emblem of feminine piety, and vows to avenge her son's death by destroying the eponymous "Indian City" (143). She becomes a figure of gender transgression and prophecy only after the tragic death of her son, and her assumption of this prophetic role transforms her into Hemans's Byronic heroine. Hemans was inspired by Byron's work, and she includes lines from *Childe Harold's Pilgrimage* in the epigraph to this poem: "*What deep wounds ever clos'd without a scar? / The heart's bleed longest, and but heal to wear / That which disfigures it. —Childe Harold*" (368). Julie Melnyk notes that out of the nineteen poems in *Records*, Hemans uses Byron in six of the poems' epigraphs (146).[10] Read in conjunction, the heroes and heroines of Hemans and Byron are made more "Occidental" and white *through* their Orientalist staging in texts like "The Indian City" and Byron's Eastern Tales.

The heroines in *Records* are influenced by Byron, yet they are less Eurocentric in terms of representation. For example, they are Greek, Italian, Native American, Indian Muslim, Hindu, and African, among others. The focalization of large, historical moments through specific female subjectivities, like that of Maimuna, is what enables Hemans to simultaneously address questions of religious nationalism and militancy while building a woman's network of white-centered solidarity. Myra Cottingham argues for the "subtle coding" of Hemans's protest of "masculine warfare" in poems like "The Indian City" (283). Cottingham sees Hemans's challenge to her readers as a sacrifice of Hemans's "own potential role as a more militantly philosophical writer in favour of a more psychologically realistic expression of futility" (283). This futility paradoxically affords Hemans the opportunity to capitalize on certain identity categories and positions of power (hero, warrior, leader, prophet) and illustrate her emboldened subjectivity.

It is not until the third and final section of the poem that Maimuna fully transforms into the hero capable of leading a nation. The sound of "the gathering of Moslem war" begins this section (146), and the previously shining city has lost its luster. The plantain plant from the idyllic first section no longer glitters "with leaves of gold" but rather, offers "shade, / As the light of the lances along it play'd" (149–50). Maimuna has ignited war:

> Maimuna from realm to realm had pass'd,
> And her tale had rung like a trumpet's blast;
> There had been words from her pale lips pour'd,
> Each one a spell to unsheath the sword. (161–4)

She is also on the frontlines of war as a "queenly foe, / [with] Banner, and javelin, and bended bow" (171–2). Rather than illustrating Maimuna's physical prowess in this battle, however, Hemans notes her "deeper power [which] on her forehead sate" (173), the mental power of vision and prophecy:

> Her eye's wild flash through the tented line
> Was hail'd as a spirit and a sign,
> And the faintest tone from her lip was caught,
> As a Sybil's breath of prophetic thought. (175–8)

Again, we see Maimuna's prophetic power, that her tale of woe has moved her Muslim brethren to war and torn the city asunder. Even if Maimuna is not literally a prophet, the power of her tale still rings "like a trumpet's blast" and is able to mobilize an army (162).

Once the war is over, however, Maimuna does not rejoice in or relish her side's victory and spoils. She feels no relief or redemption, only "[v]ain, bitter glory," which sickens her to turn "from her sad renown, / As a king in death might reject his crown" (179, 185–6). Her "wounded" heart has become "weary," and she seems to be close to death herself: "*She wither'd faster, from day to day*" (157, 198, 188). While the idyllic Indian city has been ruined and "rent" as she intended, Maimuna does not feel glory or peace. She lies supine and seemingly defeated on a "couch" murmuring "a low sweet cradle song, / Strange midst the din of a warrior throng, / A song of the time when her boy's young cheek / Had glow'd on her breast in its slumber meek" (201–4). Maimuna has transformed back into a gentle maternal figure and given up her role of warrior and heroine.[11] While it seems Maimuna has lost the will to live, one day, a "gust o'er her soul again" suddenly provokes her to start up and declare, "'Give him [my son] proud burial at my side!'" (208). According to her wishes, she is then laid to rest with her dead son where "the [Hindu] temples are fallen" (210), a last act of reprisal and trespass against those who murdered her beloved son. The poem ends with a panoramic vista of the ruined city:

> Palace and tower on that plain were left,
> Like fallen trees by the lightning cleft;
> The wild vine mantled the stately square,
> The Rajah's throne was the serpent's lair,
> And the jungle grass o'er the altar sprung—
> This was the work of one deep heart wrung! (223–8)

The once picturesque Orientalist setting is gone, all because of one mother's "deep heart wrung!" (228). Significantly, the poem begins and ends by invoking the "heart," first with Byron's epigraph, "*What deep wounds ever clos'd without a scar? / The heart's bleed longest*" (368).[12] More than battlefield prowess, it is Maimuna's ultimately "wounded" and "weary" heart that structures and frames her multiple identity roles. This heart motif can be found throughout Hemans's oeuvre, as Hemans focalizes her poetic subjectivity in affective over physical senses, as "Woman on the Field of Battle" also illustrates.

Maimuna's heroism is reinforced by her martyrdom, yet this martyrdom is fraught with contradiction, as it speaks to a woman-centered fatalism that is transgressive in terms of its implications with suicide.[13] Thus, Maimuna's martyrdom is also an act of gender transgression and performativity.[14] While many scholars have argued that Hemans reiterates nineteenth-century gender norms in her works, protagonists like Maimuna pressure this argument by inhabiting overlapping roles like mother, pious Muslim, prophet, war leader, storyteller, invalid, sentimentalist, and non-Christian martyr. The multiplicity we see in Maimuna's identity formation is what Judith Butler would call a narrative of becoming.[15] In *Undoing Gender* (2004), Butler writes of narrative becoming in terms of performative gender: "If gender is performative, then it follows that the reality of gender is itself produced as an effect of the performance" (218). Through Maimuna's own gender performativity, we see a mechanism of how

Maimuna's characterization is reproduced and altered during that reproduction.

Because of Maimuna's transformative leaps of character, she becomes a symbol of resistance and feminist agency for Hemans's imagining of global solidarity. To process the grief of losing her son and forge her own "livable existence" (Butler 206), Maimuna must transgress traditional gender roles to survive her circumstances. This transgression eventually enables her to establish her voice and place in history.[16] Maimuna's narrative of becoming illustrates Butler's paradox that "we must be undone in order to do ourselves: we must be part of a larger social fabric of existence in order to create who we are" (100–1). This is to say, Maimuna's role switching between doting mother, prophet, Byronic heroine, and religious martyr does not cause her undoing or death but, rather, weaves her more inextricably into the public consciousness and cements her identity as a legitimate subject with the rights and opportunity to participate as "outsider within" Hemans's Orientalist imaginary (Collins 14).

This Orientalist imaginary displaces Maimuna and her rebelliousness at a safe distance from British soil. This displacement also functions to appropriate and efface a racialized suffering in contrast to British white femininity. William Hazlitt writes about how the language of poetry "naturally falls in with the language of power. The imagination is an exaggerating and exclusive faculty: it takes from one thing to add to another: it accumulates circumstances together to give the greatest possible effect to a favorite object" (*Characters of Shakespeare's Plays* 4.214).[17] Hemans's narrative of Maimuna's suffering, heroism, and sacrifice uses this exaggerating and exclusive imagination to empower a certain type of implied "woman" over others: the woman who imagines and feels with domestic safety and distance from actual war and violence.

The racialized assumptions undergirding Hemans's "woman" figure turn to indeterminate symbolism in "Woman on the Field of Battle," where Hemans's "woman" remains unnamed. The "Woman" evoked in this poem elides clear markers of identity categories such as nationality, race and ethnicity, religion, sexual orientation, age, and class. The poem serves as a paradigm of womanhood not only in its larger collection, *Songs of the Affections*, but the symbolism of Hemans's "woman" across her works.[18] The poem is made up of fifteen quatrains alternating between dimeter and trimeter lines, with a limited third-person point of view. Its epigraph reads, "*Where hath not a woman stood, / Strong in affection's might? a reed, upborne / By an o'er mastering current!*"[19] The "affection" here possesses a "might" that withstands an "o'er mastering current" (3). This affection is something that empowers the woman, who stands "strong" amidst "the fierce battle-storm" (3). The lingering question of the speaker's exact vantage point is never fully answered.

The poem begins:

> GENTLE and lovely form,
>   What didst thou here,
> When the fierce battle-storm
>   Bore down the spear? (1–4)

The stark contrast between the woman's "gentle and lovely form" and the "fierce battle-storm" is further reinforced by the rhyme. The next stanza commands, "Tell, that amidst the best, / Thy work was done!" (7–8). The dead woman in this poem, like Maimuna, is immediately positioned amidst a battle scene, amongst "the best" warriors, and her "work" is equated with these (presumably male) compatriots. The poem's movement from interrogative to imperative statement asserts the command of this voiceless, nameless figure.

In the next stanza, the speaker continues to meditate on this unnamed woman:

> Yet strangely, sadly fair,
>   O'er the wild scene,
> Gleams, through its golden hair,
>   That brow serene. (9–12)

From the proud prospect of this woman's "best" work, the poem's speaker shifts abruptly with the interruptive, "Yet." This banner-strewn landscape signals not only the triumph of a war hero but also the "sadly fair" and "serene" countenance of a woman whose story is unknown to the speaker. Soon, we learn that this woman is now a "Slumberer!" whose "early bier / Friends should have crown'd, / Many a flower and tear / Shedding around" (17–20). The speaker laments that the dead woman's friends have not "crown'd" her "bier" or shed a "tear" of grief for her (18, 17, 19), and the subsequent stanzas continue in this elegiac mode of honoring and commemorating the woman.

The speaker argues that the woman should have been mourned by her "[s]isters" who "above the grave / Of thy repose, / Should have bid violets wave / With the white rose" (25, 26–8). The delicate imagery contrasts with the woman's battlefield prowess. Like Maimuna, this woman has died without fanfare and lies seemingly forgotten in the ruins of this "wild scene" (10).

After this elegiac mode, the speaker turns again to interrogation:

> Why?—ask the true heart why
>   Woman hath been
> Ever, where brave men die
>   Unshrinking seen? (37–40)

The beginning question asks "why" women have died without the same recognition as men, but it ends with an unclear dangling modifier, "[u]nshrinking seen" (40). Is it the "brave men" or the aforementioned "woman" who are/is "unshrinking seen" in battle? Regardless of the subject (who is "seen"), the "true heart" pleads for a response, to no avail (37). The speaker then ponders possible reasons for joining a war or engaging in battle. Hemans writes of "Some [who came], for that stirring sound, / A warrior's name" (43–4). Other reasons for joining the battle include "for the stormy play / And joy of strife;" and/or "to fling away / A weary life" (45–6, 47–8). These are not the reasons of the elegized "woman," however. Rather, they are the reasons of "[p]roud reapers" (42). This woman, in contrast, is described as "pale sleeper ... With the slight frame / and the rich locks, whose glow / Death cannot tame" (49–52). The woman lacks a name or specific history but is still exceptional and untamed by death. She has unknown reasons for going to battle and being found dead by the speaker. Her "pale" color and "golden hair" evoke whiteness, and as Lawrie Balfour notes, the "white presumptions of identitylessness" that function to keep histories of racialization unrecalled (795). Racialization is not always an explicit event or act, and it can occur in moments like these—"golden," "pale," "slight," and "rich"— words with racial assumptions linked to idealized whiteness.

In the final two quatrains, the speaker eventually shares this dead woman's true motive—love:

> Only one thought, one power,
>   *Thee* could have led,
> So, through the tempest's hour,
>   To lift thy head!
> Only the true, the strong,
>   The love, whose trust
> Woman's deep soul too long
>   Pours on the dust! (53–60)

This woman, like Maimuna, has been led by "love," the "one thought, one power" that propels her to "lift [her] head" and persevere. The woman's "love" reinforces the epigraph's claim for "affection's might."[20] The strength of affection is aligned with the woman's work, and this affection is not limited to sentimental passivity. Affection becomes a force of action used by Hemans's women—women who reach a symbolic order in "Woman on the Field of Battle." By implying the whiteness and affective might of this ideal "woman," Hemans links affection and its "might" to whiteness. Ahmed reminds us that "emotions do things, and they align individuals with communities—or bodily space with social space—through the very intensity of their attachments" ("Affective Economies" 119). The intensity of these attachments is seen in Hemans's imagining of white women's emotions/"affection" as equal to battlefield strength.

Through her racialized poetics, Hemans maneuvers the circuitous routes between multiple subject positions of womanhood. These positions are white dominant, Orientalist, exclude Black women, and displace race onto emotions or affective modes of subjectivity. In "The Indian City," Maimuna's Orientalist representation transgresses and transcends the privacy of "domestic affections." Maimuna represents a complicated doubling of subject position—first, as woman, and second, as "Other." This otherness forges Hemans's Orientalism as a type of racial logic distinct from the white Poetess figure Hemans herself occupies. Hemans's "Woman on the Field of Battle" idealizes a feminine subjectivity that is, like Maimuna, fearless warrior, but here, the unnamed woman is not transgressive or suicidal. She is an idealized, identityless white woman delinked from national borders and individuality. She symbolizes a white woman's affection as a universalized force beyond self, race, or place.

What does it mean to have affection or be "affectable?" What are the racial and sexual bounds of feeling and unfeeling? Lootens argues for the "definitive force of affect" in the "Poetess tradition" (75), but this affect, as the development of feminist criticism shows us, has focused on white writers like Hemans. Wheatley, as Lootens argues, has been excluded from a "Poetess" tradition, first for being enslaved and second, for the lack of emotion in her writing. In her anthology of nineteenth-century American women poets, Cheryl Walker excludes Wheatley "on grounds of both patriotism and of feeling, from [the] volume's accounts of the 'more passionate women poets'—that is, of the more qualified 'nightingale poets' or 'poetesses' of the nineteenth century" (23). This exclusion through emotion shows the racial and sexual politics of both feeling and what Xine Yao calls unfeeling—the state of being "disaffected." Yao investigates, "what we can apprehend if we stay with the negativity of unfeeling and suspend its rehabilitation. Through this provocation, I seek to excavate unfeeling occluded by the stifling imperatives of the political stakes of sympathy" (3). In this excavation, the works of Black women like Wheatley are not subsumed under the aegis of white women's feelings or sympathies. Instead, they are read as the grounds for reading and imagining otherwise. This otherwise challenges a transatlantic poetess tradition rooted in white femininity and finds new routes.

Wheatley's Poetics: Imagining Otherwise

Wheatley's poems show a transatlantic Romantic poetics reflective of non-European anglophone voices and the expansion of poetic expression to a world not oriented around whiteness. This expansion, embedded in colonialism, slavery, and racial commodification, empowers poetry as a political endeavor that comments on liberty, freedom, revolution, and tyranny not as ideas but as ongoing realities. No longer the imagined communities of suffering for Hemans's women, Wheatley lives and writes from actual bodily dispossession, violence, and cultural genocide. James Edward Ford III argues that "the African poetess who takes on the pseudonym 'Phillis Wheatley' uses *Poems* and her extant writings to oppose a doubled tyranny—of political slavery and chattel slavery—in the Age of Revolutions and to embrace blackness as a form of self-making outside the strictures of Western 'Man'" (185). Wheatley's task of opposing slavery deeply compounds the aesthetic project of self-making and embracing Blackness. In her multivalent, ambivalent use of imagination and fancy, she forges a Blackness seeking liberatory possibilities away from a white male subjectivity. Wheatley's lyric subjectivity maps a Black affective reality apart from white thinking and feelings—Black embodiment in an antiblack world.

Wheatley's poems do this with a complexity of speakers, subjects, meanings, and routes of alternative identification. My readings of Wheatley's poetry counter the tendency to read her aesthetics as purely neoclassical or imitative. Wheatley deploys the sublime language of flight and light, emphasizes certain words through italics, makes rhetorical moves of irony and double meaning—a poetics that actively structures the text with awareness of its white dominant audience. With this awareness, it seizes the opportunity to become the judging subject and not object of poetry. Becoming the subject opens up a space of non-white opacity that does not rely on racialized whiteness to exist or be seen.[21] As Édouard Glissant notes in his poetics of relation, a person has the right to be opaque, and the "opaque is not the obscure . . . It is that which cannot be reduced" (191). This irreducibility creates in Wheatley's work a counter-imagination that seeks worlds of freedom, possibility, and Black emancipation.

While critics like Phillip M. Richards, Vincent Carretta, and Rafia Zafar have done important work in reading Wheatley's literary aesthetics and print history, Wheatley's alignment with neoclassical imitation and not Romanticism has diminished the innovation of her work. Alternatively, Julie Ellison has read Wheatley's poetic idioms like "fancy" in terms of their feminist potential, predominantly through what Ellison calls the spatial inflections of Wheatley's "prospect poetry" ("Politics of Fancy"). Ellison describes Wheatley's poetic sensibility as "a form of affective hypermobility that allows the speaker to veer between the moods of power and weakness" (*Cato's Tears* 21). Although Ellison's argument engages with Wheatley's fancy through Romantic theory, my analysis of Wheatley's aesthetics departs from Ellison's in that I attend to questions of race and bring in antiracist feminist critique to reshape the disciplinary and discursive boundaries of Wheatley criticism. In doing so, I resist the white solipsistic readings that have failed to discuss the racial logics of Wheatley's poetry and poetic reception.

In the first poem in her collection, "To Maecenas," Wheatley deploys the conventions of a Homeric ode and invokes "grace" from "ye *Muses*" for Terence, a Black slave who eventually was freed and became a Roman senator and playwright.[22] The speaker asks why of Terence "one alone of *Afric*'s sable race" do these "rolls of fame" unspool? (40, 42). This contestation of Terence being the "one alone" celebrated African artist proposes Wheatley's own poems as working to join Terence in expanding the grounds of African and Black art. The poem ends in a moment of defiance where the speaker vows to "snatch a laurel" from ancient Roman patron Maecenas's head (45). This act of defiance ends in the speaker commanding, "Hear me propitious, and defend my lays" (55). Hilene Flanzbaum finds a pattern of muses in Wheatley's collection, arguing that the "muse materializes only when the ensuing poem has no designated audience, market function, or carefully planned route of reception. These poems offer no ostensible service to the white community … Wheatley exploits the typical neo-classical convention of invoking the muse to cross boundaries" (71). Nandini Bhattacharya argues that the Muse helps Wheatley "to stand outside of the picture ... and gaze in upon her own creation" (143). Wheatley's choice to invoke outside forces in the "ye *Muses*" in the first poem in her collection establishes Wheatley's right to look elsewhere and beyond the strictures of Anglo-white tradition and its antiblack conditions.

Wheatley's "Muse" figure becomes associated with Romantic modes of imagination and fancy in "On Imagination." Here, we see Wheatley representing imagination and fancy as a means to mentally escape confinement. Deanna Koretsky writes that the poem "ascribes to the imagination the power to remake the world, not merely to escape it. The imagination enables her to write herself on her own terms rather than those ascribed to her by a white supremacist society" (96). This turning away from white supremacist logic is proposed in the poem's ending. As Lootens and Kaplan note, the speaker in Hemans's poems is "primed to mourn, perform silence, and be lost" such that "hers is a speaking silence against which later feminist poetics must ring out" (Lootens 65). What makes Wheatley's "On Imagination" distinct from the imagination of Hemans is its ending directive for orality and its refusal to be silenced or lost.[23] While the universalizing tendency of the Romantic imagination can threaten to deny difference and plurality in works by Hemans, it can also level the terrain of hierarchical tradition and become a tool of agency for those excluded from white poetry, such as Wheatley.

"On Imagination" begins with the speaker's invocation of an "imperial queen" (1), who we later find out is a personification of Imagination. While Wheatley calls Imagination an "imperial queen" (1), she describes Fancy in seemingly deficient terms. She writes, "Now here, now there, the roving Fancy flies / Till some lov'd object strikes her wand'ring eyes" (9–10). Wheatley gives the Imagination a divine potency, writing how Imagination's "wond'rous acts in beauteous order stand, / And all attest how potent is thine hand" (3–4). Additionally, Wheatley also sees Imagination as a unifying force that "Measure[s] the skies, and range[s] the realms above. / There in one view we grasp the mighty whole, / Or with new worlds amaze th'unbounded soul"

(20–2). Fancy, unlike Imagination, cannot scale the prospect and is unable "[t]o rise from earth, and sweep th'expanse on high" (42). The fancy in her poem is unable to unify or "grasp the mighty whole" like the Imagination, because it is bound by "silken fetters" in a "soft captivity [that] involves the mind" (21, 11, 12). Rather than just a matter of choice, Wheatley's "Fancy" is held captive by forces outside its control. Ellison argues that Wheatley's "fancy temporarily fuses imperial and lyric consciousness" ("Politics of Fancy" 230). This imperial and lyric tension is seen in the contrast between "roving" and "raptur'd" fancy and the imperial "queen" in Imagination.

Her distinction between imagination and fancy in her "beauteous order" reminds us of Coleridge's efforts to distinguish between the two (3). For Coleridge, the imagination is a divine faculty which in the ideal poet, "brings the whole soul of man into activity . . . diffus[ing] a tone and spirit of unity" (*Biographia Literaria* 402). He writes of the imagination "either as primary, or secondary" and finally, he mentions fancy, which "is indeed no other than a mode of Memory emancipated from the order of time and space; while it is blended with, and modified by that empirical phenomenon of the will, which we express by the word choice" (313). Fancy as modified by choice corresponds with Wheatley's depictions of fancy as "roving" and "raptur'd" ("On Imagination" 9, 23).

Coleridge places the imagination in a leading role as "prime agent of all human perception" just as Wheatley calls her Imagination "the leader of the mental train" and "the sceptre o'er the realms of thought" (34, 36). These similarities show that Coleridge's celebrated theories of imagination are not as singular as they seem. Both Coleridge and Wheatley endorse imagination as a divine and unifying force, and imagination's primary or leading role in human perception and thought. John Shields uses these similarities to argue that both Wheatley and Coleridge "agree" that "the capacity to harness the productive power of imagination manifests an aesthetic indication that that true artist is a genius" (*Phillis Wheatley* 100). I would propose, rather, that their usages of imagination and fancy overlap but are distinct. Wheatley's poems reflect an aesthetics of differentiated imagination *and* fancy. For example, in

"On Recollection" Wheatley engages with "fancy" as a mental capacity of memory. The poem addresses Mneme, the Greek muse of memory, who enables "fancy's sight" within "the unbounded regions of the mind" (15, 8). The speaker tries to recollect her forgotten past in "Afric" (2), finding in fancy a means of remembering. This "fancy" is rooted in remembering the reality of enslavement, the trafficking of the speaker's body, and makes fancy a tool of identity affirmation and recovery. Wheatley's fancy is a means of feminist flight and escape, distinguishing hers from Coleridge's theories.

Wheatley's fancy does have similarities with Hemans's usage. Unlike Coleridge, Hemans addresses fancy positively throughout *The Domestic Affections and Other Poems* (1812), writing an "Address to Fancy" and calling fancy "queen of dreams" (1). Hemans clearly reflects Ellison's "imperial and lyric consciousness." She describes fancy as "creative pow'r," "sportive charmer," "lovely maid," and "[e]nchantress" (15, 25, 25, 48). As a creative, beautiful, and supernatural force, it reigns over the "fairy-clime" and can transport the speaker to "realms unknown" (50, 47). Hemans's fancy can even "call thy visions dear" (46), thus having a visionary power that Coleridge's description of fancy lacks. This visionary potential can create new worlds and transport or transcend everyday reality, offering respite or refuge. Both Wheatley and Hemans find in fancy an evocative figure of flight that reflects a spirit of enfranchisement against white male tradition. This spirit registers an affective state of creation and movement between worlds and realities.

Jeffrey C. Robinson notes how fancy is the Romantic forerunner of experimental poetry in the twentieth century and that it "has always been defined as expansive and exploratory but also reactive and contestatory" (2). This contestation is seen in "On Imagination," where the "roving" and "raptur'd" fancy contrasts with the imperial "queen" of Imagination. In "On Imagination" fancy is held captive by a "lov'd object" and never actually "rise[s] from earth" (41, 42). Despite Winter's "frowns," the "fields may flourish, and gay scenes arise" with the aid of fancy (24). Thus, fancy has an imaginative potential that is more than a mode of memory and something that sets the stage for the final lines of the poem. Wheatley's poem ends with another interruption of "Winter" which "forbids" the speaker "to aspire" and "chill[s] the tides of Fancy's flowing sea" (50, 52). What "Winter" forbids the speaker to aspire to is left unclear.

Up until this point, the speaker has invoked and praised the power of the "imperial queen" of Imagination while Fancy has been described as more capricious with "raptur'd eyes" (23). Still, Fancy has been given space to imagine "gay scenes" in spite of Winter's disapproving "frowns" (24, 23). At the poem's end, Winter finally chastens the speaker, reminding her that engaging with Fancy may be a vain endeavor, in contrast to the Imagination, which is "unequal[led]" by human endeavors to sing its praises (53). Rather than celebrating the harnessing of imagination as a mark of "poetic genius," Wheatley's poem ends with a seeming admission of the poet's inability to match imagination's divine potency. I use the word "seeming" because there is an ambiguity in the poem's ending that many critics have pointed out.[24] In the last lines of the poem, "northern tempests" (allied with Winter) have "chill[ed] the tides of Fancy's flowing sea" and the speaker has commanded herself to "[c]ease then, my song, cease the unequal lay" (51, 52, 53). McKay reads these lines as illustrative of "an apophasis, an affirmation by denial" (79).[25] The affirmation here, I argue, is of the speaker's identity and agency—her ability to command the "song" and to oppose the "unequal" lay.

A clear moment of triumph in the poem occurs when the poem's speaker pronoun shifts from "we" to "I" in the very last stanza. And here, the speaker allies herself with fancy and not imagination:

> The monarch of the day I might behold,
> And all the mountains tipt with radiant gold,
> But I reluctant leave the pleasing views,
> Which Fancy dresses to delight the Muse; (46–9, emphasis mine)

The "I" here is "reluctant" to "leave the pleasing views" that the flight of fancy has "dressed," and she evokes the "I" of a Romantic lyric—a speaker with interiority and traits of the poet's own circumstances. Wheatley's speaker, in her reflective inward turn at poem's end and oral directive to end the song on her own terms, reflects a moment of Black ontology—an affective space irreducible to white effacement. While the ending could simply be explained as manifesting Fancy's inadequacy to overcome Winter and her "northern tempests" (51), the insertion of the personal "I" and the turn inward, to the speaker's own subjectivity, complicate such a univocal reading. The poem's end offers a temporary escape into the creative interior space of the speaker's imaginative mind, hence the appearance of the "I." Thus, while the speaker orders herself to "[c]ease . . . cease the unequal lay" or song (53), she can be consoled by the fact that she has the power to will or summon her imagination, just as she can make it cease. The speaker's thoughts and senses, her affective being, are materialized and given presence, not solely for white audiences or in imitation of a white ideal.

Wheatley's use of Romantic tropes of imagination and fancy evidences her expert use and manipulation of anglophone poetic tradition. In many ways, her poems disorient the foundations of a white Romantic lyric subjectivity and show different routes of identity formation that throw into stark relief the cultural performance of Hemans's imagination. Wheatley's imagination is a means to recover her past, to affirm the subjectivity of a woman and poet who is Black and dispossessed of rights. This imagination reflects not just enslavement or Black womanhood but also anticipates Black feminist and identity discourses such as Patricia Hill Collins' "outsider within" status of Black women in literature, or bell hooks's call for the collective formation of an "oppositional world view" to countervail the centrality of white women and patriarchal tradition in feminist movements.

Thus, Wheatley's poetics always anticipates a past and future, moving beyond Romanticism and towards a decolonized global literary context. This is seen in her usage of European, American, and African references throughout her poems, which demands the right for multiple meanings and aesthetic hybridity. Her subtleties and maneuvers of language often exceed the frames of European and American conventions and find inspiration elsewhere. For example, she looks beyond a white European artistic tradition in "To S. M. A

Young *African* Painter, On Seeing His Works," a poem written for the Black painter, Scipio Moorhead. As Megan Walsh notes, this poem shows the ways that Wheatley "commented directly and at some length on black visual artistic production" and how, for Wheatley, painting and poetry were "coextensive" (88, 84). The speaker imagines when the painter "first thy pencil did those beauties give, / And breathing figures learnt from thee to live" (3–4). As creator of these "beauties" turned "breathing figures," the painter constructs new images that do not rely on white standards of beauty. The painter works in concert with "the poet's fire" so that the painter's pencil and the poet's "verse conspire" (9–10). This alliance will again be aided by a "muse" and come to fruition in the afterlife, so that painter and poet can coexist on "th' ethereal plain," where "nobler themes demand a nobler strain" (32, 31). In the context of Kant's "noble sublime" which is found in a "great height" rather than the terrifying sublime of a "great depth" (17), Wheatley's "ethereal plain" proposes an alternative sublimity of Black humanity, shared creation, and autonomy from the forces of antiblackness and erasure.

Both sublime and earthly, Wheatley's poems traverse aesthetic and physical frames through what Nandini Bhattacharya calls Wheatley's "construction of transnationalism as a strategic arena for politicizing the aesthetic" (157). This transnationalism is radically different from Hemans's "imagined transnational, multiracial, interfaith community of female suffering" (Lootens 66). It is a lived transnationalism, a trafficking of Wheatley's body across continents and sea, the voyages across the Atlantic that both enslaved her and made her a transatlantic poetic celebrity, "the African Poetess," in 1776 ("Poetical Essays," 193).[26] Wheatley's final passage to the US, a "flight" of transnational migration, brings with it the publication of *Poems* and the first recorded book by an anglophone Black writer: all, as Vincent Carretta notes, "while Wheatley [is] still at sea" (xvii).

Wheatley recalls the first of these sea voyages in "On Being Brought from Africa to America." The speaker expresses a vivid sense of being both trafficked and enslaved: "Brought" from a "*Pagan* land" without consent (1). Critics have pointed out the poem's levels of meaning dependent on the discourse through which it is read—religious, typographical, political. Antonio T. Bly notes how throughout *Poems*, Wheatley incorporates typographical choices of italics and capitalization that, "complicate the word's ability to mean" (319). For example, this poem's series of italicized words include "*Pagan*," "*Saviour*," "*Christians*," "*Negros*," and "*Cain*." This "*Pagan* land" obtains an ironic meaning in the context of Wheatley's emphasis on Christianity in the other italicized words, "*Christians*" and "*Cain*." Along with italics for emphasis, the capitalization of "AFRICA" alongside "AMERICA" in the title testifies to an equivalence between the continents.

Within its fixed verse forms of iambic pentameter and octave, the poem's tone begins with a seeming optimism: "'Twas mercy brought me from my *Pagan* land, / Taught my benighted soul to understand" (1–2). These same lines, however, also show the speaker acknowledging her existence before enslavement. MaryCatherine Loving points out the speaker's semiotic "efforts at subversion" through these moments showing the trafficking of her body from one location to another (73). These lines invoke "her capture, the voyage in the hull of a ship, and the change in her status at the end of that voyage" (Loving 69). This change is her enslavement, not just her "benighted soul" being taught Christianity. On one level, the poem reads like a paean to Christian redemption: how "mercy" brought the speaker from a "*Pagan* land" (Africa) and saved her "soul" (1–3). Cedrick May, however, notes the poem's critique of slavery through its "use of a positive theological system emphasizing the benevolent God of love over the irascible spirit of an older Calvinist tradition" (59). This critique is indirect, using irony and the speaker's own ambiguity of religious beliefs.

The poem continues, "Some view our sable race with scornful eye, / 'Their colour is a diabolic die'" (5–6). This "scornful eye" is amplified through the direct dialogue of an anonymous "Some" who equate Blackness with the "diabolic." Forcing her white readership to confront the limits of their gazes and religious beliefs, Wheatley questions the legitimacy of slavery to Christian theology. The speaker urges the reader to "Remember, *Christians*, *Negros*, black as *Cain* / May be refin'd, and join th' angelic train" (7–8). The parallelism and shared italics for "*Christians, Negros*" proposes their shared possibility for worldly transcendence in the religious sublime. Thus, the closing "train" imagery reminds the reader of the speaker's trafficking and movement, but also the possibility of flight or ascent.[27] This duality of meaning can be taken as an irony that buttresses the speaker's continued trope of Blackness—"sable race," "black as *Cain*"—an assertion of Blackness that is ineradicable, not "benighted," and deliberately opaque. As Glissant notes, "opacity" is "an alterity that is unquantifiable, a diversity that exceeds categories of identifiable difference" (189). For Wheatley, this opacity is the grounds from which her poem forges an alternative route of Black identity sustained throughout centuries of a transatlantic slave trade of immeasurable violence and genocide. In doing so, Blackness as opacity resists inscrutability and finds agency in its alterity. This alterity disrupts the whiteness of the Romantic lyric subject and exceeds the frame of a Romantic ideology founded on white supremacist logic. By exceeding, Wheatley's work forges a poetics that cannot be read solely through pre-existing theories and demands its own theorization apart from one field or period such as Romanticism.

Conclusion

Looking at Wheatley's poems has been an act of disorientation in this book. This disorientation helps decenter a white feminist account of the period and begins to trace the fraught relationship between race, gender, Orientalism, and antiblackness in Romantic poetics. As Ahmed asserts, the real hope for feminist solidarity "might lie in taking a feminist orientation, a way of facing the world, which includes facing what we might not recognize, with others we do not yet know" (*Cultural Politics* 189). By moving from Hemans to Wheatley, I turned away from a transatlantic poetess tradition rooted in whiteness, gathering around Wheatley's poetics instead as the grounds for an alternative route. This route is one that begins to unsettle the boundaries of Romanticism and remakes it in the image of those it has excluded.

This chapter began by tracing Hemans's cultural and racial representations to interrogate the power dynamics embedded and reproduced in entanglements of womanhood, race, place, and culture. Hemans's poems reflect a type of white women's poetry written through a British imperial gaze. This gaze replicates and reproduces many of the poetic devices of Coleridge, Byron, and the other authors in this study—devices such as dislocated setting, racial others, and a universalizing imagination. In "The Indian City" Hemans's Orientalist representation of Maimuna transgresses and transcends the privacy of "domestic affections," asserting the affective "might" of a woman. Hemans engages in rhetorical subversions and resistances to fixed conceptions of womanhood. At the same time, however, this woman is othered, displaced, and inscrutable at safe distance from British soil. Thus, Hemans transgresses while consolidating a white woman's subjectivity. In "Woman on the Field of Battle" Hemans continues to valorize the affection of a "woman" as strength suited for military battle. This symbolic woman is idealized both for her whiteness and for dying nameless, lost, and silenced. This woman's death reinforces a patriarchal nationalist ideology promoting the valor in a white women's death as sacrifice.

Hemans's racialized poetry imagines a feminist solidarity but in doing so, suppresses non-white perspectives and centralizes white women. This white womanhood displaces race and ethnicity onto emotions or affective states, avoiding the naming of whiteness as fundamental to Hemans's poetic speakers. By centering affective states of white womanhood, Hemans's poems suppress the female consciousness or affective reality of non-white women. This suppression is the point from which I turned to Wheatley's poems as a response to white femininity and the antiblackness of British anglophone poetry. Wheatley's poems refuse a singular tradition, meaning, or audience. They deploy and subvert Romantic tropes of imagination, fancy, and lyric subjectivity, but also expand beyond Romantic frames to think, feel, and visualize otherwise. This otherwise is a place of autonomous Blackness, womanhood, opacity, affect, transnationalism, and scenes of liberation—a place essential to forging a world not oriented around whiteness.

Notes

1. Laura Mandell edits a special issue of *Romanticism on the Net* on the transatlantic poetess. No. 29–30, February–May 2003. <https://doi.org/10.7202/007712ar>.
2. As bell hooks writes, "[t]o be in the margin is to be part of the whole but outside the main body" (1). Hooks's theory seeks a fuller, more encompassing feminist praxis that includes a "larger number of experiences, that serve to unify rather than to polarize" (2). This unifying gesture amidst multiplicity "will emerge from individuals who have knowledge of both margin and center" (2).
3. In "we" I am thinking of Kandice Chuh's "we" usage in *The Difference Aesthetics Makes*. We as in "those committed to the minoritarian project of mobilizing knowledge to transform the social field by, in part, attending to the arrangements and practices of knowledge production" (124).
4. In the rest of the chapter, I will refer to Phillis Wheatley Peters as Wheatley for succinctness.
5. One example of what engages Wheatley's poems with Romanticism is John Shields's work, *Phillis Wheatley and the Romantics*.
6. One of Hemans's first published works, *England and Spain; or, Valour and Patriotism* (1808), is a nationalist call to action arguing for England to help Spain resist Napoleon's invasion of their peninsula.
7. It is worth noting that of the major British Romantic authors we study today, Hemans offers many translations in her works, with poems and paratexts translated from French, Spanish, Portuguese, Italian, and German. Cf. David Simpson's "The limits of cosmopolitanism and the case for translation."
8. For more on the Orientalist setting of "The Indian City," see Pramod K. Nayar's "The Imperial Picturesque in Felicia Hemans' 'The Indian City.'"
9. Whether this defiance is intentional or not is left unclear.
10. Osman also recounts Byron's influence on Hemans's heroines in *Records of Woman*, arguing that Hemans was spurred by "Byron's propagandistic appropriation of the orientalized Greek heroine as a symbol of revolutionary freedom, and even composed several poems on philhellenic themes, namely 'Modern Greece' (1817), 'The Suliote Mother' and 'Greek Funeral Chant' (from *The Forest Sanctuary*, published in 1825), 'The Bride of the Greek Isle' (from the 1828 *Records of Woman*), and 'The Sisters of Scio' (from the 1830 *Songs of the Affections*)" (para. 3).

11. Susan Wolfson astutely observes that "the imagination of [Hemans's] women with violent political agency had to take routes into a supernatural idiom . . . and return routes to domestic spheres and affections" ("'Something must be done'" 119). These routes and returns are traceable in Maimuna's story. By poem's end, Maimuna is a far cry from the Byronic hero of the battle scenes.
12. The heart imagery recalls the ending of Wordsworth's "The Ruined Cottage" as well, when the woman's "hope endeared, / Fast rooted at her heart, and here, my friend, / In sickness she remained, and here she died, / Last human tenant of these ruined walls'" (525–8).
13. Deanna Koretsky discusses Romantic suicide and modern liberalism in *Death Rights*.
14. Helen Luu writes about the deconstruction of "femininity" in *Records of Woman*.
15. By "performativity" I am engaging Judith Butler's term as discussed in *Gender Trouble, Bodies that Matter,* and *Undoing Gender*. She first coins it in *Gender Trouble* (1990), when she writes about the process of performing gender: "There is no gender identity behind the expressions of gender; identity is performatively constituted by the very 'expressions' that are said to be its results" (25). The phrase "narrative of becoming" refers to Butler's description of the body in *Undoing Gender*: "As a consequence of being *in the mode of becoming,* and in always living with the constitutive possibility *of becoming otherwise,* the body is that which can occupy the norm in myriad ways, exceed the norm, rework the norm, and expose realities to which we thought we were confined as open to transformation" (217, emphasis mine).
16. Wolfson asserts that Hemans's portrayal of the "death of the rebellious female" is characterized by hesitation "before violent revolution as a fatal course" and yet, it is still "caught up, in a shadowy context: the historical persistence of gender symbolism in the dark havoc of injustice and oppression" ("Something must be done" 119). Judith Butler would consider this "gender symbolism" a type of restrictive and even compulsory norm that limits and even damages the opportunities for a "livable existence" (*Undoing Gender* 206).
17. This rhetoric of exclusivity and power is something that, according to David G. Riede, made Hazlitt "suspicious of poetry and its natural tendency to side with power, its 'right royal' tendency to put 'the one above the infinite many, might before right'" (*Oracles and Hierophants* 247). Yet, Hazlitt still loved poetry and its countervailing power of democratization.

18. Wordsworth has a similarly titled "Poems Founded on the Affections" in his collected works of 1815.
19. Cf. Matthew 11: 7, "reed shaken with the wind" (*Selected Poems* 457).
20. Of the sixty-one poems in *Songs*, eleven include the word "affection." These usages predominantly anthropomorphize the word into an agential character, twice giving it strength or "might."
21. Wheatley's "sublime" describes skies, grief, the "king or mighty God," and the "Muse" figure. The poems where the words "sublime" or "sublimity" appear are as follows: "To the University of Cambridge, in New-England," "To a Clergyman on the Death of his Lady," "On Isaiah lxiii. 1–8," and "To a Gentleman on his Voyage to Great-Britain for the Recovery of his Health."
22. For more on the paradox of the Muse in Wheatley's "To Maecenas" and elegies, see Paula Bennett's "Phillis Wheatley's Vocation and the Paradox of the 'Afric Muse.'"
23. It also veers away from dedicatory odes to patrons, religious eulogies, and purely neoclassical style, asserting the potency of Wheatley's "imagination" as an act of poetic expression and creation.
24. Michele McKay and Ellison, for example.
25. McKay sees these lines as expressing "dissent from an inadequate model. They may be read, in other words, as dismissive not of the poet's inherent poetic capacity but of any attempt at a mode of song (lay) unsuitable (unequal) to her peculiar genius" (79).
26. For more on Wheatley as "African Poetess," see Laura Mandell's "Introduction: The Poetess Tradition" in *Romanticism on the Net*.
27. Wheatley's ending "train" evokes, as in "On Imagination," a sublime prospect unbounded by earthly concerns.

Chapter 4

Disorienting Romanticism: William Blake's Orientalist Poetics

> West, the Circumference: South, the Zenith: North,
> The Nadir: East, the Center, unapproachable for ever
>
> William Blake, *Jerusalem*

The writers in this study envisage themselves in an expanding world of others. This is a world that requires turning towards and away, pushing beyond, decentering, delimiting, and traversing boundaries. A poetics of orientation traces this expansion through the construction of the Romantic lyric subject and its global coordinates of race, place, and culture. Returning to Omar F. Miranda, he considers the concept of the "global lyric" in the Romantic era, noting Coleridge's "Kubla Khan" and Sir William Jones's "Hymn to Surya" as variations of the global lyric form. Miranda finds Wheatley's "On Being Brought from Africa to America" as an important precursor to variations of the global lyric, a form which has "multidirectional pathways and diverse cultural and temporal orientations" (323, 310). Multidirectional, diverse, world-facing—Wheatley's orientations embrace ambiguity, paradox, experimentation, and unfixity. These orientations imagine a world that affirms a Black woman's subjectivity, a world that turns away from the "scornful eye" of the white gaze (6).

This chapter turns to William Blake's genre-crossing works that visualize queer forms and offer new frameworks for the world and its hemispheric divisions. As Katie Trumpener notes, Romantic writers, in situating themselves in a globalized idea of Britain, create "mental cartographies" of "conceptual, emotional, and perceptual frameworks of place and world making" (223). William Blake's mental and psychological realms of place and world-making are fundamentally different from the other authors in this book. His idea of East/West relations is not the hegemonic Orientalism of clear division and conquest. James Watt describes Blake's Orientalism as "plebeian" (146), and this sense of common people turns away from centering the poet as aesthetic center. Blake's Orient is concerned with freedom and creation unbarred from cultural norms. He departs from the scholarly Orientalism of Sir William Jones, the universalizing idealism of Percy Bysshe Shelley's shapes, the cosmopolitan raconteur of Byron's tales, and Hemans's poetics of affection.[1]

Blake's Orient is an always future realm rooted in both biblical and sensual prophecy. In 1793, Blake writes in *The Marriage of Heaven and Hell*, "*The philosophy of the east taught the first principles of human perception, we of Israel taught that the Poetic Genius (as you now call it) was the first principle and all the others merely derivative*" (Pl. 12).[2] These "first principles of human perception" herald a model of human perception rooted in the Bible as "Eastern" document. As the Bible is the foundational text for Blake's "Poetic Genius" and its narrative takes place in the imagined Orient, Blake's Orientalism peddles mythic and allegorical tropes of human, animal, and spiritual bodies as divine.[3] Through the cartography of the "East" as a symbol of perception, Blake disrupts a colonial imagination with forms of otherness that turn away from Orientalist imitation.

This turn away from imitation shows Blake's refusal to imagine a fixed "Orient" and instead, his openness of directionality. This openness is seen in his visual forms and structures including handwriting, illustrations, and representations of the human body that deny fixity. In turning away, Blake moves toward new textual and visual representations rooted in phenomenology and futurity.[4] For Blake, it is not only the human body but the *idea* of embodiedness, that structures the spaces and modules of his art.[5] By "body" I refer to both material and abstract forms; that is, any fundamental or united whole of some common attribute (*OED*). For example, the non-binary, human-like bodies in Blake's illustrations become differently envisaged in later works, posing a connection between Blake's conception of gender/sexuality and Orientalism as a shared body of "others."[6]

Thus, I argue that Blake's composite art—calligraphy, illustration, and printing technique—disorients the literary map of Romantic Orientalism through a phenomenological and modular expression of individual and embodied subjectivity. In his prophetic works, Blake's textual and visual representations of life forms also disorient common conceptions of the Romantic lyric speaking subject. Unlike Jones, Shelley, Byron, and Hemans, Blake's works envisage unfixed forms of relation beyond human, gender, and racial classification, rewriting a literary cartography of Romanticism and Orientalism. While there is not a clear, logical map for Blake's cosmos, his composite art offers a site of imaginative multimodality that moves Romantic poetics toward new paradigms, contours, and shapes of relation. In doing so, Blake's works propose alternative aesthetic horizons beyond the lyric poem and an openness to new, shifting orientations beyond an East/West binary.

Blake's mode is one of de-familiarization and de-personalization. In Blake's poetic and pictorial bodies, we find a heuristic for reading and seeing in new ways—alternative visualities of shifting self/other orientations—mixed orientations that embrace difference. This heuristic is sensual, ephemeral, and revelatory in the way it juxtaposes lines and curves, both textual and pictorial. Carol Bigwood reminds us that "[t]he non-linguistic, . . . never fully yields its meaning" (312). This withholding of complete meaning in multimodal art yields Blake's *avant la lettre* queer futurity on the material page.[7] By "queer" I am thinking of Ahmed's two uses: what is "oblique" and "off line" as well as "nonnormative sexualities" (*Queer Phenomenology* 161). In Blake's work, I use "queer" to signal a disavowal of normative literary forms and his representations of otherness within and beyond identity markers of human/spirit, race, gender and sexuality, class, religion, and politics.[8]

Blake's model of orientations is one in which binaries of good and evil, male and female, word and image, poetry and prose, and body and mind are destabilized and re-enacted in new formations.⁹ These formations are culturally ambiguous. I trace both formal and content choices in works that mark the start and end of Blake's prophetic books, *The Marriage of Heaven and Hell* (1790–3) and *Jerusalem: The Emanation of The Giant Albion* (1804–20). Many argue that *Jerusalem* represents the "Bible of Hell" alluded to in the *Marriage*.¹⁰ In looking at Blake's religious satire in the *Marriage* and apocalyptic prophecy in *Jerusalem*, this chapter also traces Blake's poetics as a disorientation of Orientalist norms. This disorientation is a type of becoming oblique to the world of East/West thinking, refusing any orientation toward a fixed Orient.

Like Samuel Taylor Coleridge, Blake can piece together his own cosmic system through a syncretic mode of culturally heterogeneous mythologies. Stuart Curran writes that the "continuing readjustments" of the various mythological human attributes in *Jerusalem* "take place independent of an external space-time continuum. Its form departs radically from the customary epic depiction of a culture's organizing mythology" (344–5). Whereas Coleridge's system culminates in autobiography in *Biographia Literaria*, Blake's system turns toward prophecy and hemispheric divisions in *Jerusalem*. In biblical scripture, the Apocalypse is often compared to a wedding, and in Blake's mythology the bride is Jerusalem herself.¹¹ In turn, Blake's concept of matrimonial union in the *Marriage* is apotheosized into spiritual emanations of filial union in *Jerusalem*. What unites both of Blake's works is the spiritualization of human marriage as a type of divine union of the poetic imagination.

By the time we get to *Jerusalem*, all his characters—the mass public, the deists, the Jewish people, and Christians—are part of a fourfold structure of which *Jerusalem* has twenty-six correspondences, according to S. Foster Damon in *A Blake Dictionary*.¹² These fours appear in Blake's repeated use of the cardinal directions—north, south, east, west—to orient the reader in his modular world of shifting settings, characters, and geographical coordinates. Scholars have tried to map out a logical system of cultural and gender representation in Blake's works, with one consistency being found in this four-point system of life. This system is found in different iterations across his works, most concretely in *Jerusalem* and its purported palimpsest, *Vala, The Four Zoas* (c. 1796–1807).

Blake's fourfold system of life and energy is marked by his naming of the four cardinal points. Critics have long studied the four-point planetary system that is found in Blake's works as the imaginative compass of his inner world. In *Jerusalem*, Blake writes of the gates of Los's children, "thereby the gates / Eastward & Southward & Northward, are incircled with flaming fires. / And the North is Breadth, the South is Heighth & Depth: / The East is Inwards: & the West is Outwards every way" (Pl. 14). The eastern gate is curiously "inward," raising the idea that inwardness and in turn, interiority, can be associated with the East/"Orient." Like Byron's Eastern Tales, Blake directs his Orientalist gaze self-referentially inward. In linking inwardness to "oriental" art, the Romantic orientation toward interiority locates the possibility of self-discovery in the East. With this inward directedness, the East and its typified "oriental" aesthetic of curves and arabesques offers for Blake a route of self-discovery and expression displaced from the limits of realism.

This East, is also, as Blake notes in the *Marriage*, the birth of human perception and "Poetic Genius" as its first principle. The East is the beginning of an uncorrupted poetic genius—a genius that has been tainted by human civilization. In this Orientalist staging, Blake conceives of the East as an Edenic space of liberty for all, which Jerusalem represents. "Jerusalem" can mean many things, and her emanative presence is the most consistent symbol in the work. In terms of symbolism, she is often referred to as "Liberty" (Pl. 26, 54). Rather than wanting us all to be "other," as many Orientalists gesture toward, Blake argues through the figure of Jerusalem that the universal pursuit of liberty is the ultimate purpose of his cultural prophecy. In Blake's Jerusalem, everyone is guaranteed eternal freedom and toleration, regardless of class, sex/gender, race/ethnicity, or species. This egalitarian ethos is one of "Universal Toleration" (Annotated to Boyd's *Dante*, *CPP* 635). This toleration is a space where "Humanity knows not of Sex" (Pl. 30) and therefore, "Sexes must vanish & cease / To be when Albion arises from his dread repose" and reaches the Holy

Land (*Jerusalem* Pl. 30, 92).[13] Through this vanishing, Blake opens the "Possibility" of "Mutual Forgiveness forevermore" so that "we may Foresee & Avoid / The terrors of Creation & Redemption & Judgment" (92). This vanishing of the sexes shows Blake's queer futurity—a future in which the "terrors" of human-made systems no longer divide and judge.

Blake's Handwriting

The human-made divisions that Blake decries are also divisions on the page, including image/text, poetry/prose, and handwriting choices. Blake's choices of handwriting are fundamental yet overlooked principles of his composite art. His use of both cursive and print handwriting mimics typographic conventions of roman and italic script. As a pictorial *and* typographical representation in his works, Blake's handwriting fuses word and image. By focusing on his handwriting choices, I argue that Blake's italic script constitutes a graphic form of modulated expression. This modulation relates to Blake's technique both at the levels of production and expression. Through this modulation, Blake's handwriting takes on a communicative function next to and interfused with his illustrations and words. It reinforces and subverts the semantic content, offering another mode of reading Blake.

Blake's italic lettering is a semi-cursive penmanship demonstrating the running hand, while his roman lettering mimics historical print type as seen in the Bible. Complementing what W. J. T. Mitchell calls Blake's "imagetext," Blake's style of handwriting is an aesthetic choice that should be considered alongside the linguistic and pictorial elements on the page.[14] For example, on the center of plate 54 of *Jerusalem*, the words "Reason / Pity Wrath / This World / Desire" are written in italic handwriting and enclosed by a sphere, most likely meant to represent the planet Earth (see figure 4.1). The words "Pity" and "Wrath" merge with the pictorial line of the globe, and the globe is surrounded by "a concentric arrangement" of various nude figures, flying mid-air against the sky backdrop of the plate (Pl. 54). This marriage of image and text is common in

Figure 4.1 *Jerusalem*, copy E, obj. 54, c. 1821. Yale Center for British Art. The William Blake Archive. Public Domain.

Blake's visual poetics, showing his mixed orientations—Blake's art of looking more than one way at the same time, creating lines of connection/meaning that are not linear, straight, or have an intended or fixed endpoint.

Romantic-era manuscript production and Blake's unique printing process can help to contextualize Blake's handwriting and pictorial choices on a material level. During Blake's life, manuscript and art production was becoming increasingly mechanized, imitative, and profit-driven, so Blake's choice of handwritten and hand-drawn work rejects the mechanistic engraving practices that he openly disparaged. Morris Eaves writes that engraving during Blake's time was modified due to moveable type, thus "alter[ing] the outlook for letterpress printing so favorably that the technological basis common to the reproduction of both words and pictures became hard to discern: words were 'printed,' pictures 'engraved'" (*Counter-*

Arts Conspiracy 186). In essence, pictures were still produced as wholes whereas type was now moveable.[15] This distinction is something Blake avoided. As many scholars note, Blake's printing process allowed for simultaneous printing of image and text from the single copper plate. He used "quill pens, brushes, and a homemade liquid 'ink' impervious to nitric acid" to write and draw each page individually (Viscomi "Blakes Invention" para 1). This method allowed for an amount of artistic control and freedom which was unparalleled by the modern commercialist practices of Blake's day, specifically those of book dealers and the Republic of Scholars, a noted group of mechanizers who Blake critiqued for instructing students in imitation over innovation.[16] Through his invention of new production methods and illustration, Blake's printing process disrupted the conventions of illuminated manuscripts.

Blake's illuminated works disrupted but also adapted traditions that had been dormant since the Middle Ages. Whereas usually the business of illuminated printing required many hands, for Blake all the work could be done by him and his wife, Catherine. Together, they could "unite the labors of both the craftsman and the artist" (Mitchell *Blake's Composite Art* 15). In addition, instead of manuscripts being copied individually, Blake's printing practice allowed him to create copper plates that could be reused repeatedly. In terms of lines and style, Blake's illustrations were rather conventional for the period. Mitchell, however, makes an important distinction between the eighteenth-century concept of "*ut pictura poesis*" and Blake's mode (33). While there was a concerted effort to make poetry more painterly and paintings more poetic, the effort generally ended up "making poetry and painting more similar, adding them together as complementary representations, or reducing them to their common denominator, nature" (33). David B. Morris notes how Blake's word and image fusion in the *Marriage* "creates a visual/verbal natural landscape unique in the pre-modern poetry of natural description: not nature methodized (as for Pope) nor nature moonlit (as for Wordsworth and Coleridge) but nature dreamed and weirdly dissoluble" (277). Blake's images are imaginative and dissoluble, not realistic, or necessarily related to the primary words on the page. They evoke and supplement rather than conventionally illustrate what is happening in the text.

Through his innovations in printing, textual, and visual production, Blake changes the experience of engaging with his text. Carol Bigwood explains:

> Our eye is helped to rediscover its natural, prelinguistic mode of relating to language as line by the fact that we see Blake's hand in the handwritten words. Whereas the usual uniform type encourages the eye to pass through the concrete language lines to the abstract meaning signified, with Blake's print we notice the words themselves as unique writing lines that vary in size, density, color, and style. (310)

Blake's handwritten lines are visual, prelinguistic, and linguistic signifiers, offering new ways in which to interpret the dialectical relationship between opposing forces, images, and perspectives in his work. If, as poet Charles Bernstein notes, "*All language is visual when read*," an approach to Blake's visuality that considers his handwriting style can link the often-bifurcated study of literary and visual signs (xiii).[17] From this premise, I argue that Blake's pages in effect become modular forms beyond picture and word, deconstructing the image/text binary with their own internal logic of signs and curvature.[18]

Only two sections of the whole of the *Marriage* use non-italicized writing: The beginning "Argument" and the "Proverbs of Hell" (see figures 4.2 and 4.3). The titles of the "Argument" and the "Proverbs of Hell" sections are separated from the pictorial elements on the page, unlike the other titles that are in italic script. The rest of the work's titles and body text are in italics. These italic sections include "The Voice of the Devil," five "Memorable Fancy" sections, "A Song of Liberty," and the "Chorus." The italic sections are imaginative, narrative, and aural—departing from the exposition of the "Argument" and the parodic doctrine of the "Proverbs of Hell." Like the *Songs of Experience* (not *Innocence*), the majority of the *Marriage* is written in italic script. Blake's significantly heavier use of italics in the *Songs of Experience* (compared to the *Songs of Innocence*) offers a clue to his script choices in the *Marriage*. This correlative trend of italics links Blake's aesthetics of curvature and movement with "experience" and self-awareness, suggesting the inwardness Blake associates with the "East."

The handwriting choices in *Songs of Innocence and of Experience* (1789, 1794) illuminate the possibility of a certain inner logic to Blake's use of both italic and roman handwriting, especially because *Songs of Innocence* was published a year before the *Marriage*. W. J. T. Mitchell briefly examines the typography of the *Songs* in his book, *Picture Theory*. He argues that after the *Songs*, Blake used italics much more heavily than roman script (148). In *Songs of Innocence* italics are used irregularly, with some poem titles italicized and others not. The introduction to the set of poems, however, is in roman script. All the actual text of the poems (except for "The Voice of the Ancient Bard") is roman. In *Songs of Experience*, which was published in 1794, however, the introduction is in all italics. This is a marked shift from *Songs of Innocence*. In addition, *Songs of Experience* uses italics more frequently in general, with most of the text of the poems themselves in italics. This contrasts with most of the text in *Innocence* being in roman script. The significance of these choices becomes more apparent in the *Marriage*.

"The Argument" serves a prefatory function, serving as a type of prelude to the prophetic fury of the sections to come (see figure 4.2). The image of a "perilous path" is introduced, and it is the "just man," not the "villain" who follows this path. The villain, on the other hand, originates in the "paths of ease" (Pl. 2). This alignment between "ease" and evil suggests that the choice between a "perilous" or "eas[y]" path is a moral one as well. This section situates the reader in a subversive space from where the rest of the work will build its new prophecy and religion. A "sneaking serpent" is mentioned, an expression of curvature in contrast to the just man, but it is the just man, not the serpent, who traverses the "perilous path." By connecting the "just man" and his journey to peril, Blake diverges from the straightforward logic of straight/good, crooked/evil.

"The Argument" ends with the same two lines it begins with: "Rintrah roars & shakes his fires in the burdend [sic] air / Hungry clouds swag on the deep" (Pl. 2). This circularity creates a type of confinement or fixity of argument. By writing

Figure 4.2 *The Marriage of Heaven and Hell*, copy D, obj. 2, 1790. Lessing J. Rosenwald Collection, Library of Congress. Copyright © 2022 The William Blake Archive. Used with permission.

in roman and not italic handwriting, Blake visually reinforces this inertia. This section makes way for the italicized and untitled section that comes next. We see Blake's law of contraries and the first appearance (outside of the title page) of the words "heaven" and "hell" (Pl. 3). It is noteworthy that the eponymous "heaven" and "hell" are first used in the work in italic script—the forward slant evoking movement and a propulsive futurity to Blake's world. This italicization of "heaven" and "hell" could reinforce the satirical tone of the work, upending it from traditional Christian doctrine. The section culminates in Blake's assertion that "Good is Heaven. Evil is Hell" (Pl. 3). This line is also written in italics, connoting a lack of direct meaning.[19]

The next plate, in shifting to italic script and being left untitled, is anomalous in terms of the modularity of the text. This plate famously ends, "Without Contraries is no progression. Attraction and Repulsion, Reason and Energy, Love and Hate, are necessary to Human existence. From these contraries spring what the religious call Good & Evil. Good is the passive that obeys Reason. Evil is the active springing from Energy" (Pl. 3). With this, Blake sets up the fundamental principle on which the *Marriage* operates—his *"episteme of the contraries"* (O'Gorman 61). Blake's episteme is built on the energetic display of oppositions, and the script difference is another opposition that Blake uses to push the limits of the material page.[20] Blake's shifts in handwriting, too, symbolize the contraries of energy and reason, the prolific and devouring, and the straight versus crooked paths of Blake's "original derivation from the Poetic Genius" ("All Religions are One" *CPP* 1–2).

The "Proverbs of Hell" section is the only other section of the work in roman script (see figure 4.3). Through its heterodox list of proverbs, this section's irony and satire is reinforced by the upright graphic text. Blake's tone is inconsistent here, too, at times possibly earnest or direct. For example, Blake writes, "The thankful reciever [sic] bears a plentiful harvest" (Pl. 9). This contrasts with more ironic proverbs, such as "Listen to the fools reproach! it is a kingly title!" (Pl. 9). What can be concluded from these shifts in tone in the proverbs? When one considers this section's relative lack of illustration and pictorial elements, the words focalize as the central locus of meaning. The fact that the whole section is in roman script adds to the ironic prescriptiveness of this section and links upright handwriting to verbal over visual semantics.

Blake's prose polemics in "The Argument" align rigidity and scientific exactitude with a lack of genius, while irregularity and crookedness are associated with genius. Correlatively, the ironic and didactic "Proverbs of Hell" section, by being written in roman script, graphically mirrors the "Argument" section. As previously noted, italic script is used for sections of song, poetry, persona, and narrative, most notably Blake's "Memorable Fancy" sections. Blake's handwriting shifts are in conversation with his effort for a more original, natural style, not an aesthetics of smoothness and consistency. For Blake, it seems, genius is possible only out of a "crooked" path, a path that is mutable and embedded in direction over essence,

130 Romanticism and the Poetics of Orientation

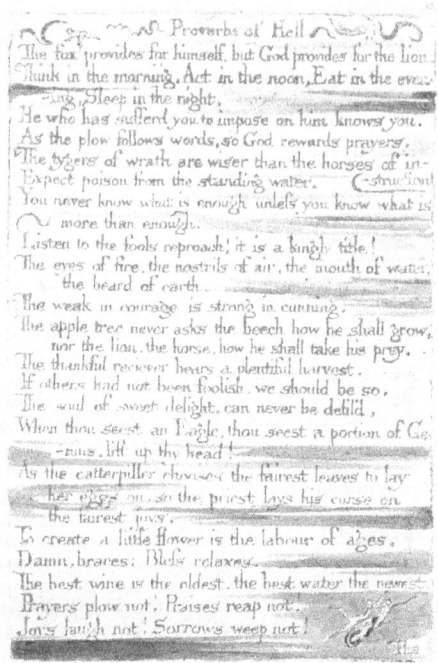

Figure 4.3 *The Marriage of Heaven and Hell*, copy D, obj. 9, 1790. Lessing J. Rosenwald Collection, Library of Congress. Copyright © 2022 The William Blake Archive. Used with permission.

which is visually embodied in the italic script of much of the *Marriage*. Returning to the "The Proverbs of Hell" section, Blake writes that "Improvement makes strait roads, but the crooked roads without Improvement, are roads of Genius." Blake's "crooked" genius involves a shift away from the poet as center or arbiter of imagination. This change in direction does not idealize "improvement" or linearity.

In terms of the historical context of Blake's choices of handwriting and focus on "crooked" form over linear progress, his typographic influences for the *Marriage* should not be overlooked. The Bible and John Milton's *Paradise Lost* serve as the clearest forerunners of Blake's *Marriage*. Although Swedenborg's religious doctrines like *A Treatise Concerning Heaven and Hell* are the most immediate or recognizable sources of Blake's parody, the lasting relevance of biblical narrative and Milton's works can be traced throughout Blake's oeuvre. Blake directly references Milton in the *Marriage* and continually adapts Miltonic themes like *felix culpa* in his prophetic books. In *The Counter-Arts Conspiracy*, Morris Eaves writes of the Romantic period's "three-part pattern of identity, loss of identity, and recovery of identity," exemplified in Wordsworth's *Prelude* and Blake's *Jerusalem* (111). Eaves concludes that "[i]f we want to take the romantic view, it will be truer to call *Paradise Lost* the historical or external version of the romantic myths found in *The Prelude* and *Jerusalem*" (111). As antecedent to *Jerusalem*, the *Marriage* poses the fundamental dialectic of contraries as the basis for this romantic myth. The *Marriage*'s "Bible of Hell" section mentions:

> *But in Milton; the Father is Destiny, the Son, a*
> *Ratio of the five senses. & the Holy-ghost, Vacuum!*
> *Note: The reason Milton wrote in fetters when*
> *he wrote of Angels & God, and at liberty when of*
> *Devils & Hell, is because he was a true Poet and*
> *of the Devils party without knowing it* (Pl. 6)

In aligning Milton with "*the Devils party*," Blake ironizes Milton's Christianity while introducing a new "infernal" method of creation and existence (Pl. 14).[21] The "*fetters*" which Blake writes of are aligned with "*Angels & God*," while "*liberty*" is attributed to "*Devils & Hell*" (Pl. 6). This entire section is written in italics, visually reinforcing its distinction from the "Argument" and "Proverbs of Hell" sections.

The theme of a spiritual marriage is something Blake also adapted from scriptural text, most singularly the carnal and ideal love depicted in the Bible's Song of Solomon/Song of Songs. In a 1793 Blayney edition of the Bible, the italicized gloss headings of the Song of Solomon summarize the upcoming love poem as between "Christ" and "church," rather than the earlier Judaic allegory of God and his bride, Israel. This King James rereading is something Blake ultimately reroutes back to Israel in his persona of Jerusalem, who represents both bride of and eternal emanation of all religions. In doing so, Blake locates his concept of marriage in a polysemic world of sensual spirituality and fecundity that is familial but not necessarily generative of filial offspring. As was common practice in biblical translation, italics are also used within the verse translations themselves to note editorial intervention and added words. This italic/roman distinction is something that Blake could have had in mind when experimenting with his own handwriting.²²

In addition to the Bible, *Paradise Lost* and Blake's works share similar typography. The 1769 King James Version Bible, revised by Dr. Benjamin Blayney, and commonly regarded as the standard from which modern Bibles are printed, was printed when Blake was twelve years old. It maintains the precedent of italicizing foreign, emphasized, and heading/title words, and italicizes the prefatory glosses at the beginning of each chapter.²³ It does not, however, use italics to denote the word(s) of God, which is a continuation of the precedent set by the 1611 Authorized King James Version. The 1769 version uses roman type while the 1611 version uses Gothic type. It is safe to assume that Blake had seen the 1769 or a similar version, with its modernized writing style that was more easily imitated by his own handwriting. When the 1769 version switches to italics it is for an organizational and editorial function, not a thematic one. This use of italics is the standard of Blake's day. For Blake, the choice between roman and italic handwriting does seem more idiosyncratic and irregular than printing practices of his day, as it is not usual for whole sections of a work like Blake's to be in italic handwriting. Whereas in works by his contemporaries, italics are more sparingly used, most of the *Marriage* is in italic script.

Blake's interest in being the next Milton influenced his poetic development. While writing his unfinished poem *Milton*, Blake illustrated the twelve books of *Paradise Lost* with two sets of watercolor illustrations containing scenes evocative of the illustrations in the *Marriage*. The italics in the first version of *Paradise Lost* do not diverge markedly from the usage in standardized versions of the Bible. Milton italicizes foreign, emphasized, and heading words, as well as Satan's name, but he does not italicize the speech of God or Satan. At the end of each book, "*The End of the [numbered] Book*" is italicized as well. Thus, like the 1611 and 1769 versions of the Bible, the italics here perform an editorial or organizational function. In 1770s British editions of *A Treatise Concerning Heaven and*

Hell (1778), Swedenborg follows the conventions of the Bible in italicizing foreign words and not italicizing the word of God. He does seem to use italics more sparingly than the Bible and *Paradise Lost*, however, eschewing its use in titles, headings, and organizational roles. He does use italics in the specific catalogues of his own religious doctrine.[24] Blake may have been experimenting with Swedenborg's convention of italicizing doctrine in his wide use of italics in the *Marriage*.

Like many of his other works, the *Marriage* has varying copies with different sequences and numbers of pages. As scholars like Makdisi have noted, there are three distinct versions of the *Marriage*, one of which is just the "Song of Liberty" (plates 25–7) in a monochrome stand-alone pamphlet version.[25] Makdisi notes that because these monochrome pamphlet versions of the *Marriage* were each printed on a single folded piece of paper, they mimic the innumerable handbills printed by radicals in the revolutionary 1790s. Makdisi concludes that Blake conceived of the work "either as a modular book . . . or, the other way around, as an amalgamation of different constituent elements that, even in the 'complete' version of the text, never really cohere into a single, straightforward narrative" (*Reading William Blake* 59). This modularity demonstrates how Blake's work is an active material network of flux and futurity. It is meant to be disassembled, read non-linearly, and not cohere into a uniform narrative. In this modular work consisting of an array of handwriting, image, text, tone, and theme, Blake reorients conceptions of the Romantic subject toward questions of visuality, phenomenology, and alternative aesthetic horizons.

The Italics: Finding an Internal Logic

As I have established, other than the "Argument" and "Proverbs of Hell" sections, all the text in the *Marriage* is italic. Whereas italic handwriting lines often fuse with image, the roman script titles of the "Argument" and the "Proverbs of Hell" are visually separated from the other elements on the page. The spaces between roman text and image reinforce the associations between roman script and fixity, italic script and movement. Unlike the Bible and *Paradise Lost*, Blake's use of italics is not for organizational so much as expressive purposes. Johanna Drucker writes, "the visual performance on the page ... can also be seen and understood as a schematic form, structurally logical and meaningful even when it has no analogue to a pronounceable form" (103). This lack of analogue opens Blake's work to a communicative function outside of narrative causality and plot structure, and Blake's resultant structure is a series of modules/plates with various routes of pictorial and textual engagement.

The italics of the "voice of the Devil" section links Blake's italic text with the prolific energy of "Eternal Delight" (Pl. 4). The five "Memorable Fancy" sections visually reinforce this energy with italic handwriting as well. These sections parody Swedenborg's "Memorable Relations" which consist of "circumstantial accounts of conversations and adventures with angels and devils" (Johnson and Grant 81). Blake's parody is supplemented by the curved pictorial and handwritten lines, offering the reading and seeing eye mutually reinforcing modes of engagement. All the titles of the "Memorable Fancy" sections exhibit Blake's union of image and text, with the letters joining pictorial curves and elements seamlessly at the top of the plates (see figure 4.4). By connecting text and image, Blake reinforces a visual marriage as a fecund union of opposites or non-traditional pairs. The title "Memorable Fancy" also reminds us of Wheatley's engagement with "fancy" as a productive mode of memory in "On Recollection." Like Wheatley, Blake's fancy is linked to memory but also creation and transformation.

In the third "Memorable Fancy" section, Blake writes about a "printing house in hell," where the speaker sees "printing in the infernal method, by corrosives, which in Hell are salutary and medicinal, melting apparent surfaces away" (Pl. 14). This printing house inverts the practices of the typical printing presses of Blake's day, stripping away surfaces to display what is "infinite" behind them. Blake's echoes his own printing method here in that he reverses the normal method of etching. Blake worked directly on a copper plate and wrote the text and illustrations in reverse. He then etched the plate with acid to eat away the copper and leave the design standing in relief,

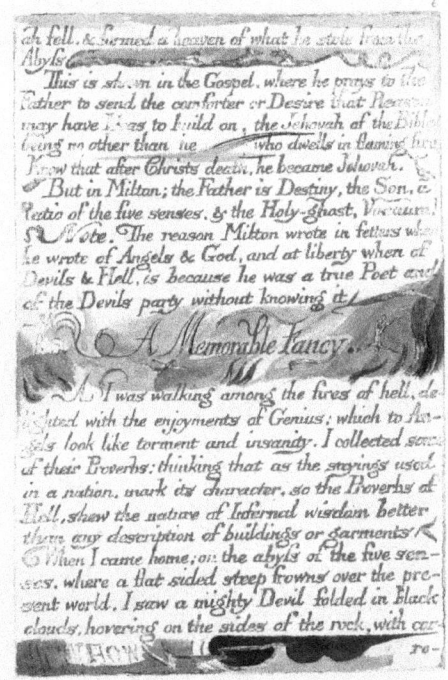

Figure 4.4   *The Marriage of Heaven and Hell*, copy D, obj. 6, 1790. Lessing J. Rosenwald Collection, Library of Congress. Copyright © 2022 The William Blake Archive. Used with permission.

what is called "relief etching."[26] Blake's method allows for the convergence of invention and execution, a level of control and creativity that avoids more systematized letterpress printing of his day. In letterpress printing, text is written on paper and then set in type, moving, as Viscomi notes, "unidirectionally—from author to compositor" (*Blake and the Idea of the Book* 286). Blake's printing method affords an opportunity to subvert the letterpress method and work from a new "infernal" method of production in the *Marriage*.

After the printing-house scene, the "Fancy" sections become more and more propulsive, with Giants, fires, a Hellish Bible, and a curious Angel friend. By the end of the narrative the Angel has been converted. "This Angel, who is now become a Devil, is my particular friend; we often read the Bible together in its infernal or diabolical sense which the world shall have if they behave well" (Pl. 24). This religious conversion is written

Figure 4.5 *The Marriage of Heaven and Hell*, copy D, obj. 27, 1790. Lessing J. Rosenwald Collection, Library of Congress. Copyright © 2022 The William Blake Archive. Used with permission.

in italic script and is a turn to the "crooked roads," the ones which lead not to "Improvement," but instead, lead to "Genius" (Pl. 10). Genius, the alternative to linear improvement, is possible only out of a "crooked"/curved path, as visually embodied in the italic script of much of the *Marriage*.

In the final sections of the *Marriage*—"A Song of Liberty" and "Chorus"—the script is again in italics yet there is also a noticeable shift in tone and theme (see figure 4.5). In the "Song," we have orality and a high "odic or Ossianic style" (Pechey 68). This orality is a polyphonous space and not just "The Voice of one crying in the Wilderness" ("All Religions are One" 1). Blake mentions a range of people and places, including "Albions [Britain's] coast," "American meadows," France, "Golden Spain," "O Rome," O citizen of London, "O Jew," and the "O African! black African!" (Pls. 25–6). This list is a type of cultural "allo-identification," what Eve Sedgwick notes as "identification with" instead of "as" along the lines of gender, sexuality, race, class, nation (59). These paths are "likely to be strange and recalcitrant," and Blake's song proposes a collective group of liberty that is united while different (Sedgwick 59). The plurality of voices in this song includes humans, animals, and nature, and they all call for the end of "Empire." Near the end of the song comes "the son of fire in his eastern cloud," beckoning dawn and the "East" of Blake's later works.

The italicized "Chorus" section that comes next shifts to censure. Unlike the "Song," the chorus uses a series of negatives, making assertions through contraries:

> Let the Priests of the Raven of dawn,
> *no* longer in deadly black, with hoarse note
> curse the sons of joy. *Nor* his accepted
> brethren whom. tyrant, he calls free: lay the
> bound or build the roof. *Nor* pale religious
> letchery call that virginity. that wishes
> but acts not! (Pl. 27, emphasis mine)

There is no clear narrative progression between the "Song" and "Chorus." The association between Blake's italics and dynamism takes on a new oral quality through these closing sections that are meant to be sung. The italics thus reflect text that will be sung or read out loud, showing the multiple functions of Blake's handwriting choices.

Linking Word and Image: Blake's Bodies

Returning to the title plate of the *Marriage* uncovers some of the fundamental attributes of Blake's composite art (see figure 4.6). These attributes result from traditional techniques—engraving, illustration, and painting—that are amended by Blake. Blake's pictorialism incorporates handwriting, which is Blake's playful mimicry of typography as another pictorial form.[27] On the title plate, the word "*Marriage*" is written in italics and merges with the pictorial elements on the page. As in the "Memorable Fancy" sections, the lines of the lettering

Figure 4.6 *The Marriage of Heaven and Hell*, copy D, obj. 1, 1790. Lessing J. Rosenwald Collection, Library of Congress. Copyright © 2022 The William Blake Archive. Used with permission.

meld with the pictorial borders. It is telling that the romantic word of union, "marriage," is the point of convergence between image and text. The fact that this "marriage" happens via italic script reinforces Blake's larger pattern of italics/roman usage. In unifying picture and typography, the choice of italics can be seen as deconstructing or destabilizing the very boundary between both modes of representation. In essence, the imagetext creates while deconstructing, "enacting [Blake's] vision of a liberated social and psychological order" (75).[28] Mitchell's connection between Blake's aesthetics and ethics gives Blake's visual enterprise a philosophical symbolism that continues in *Jerusalem*. Like *Jerusalem*'s apocalyptic ending, the *Marriage* indicates that an end to the world can happen at any time.

This millenarian impulse is pictorially represented in the sensual bodies that populate Blake's illustrations. The sexuality of Blake's bodies is transmogrified when viewed as also heavenly bodies of cherubs and emanations. Pictorially, the title page displays two naked bodies embracing in a kiss right below the title. They are horizontal and although scholars often describe them as feminine, their gender is not certain. What is more certain is that they mirror each other in their appearance and gestural desire. In terms of embodiment, these two figures are similar in body size and shape, not diametrically opposed or evocative of heteronormative marriage and gender representations. The ambiguity and corporeal similarity of these two figures is echoed in other images of the work. On plate 3 (see figure 4.7), the *William Blake Archive* describes the top image as "an apparently nude female," yet this denotation is not verifiable. What is clear, however, is that the figure is nude and muscular. There are also two horizontal bodies of unclear gender at the top of plate 14 (see figure 4.8). Scholars have persisted in maintaining the gender binary in describing these images when, in pictorial reality, this binary is ambiguous. The illustration description of this plate 14 states, "Hovering in flames over the dead male is a nude(?) [sic] female figure with her arms raised horizontally" (*The William Blake Archive*). This heteronormative guess is arbitrary to the point of obscuring the non-binary or genderqueer potential of these pictorial representations. These

Figure 4.7 *The Marriage of Heaven and Hell*, copy D, obj. 3, 1790. Lessing J. Rosenwald Collection, Library of Congress. Copyright © 2022 The William Blake Archive. Used with permission.

figures question not only gender, but also pictorial representations of angels, devils, and spiritual bodies. As in Blake's handwriting choices, all is not meant to be straight, narrow, and/or normative. The fluidity of gender and corporeality animates the images and their evocative queerness, a queerness furthering Blake's claim for the "improvement of sensual enjoyment" (Pl. 14).

Throughout his oeuvre, critics have noted the centrality of the human body in Blake's illustration.[29] In *Jerusalem*, Blake writes of the mutuality between Los and Enitharmon, "When in Eternity Man converses with Man they enter / Into each others [sic] Bosom (which are Universes of delight) / In mutual interchange" (Pl. 88). The human as divine form seeks interaction with other forms of "Man" in order to feel "delight." In terms of visual representation, Blake's human form is a "structural principle of space" that serves as a paradigmatic

Figure 4.8 *The Marriage of Heaven and Hell*, copy D, obj. 14, 1790. Lessing J. Rosenwald Collection, Library of Congress. Copyright © 2022 The William Blake Archive. Used with permission.

shape of life (*Blake's Composite Art* 34).[30] The human body complements Blake's handwriting choices and unites verbal and graphic forms through a phenomenological and modular understanding of Romantic subjectivity.

In starting my analysis of Blake with *The Marriage of Heaven and Hell* and its handwriting choices, I initially set out to find an internal logic or pattern to the work's calligraphic choices. What I have found is that Blake's orientations—linear, pictorial, sexual, semantic—offer a mode of reading that embraces fluidity, dynamism, and recursive engagement. The upright handwriting in the "Proverbs of Hell" section sometimes belies the obliqueness of what is being said, and the italic sections of the *Marriage* are not consistent in tone, style, or visual representation. The italics offer a way to unite text and image and visualize movement and transformation, such as on the title page.

In the last line of the *Marriage*, Blake writes, "For every thing that lives is Holy" in italic script (see figure 4.6). Not only are all religions one, but every living "thing" is "Holy." The word "Holy" extends from italic handwriting into a pictorial curve upward, a stylistic mark of Blake's moveable art. What does Blake mean by "Holy" here? The religious denotation may seem foremost, but "Holy" here is infused with Blake's visual-semantic mode. Semantically, this ending opens the realm of the Holy to include all forms of life, not just human. Taken as a whole, the *Marriage* alludes to the potentially awe-inspiring "animacy" that Mel Y. Chen describes "as an often racialized and sexualized means of conceptual and affective mediation between human and inhuman, animate and inanimate, whether in language, rhetoric, or imagery" (9–10). Chen's exploration begins at the level of language and grammar and asks, if language "helps to coerce certain figures into nonbeing . . . then what are the modes of revival, return, or rejoinder?" (14). These "re-" terms contain, at their root, affinitive ideas of life (re*vival*), movement (re*turn*), and union (re*join*der). These ideas foreground the *Marriage* and its ricocheting rhetoric of image and text. Grammatically, the "every thing" in this closing statement has dual meanings. The first is the indefinite pronoun, "everything," but Blake's choice of splitting this noun phrase with a visual and grammatical gap (determining adjective plus noun), echoes what Coleridge would call a "unity in multeity" in Blake's aesthetic universe ("On Poesy or Art"). By separating "every" and "thing" with the blank space, Blake's system of unity through division is reinforced for the visual and reading eye.

From Handwriting to Emanated Form: Blake's *Jerusalem*

Jerusalem has been called Blake's most difficult and mysterious work. Joanne Witke, Paul Youngquist, W. J. T. Mitchell, and others have agreed that *Jerusalem* has no consistent narrative across its 100 plates and is a work of confusion yet possibility. As a "prophetic" and Orientalist work, its amalgamated unfixity of form, content, and style disorient the reader. *Jerusalem* as a text is less amenable to a heuristic of handwriting because the entire work is written in italic script without pause. Due to the length of *Jerusalem* and its more uniform handwriting, I will focus on its fourfold structures as one organizing force.[31] Through this focus, I will identify Blake's turning away from a fixed East and his ultimate disorientation of a fixed lyric subject. What results is Blake's rupturing of binary systems of classification, including East/West, male/female, and earth/heaven, reorienting Romantic poetics toward visuality, phenomenology, and alternative aesthetic horizons beyond the lyric poem and the page.

By reading *Jerusalem* through its fourfold modular system, I counterbalance the reading experience of "confusion and obscurity" that Bernard Blackstone attributes to Blake's symbolic books (69). As Joseph Wittreich notes, the four eras of the book of Revelation are roughly consistent with the four chapters of *Jerusalem* and the four periods mentioned in the "Argument" section of the *Marriage* (44). At the beginning of *Jerusalem*, the "Four Points" of "Great Eternity" are described as "West, the Circumference: South, the Zenith: North, / The Nadir: East, the Center, unapproachable for ever. / These are the four Faces towards the Four Worlds of Humanity / In every Man" (Pl. 12). As "Center, unapproachable for ever," the East becomes the continually retreating axis for Blake's vision and throughout the work, the East is the motif of not only dawn and Jerusalem, but interiority and subjectivity. The movement inward is the source of life and energy for Blake's eschatology, and the East is the origin point for the life cycle of humanity. The narrative movement comprises a series of nested circles of creation and destruction, apocalypse and regeneration, moving the vision of Blake's universe toward infinity and futurity.

Divided into four parts like *The Four Zoas*, *Jerusalem* is a story of the end of the world superimposing English mythic history onto the Hebrew history in the Bible. *Jerusalem*'s biblical narrative starts with the fall of man, the struggle to live in a fallen world, self-destructive redemption, and finally, paradoxical apocalypse. Its four parts are addressed to different groups, the Public, Deists, Jews, and Christians, with sections that can be read synchronically as much as diachronically. Paul Youngquist argues that *Jerusalem*, "is best read as a garden of forking paths, an open array of possible narrative trajectories that the activity of reading substantiates" (621). Susanne M. Sklar proposes that *Jerusalem* can be read either "holistically, like a painting" or "sequentially, like a story" (251).[32] A synchronic reading helps to notice structures of setting, characters, and motifs in Blake's scenes and show us how they interconnect and move us from Ulro, the land of spectral order, to Eden and eternity. For example, on plates 84–100, the messiah figure of Los transfigures destruction into a generative apocalypse. Los is called forth by the spectral order of Daughters of Albion for salvation, and he converses with Enitharmon, his female emanation, telling her, "For Man cannot unite with Man but by their Emanations / Which stand both Male & Female at the Gates of each Humanity" (Pl. 88). Rather than reading this dialogue as part of a linear narrative, it is useful to see this scene as repeating Blake's tropes of gender-fluid spiritual bodies. Rather than emanations being male or female, Blake's fluidity of gender is proleptically expressed in the *Marriage*'s illustrations and manifested clearly in *Jerusalem*'s more colorful, populated plates, such as the unclearly gendered bodies on the title page (see figure 4.9).

The title page of *Jerusalem* is comparatively less human and more intricately detailed than the title page of the *Marriage* (see figure 4.6). On *Jerusalem*'s title page, five flying creatures are depicted in varying poses and expressions. While the *Marriage* title page depicts two non-gendered bodies embracing, the creatures here are a type of anthropomorphized butterfly/flying insect creature with a human head, thorax, and abdomen, presumably the "emanations" themselves. All the handwriting is in a modified italic handwriting that is neither fully cursive nor block lettering. This distinctive handwriting is embellished by its visual joining with pictorial lines in certain instances.

After the frontispiece and title page, the work's opening is addressed "To the Public" and the speaker/"Author" writes of the work's literary style as having "a variety in every line. Both / of cadences & number of syllables. Every word and every letter is studied and put into its fit place" (Pl. 3). This fitness of place deems poetry as superior to the "inferior parts" of prose and refuses rhyme as a type of "a bondage" (Pl. 3). Blake concludes

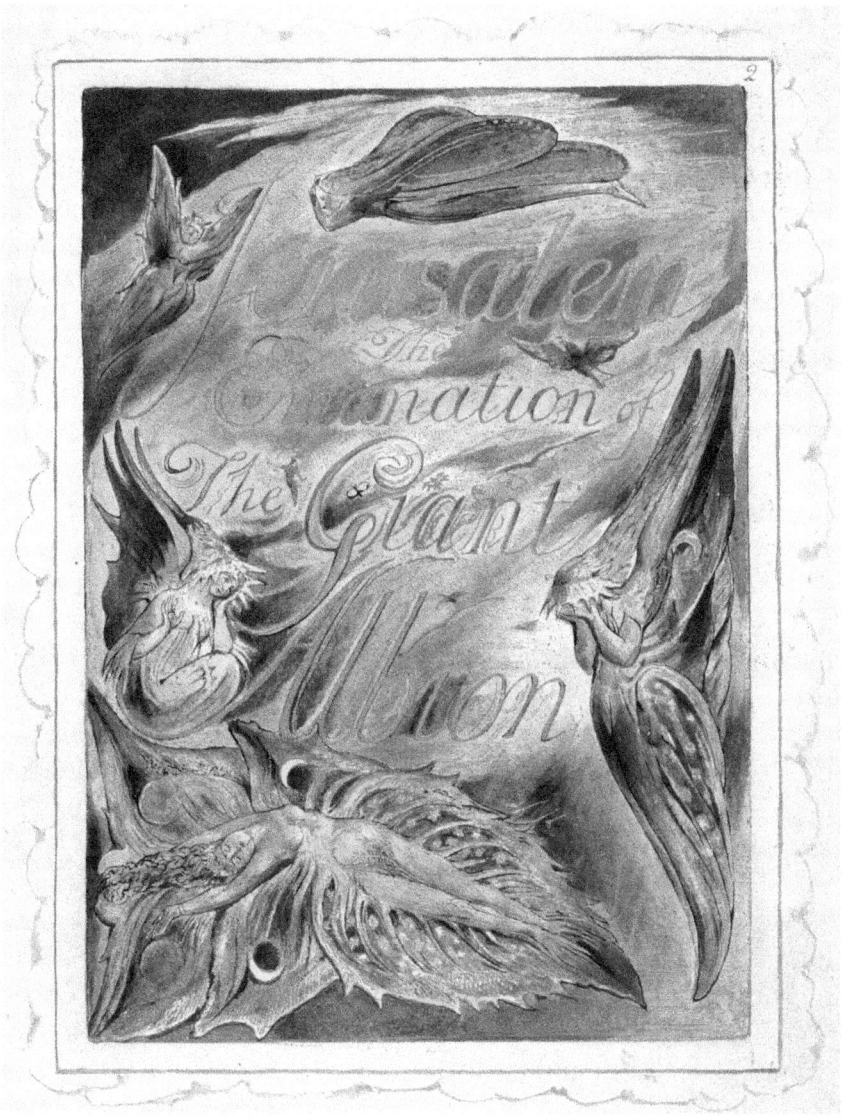

Figure 4.9 *Jerusalem*, copy E, obj. 2, c. 1821. Yale Center for British Art. The William Blake Archive. Public Domain.

this plate by asserting:

> Poetry   Fetter'd.   Fetters the Human Race.
> Nations are Destroy'd, or Flourish, in proportion as Their Poetry Painting and Music, are Destroy'd or Flourish! The Primeval State of Man, was Wisdom, Art, and Science. (Pl. 3)

The problems of bondage and the loss of originary states of being are common in Blake's corpus, and the possible parallelism of the tripartite "Poetry Painting and Music" and "Wisdom, Art, and Science" positions poetry alongside wisdom, painting with art, and music with science. This parallelism can serve as a dictum for the entire work; that is, the work's purpose of spiritual forethought through poetic expression. As Bloom notes, *Jerusalem* "has a strong taste for intellectual symbolism" (*Blake's Apocalypse* 929). This symbolism, particularly between Los and Spectre, is a move toward individuation, as Blake pushes aside Christianity's collective guilt to argue for "an individual [and solitary] prophetic stance for salvation" (929). Blake centers the individual "I" of Los over the "we" of "Nations," focalizing the struggle for salvation, a type of non-violent revolution for Blake, within individual subjectivities.

Jerusalem folds inward and around itself often, and the four-fold structure is the only organizing principle that maintains itself throughout the work. One of the work's most intriguing uses of "four" occurs in this opening section. The speaker starts with an abstract idea and moves into describing the borders of human identity and its affective and physiological cues. Blake writes, "From every-one of the Four Regions of Human Majesty / There is an Outside spread Without & an Outside spread Within, / Beyond the Outline of Identity both ways, which meet in One, / An orbed void of doubt, despair, hunger & thirst & sorrow" (Pl. 18, see figure 4.10). The metaphysics of "Human Majesty" take the shape of an "orbed void" of affective and physical needs—this amalgamation of thoughts, feelings, and bodily urges are the constitutive traits of the "Human Form Divine" ("A Divine Image" 3). The human form is majestic despite its vulnerability—an acknowledgment of precarity—the intersectional condition in which certain groups are exposed to unpredictable suffering, injury, and/or death. This precarity acknowledges human suffering and its pursuit of a life beyond normative or linear routes of relation and identification. On this plate, there are two contrasting pairs of figures. The inner pair evoke the embracing cherubim of the title plate of the *Marriage* while the larger, bordering figures are depicted as moving away from each other. This tension

William Blake's Orientalist Poetics   147

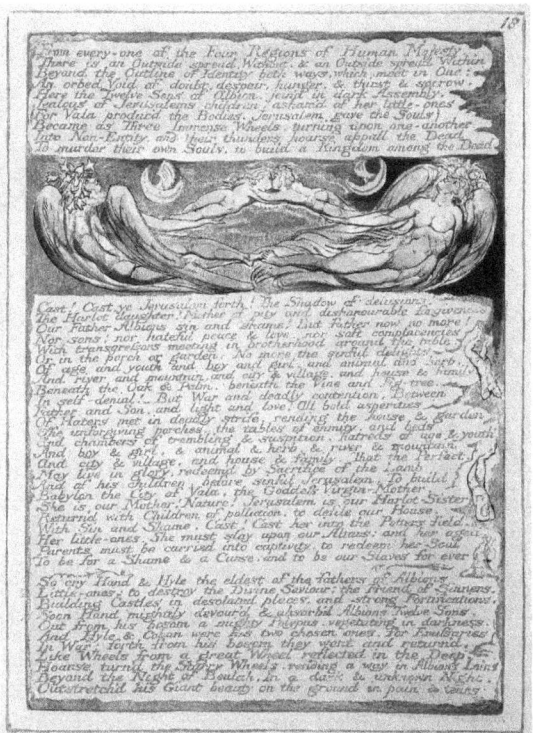

Figure 4.10 *Jerusalem*, copy E, obj. 18, c. 1821. Yale Center for British Art. The William Blake Archive. Public Domain.

between towardness and departure visualizes the movement of Blake's bodies within a world wherein the "Center" is "unapproachable for ever"— a haven of interiority and subjectivity often linked to Blake's "East."

The work culminates in an apocalyptic rebirth of the "New Jerusalem" on a planetary and geographically unbounded stage—a type of visual theatre for the human imagination. Instead of wanting to name or represent gender or human life concretely, Blake reinforces the idea of queer bodies—those that are oblique, non-normative, nongendered. The ironic imagination of Blake's *Marriage* has been supplanted by the prophetic imagination of Blake's new Jerusalem, a world that tests the limits of poetic representation. Blake takes up Sir William Jones's poetic task of expression over imitation to a level beyond the other authors in this study. Anticipating reader response, Blake writes, "Therefore [*Dear*] Reader, [*forgive*] what you do not approve, & [*love*] me for this energetic exertion of my talent" (Pl. 3).[33] The effortful physicality of this "talent" foreshadows the artisanship of the sentient forms of Blake's fourfold cosmos—emanations tasked with building Blake's new Jerusalem.

The work of building this new Jerusalem is led by Los, who is a blacksmith.[34] Standing in London while building Golgonooza against the rebukes from his "Spectre," Los declares, "'I must Create a System or be enslav'd by another Man's. / I will not Reason & Compare: my business is to Create'" (Pl. 10). Los is a symbol for creative energy that "englobes" the human form within a host of spectral forces, both good and evil.[35] In creating a new system in Golgonooza, Los eventually becomes, like all the forms inhabiting Blake's cosmos, part of eternity as well. Los and Jesus eventually co-inhere in the final section, together embodying the Man/God duality of one of Blake's ideal forms.

Whereas the masculine Los is Jesus's "Friend" (96), the feminized "Jerusalem" is an emanation and continually exists apart from Jesus's identity. She is introduced in the work on plate 11, as "lovely" and "mournful Jerusalem," a city lacking a "Body whose life is but a Shade" (Pls. 11–12). This lack of "Body" creates an object through which Blake anthropomorphizes Jerusalem as various conflicting personas, including "youthful girl," "Harlot daughter!," "Mother of pity and dishonourable forgiveness," divine "Bride," and enslaved "outcast" (Pls. 83, 18, 12, 59). This objectification of the "Eastern" woman culminates in the final section, where Jerusalem becomes an emanation again. The Vision of Albion awakens Jerusalem, "'O lovely Emanation of Albion, / Awake and overspread all Nations as in Ancient Time; / For lo! the Night of Death is past and the Eternal Day / Appears upon our Hills'" (Pl. 97). Jerusalem descends from heaven and animates every forgiven and living form (Pls. 98–9). That Albion must awaken the "East" shows the contradictory logics of empire and alliance embedded in Blake's prophecy.

As a figure and symbol, Jerusalem exists both inside and outside of British identity. Jerusalem's paradoxical position as center and periphery places her at the juncture of the "Truth" of existence for Blake's phenomenology. Blake writes,

"Jerusalem the Emanation of the Giant Albion! Can it be? Is it a / Truth that the Learned have explored? Was Britain the Primitive / Seat of the Patriarchal Religion?" (Pl. 27). Jerusalem as "Giant Albion" shows that she is a source of derivation for Britain/"Albion." In asking Jerusalem about Britain's "primitive" origin, Jerusalem functions as the prophetic authority who knows a history of "Albion" aligned with the East. *Jerusalem* folds inward and around itself often, seeking "Truth" in circular, circuitous, and recurrent movement between East and West. Within this ever-unfolding future space, the fourfold structure is the only organizing principle that maintains itself throughout the work.

Mapping Blake's Fourfold *Jerusalem*

The four cardinal points of north, south, east, and west refer to various, oftentimes inconsistent locations and things in Blake's works. Makdisi argues that Blake offers "a simultaneously and inextricably multidimensional and inter-referential map of the world . . . a series of simultaneous superimpositions, in which these 'different' geographies no longer remain separable but become interlocking and even indistinguishable" (*Romantic Imperialism* 167). This lack of differentiation between spaces shows Blake's building of one world that is intensely disparate and dynamic. The fourfold modularity is the key to unlocking any sense of order.

Fourfold structures abound in the work. Blake writes on plate 13 that "every part of the City is fourfold; & every inhabitant, fourfold. / And every pot & vessel & garment & utensil of the houses, / And every house, fourfold" (Pl. 13). Jerusalem is "eastward bending / Her revolutions toward the Starry Wheels in maternal anguish" (Pl. 14), so not only is she pointed east, but she is in continual orbit—a type of planetary form. When Jerusalem has finally descended from heaven, there is a "Fourfold Annihilation" and "every Man stood Fourfold. Each Four Faces had. One to the West / One toward the East One to the South One to the North" (Pl. 98). Every "man" has an expanded, inclusive gaze that includes all parts of the world.

With this inclusive expansiveness, man has been forgiven, a type of "Self Annihilation," and his form is an ambiguous "Body" of "Four Senses" (sight, smell, taste, hearing). Blake ends by describing senses over physical form, evoking the sentience of human form more than its corporeality. This reminds us of Blake's queer future, one in which "Sexes must vanish & cease" (Pl. 92).

In this future, the fourfold structure of *Jerusalem* carries through to "Eternity." On Plate 98, Blake describes Eternity in multiples of four: "the Four Rivers of the / Water of Life," "Four Senses in the Outline the Circumference & Form," "Four Living Creatures Chariots of Humanity Divine / Incomprehensible," "Four Rivers of Paradise," "Four Faces of Humanity," and finally the "Four Cardinal Points / Of Heaven going forward forward irresistible from Eternity to Eternity" (Pl. 98). The "forward forward" motion of the four cardinal points creates "Space ... [and] Time according to the wonders Divine" (Pl. 98). The series of eternities reached by this forward motion of North, South, East, and West is a dynamism that propels futurity.

Blake etched onto the back of one of his copper plates, "I labour upwards into futurity" (*CPP* 890). This effort "upwards" as a transcendent futurity interacts with the Orientalist yearning eastward—a yearning graphically captured by Blake's right-leaning italic writing and his repeated use of "East" in this geographic imaginary. Blake's four-directional attention to the space of the printed page as a "world" allows him to distinguish between "upward" and "eastward" movement without entirely separating them. It is in this correlation of up ("north") and east that Blake disrupts the separateness of the cardinal directions, dislodges binary thinking of East/West relations, and proposes a turn away from fixed constructions of the East as always apart or distant from center.

The upward futurity Blake seeks is one in which all life forms can participate, making his subjectivity a democratized space turning away from Orientalist difference. The work of "labour[ing] upwards" gives an altitude of perspective, a view of the whole from above. It is from this elevated vantage point that East/West comparisons dissolve, making way for an

Figure 4.11 *Jerusalem*, copy E, obj. 99, c. 1821. Yale Center for British Art. The William Blake Archive. Public Domain.

openness of directionality and elevated sense of a shared vision of the whole. By the penultimate plate, "All Human Forms identified" are now named Jerusalem (Pl. 99), combining Blake's prophetic symbols, figurations, and motifs under the umbrella of the feminine Jerusalem. The bodies on this closing plate are an elderly person embracing a muscular, younger person in an intimate embrace of erotic energy (see figure 4.11). Both forms are in motion and swooning in dynamic lines. The pair most likely resemble Albion and Jerusalem, but it is unclear. Like many of the forms that populate Blake's cosmos, these bodies are open to gender interpretation. Karl Kroeber notes how Blake views the "[a]pprehension of sexual categories as evidence of disorganized perception" and thus sexuality as "the ultimate codification of division" (360–1).[36] Through its system of division, sexuality is "temporarily enervating" and stokes the energy needed to form the "Divine Vision" of Jerusalem and "Great Eternity" (361, *Jerusalem* Pl. 54). This eternity is Blake's "expansion through interiorization" that is stoked by sexuality and an upward-eastward orientation (Kroeber 363).[37]

This plate has the final text of the work, and both *The Marriage of Heaven and Hell* and *Jerusalem* end in a "song" of rhizomatic fecundity.[38] The *Marriage*'s ending "chorus" orally invokes the holiness of "every thing." *Jerusalem*'s ending song, however, does not have the same orality or seem meant to be sung. The work ends:

> All Human Forms identified even Tree Metal Earth & Stone, all Human Forms identified. living going forth & returning wearied Into the Planetary lives of Years Months Days & Hours reposing And then Awaking into his Bosom in the Life of Immortality.
> And I heard the Name of their Emanations they are named Jerusalem
>
> The End of The Song
> of Jerusalem (Pl. 99)

Visually, this ending is a union of text and image occurring at the beginning of the closing phrase, "The End of The Song / of Jerusalem" (Pl. 99, see figure 4.11).[39] The final word "Jerusalem," however, is set apart from the pictorial elements on the page, written in italic but not cursive script—a Blakean fusion of italic and roman script. Unlike the word "holy" that ends the *Marriage*—where holy's ending "y" joins with the pictorial elements in a filigreed union—the word "Jerusalem" is completely set apart from the pictorial realm. The separation of text from picture at the end of *Jerusalem* signifies a finality or breakage. This breakage clearly distinguishes the text from the bodies below. Through this breakage, the "song" ends with "All Human Forms" named "Jerusalem."

The work's next and final plate lacks text and shows three unknown figures (see figure 4.12). The *William Blake Archive* hypothesizes Los to the left and Enitharmon on the right, with a flying figure holding the sun on their shoulders to Los's left (see figure 4.12). Rather than try to identify them, I want to focus on their embodied, visual signs. These fleshy, nude, human-like figures suddenly tower over the temple and landscape.[40] They command presence beyond the temples of religion. The figure on the right is darker than the other two figures, turning away

William Blake's Orientalist Poetics   153

Figure 4.12 *Jerusalem*, copy E, obj. 100, c. 1821. Yale Center for British Art. The William Blake Archive. Public Domain.

from whiteness and its racial logics. By holding the sun, I am reminded of Shelley's lines in *The Revolt of Islam*, "the orient sun in shadow:—not a sound / was heard" (I.12–16). Blake shows the sun lifted by this figure who is human-like, fleshy, embodied with Blake's "fibres" of corporeal existence. It is not Shelley's "shapes" of life but a human, gender-ambiguous presence. Blake embraces gender fluidity as constitutive of his ideal Human/"Man and shows that "All Human Forms" are not restricted by gender or racial categories.

In Blake's world, everyone, regardless of class, sex/gender, race/ethnicity, or species, can represent and be a part of Jerusalem. The clearest message of Blake's prophecy is the universal pursuit of liberty for all—which is what Jerusalem represents. This inclusiveness is a break from Orientalist logics of separation, exclusion, and control. It finds in the East a means of union and a shared world of non-normative, as of yet unmapped life. This shared world asserts Blake's seventh and final principle in "ALL RELIGIONS are ONE"—that "all men are alike (tho' infinitely various)" (*CPP* 2).[41] This infinite variety of the human articulates a revolutionary idea of divinity which exists in the realm of human experience, earthliness, material reality, and sense perceptions, but is no less awe-inspiring, for "[a]ll deities reside in the human breast" (*The Marriage* Pl. 11).

Conclusion: Blake's Disorientation

Ending his prophetic books in the literary "East," Blake's works transport the literary topography of British Romantic Orientalism to speculative futures. By paying attention to the structures of handwriting, bodies, and fourfold structures in Blake's composite art, this chapter proposes Blake's disorientation of Orientalist norms, and a turning away from fixed directions. This turning away disrupts normative ideas of poetry, narrative, and aesthetics. It hopefully yields new directions and futures for Romantic poetry. As Sara Ahmed notes, "moments of disorientation are vital. They are bodily experiences that throw the world up, or throw the body from its ground" (*Queer Phenomenology* 157). Blake's dynamism of text, images, and their relation on the page disorient and throw the world up, reimagine it from a slant, and position it "upwards into futurity."

In Chapter 1, Shelley's revolutionary impulse in *The Revolt of Islam* proposes an aesthetics of shapes delinked from human attributes. Shelley aestheticizes the Orient and its subjects into a space of British imaginative projection. In Blake's works, however, bodies are bodies, corporeal and fleshy, gathering around the page in lines and colors that challenge the reader and viewer to think and see otherwise. While Byron gestures eastward to the point of solipsistic self-referral and containment, Blake's facing the East absolves itself of worldly and human norms or constraints. Blake's modular and modulated expressions—printing technique, handwriting, images, fourfold systems of the universe—disorient any fixity of position or expression. Blake embraces difference, queerness, and inclusiveness. He resists East/West differentiation and division, discarding the logics of Orientalist control for the purpose of holistic world-building. At the end of *Jerusalem*, Blake writes of the "living creatures" in Eternity who have four faces of North, South, East, and West. These "Four Faces of Humanity" "conversed together" and "walked / [t]o & fro in Eternity as One Man reflecting each in each & clearly seen / [a]nd seeing" (Pl. 98). In his ideal world, Blake imagines empathetic relationships between all forms of life who can see and be seen. This is not mere coexistence but mutual understanding and connection. It is with this generous spirit of belonging that Blake's world continually expands "forward to Eternity" with a humility to all directions. In doing so, Blake faces our gazes beyond ourselves—towards who or what is next to, behind, and awaiting us.

Notes

1. Like Jones, Blake does express an Orientalist alignment of primitivism or origin with "eastern" poetry and themes. David Weir suggests that Blake may have encountered Jones's work through reading Joseph Johnson's *Analytical Review* or via his friends John Flaxman and William Hayley.
2. I will be citing plate numbers for all of Blake's works, using *The Complete Poetry and Prose of William Blake* (1982), hereafter *CPP*. I italicize the quotes that are italicized in the work, to mirror the visuals of the original work.
3. For more on Blake's "Orient" in terms of geographical references across his works, see Edward Larrissy's "Blake's Orient." Larrissy conjectures that Blake was also influenced by Charles Wilkin's Gita, drawing cherub and bard figures with "oriental" connotations in mind (12).
4. For more on queer phenomenology, see Sara Ahmed's *Queer Phenomenology*. In *Blake's Composite Art*, W. J. T. Mitchell calls Blake's work as a whole a "composite art."
5. Cf. Mitchell writes that Blake's poetry is affirmative of the human imagination and Blake's painting affirms "the centrality of the human body as the structural principle of space" (*Blake's Composite Art* 34).
6. Blake is known for depicting male and female genitals in certain illustrations.
7. Garry M. Leonard writes of how "One of Blake's many contributions in the extraordinary combinations of illustration and text is his unabashed offering of an alternative way of seeing . . . Such a perception . . . 'authorizes the production of alternative ways of projecting mind into a world" (920).

8. Blake's queerness has been recouped by scholars including Helen T. Bruder, Tristanne J. Connolly, and Steven Clark.
9. For the visual archive of my research, I am using *The William Blake Archive*, edited by Eaves et al.
10. After *Jerusalem*, Blake's prophetic mode declined, at least in terms of complete illuminated books Blake worked on three more illuminated books, *Laocoön*, *On Homers Poetry*, and *The Ghost of Abel* afterwards, and continued with commercial illustrations. His earlier epic, *Milton*, was composed c. 1804–11.
11. See also Northrop Frye's *Fearful Symmetry*, p. 196.
12. "Correspondences" refers to Blake's characters and places categorized into his fourfold system of North, South, East, and West.
13. Blake ends *MHH*, "For every thing that lives is Holy" (Pl. 27).
14. Mitchell coined the term "imagetext" in *Picture Theory* (1994), arguing for "the typographic conventions of the slash to designate 'image/text' as a problematic gap, cleavage, or rupture in representation. The term 'imagetext' designates composite, synthetic works (or concepts) that combine image and text. 'Image-text,' with a hyphen, designates *relations* of the visual and verbal" (89). Blake's method of combination, however, "was to transform the dualism into a dialectic, to create unity out of contrariety rather than similitude or complementarity" (*Blake's Composite Art* 33). Mitchell's distinction marks Blake's handwriting choices as useful evidence for the formal structures underlying Blake's composite art. By arguing for Blake's unifying, not reductive, impulse in using both verbal and pictorial/graphic arts, Mitchell is arguing that Blake's writing *and* drawing serve ideological and thematic purposes.
15. Eaves explains that "The success of letterpress print technology relied heavily upon uniformities and simplifications that yielded great gains in efficiency. All printable expressions in languages written in the Latin alphabet combine those twenty-six letters, the meanings of which do not depend on unique characteristics but on general configuration . . . Hence we reflect separately on the aesthetic sense represented through book design and the aesthetic sense represented through the text, which is a general or abstract entity located in all particular instances" (*Counter-Arts Conspiracy* 189–90).
16. Joseph Viscomi's work on Blake's illuminated printing, *Blake and the Idea of the Book*, offers a diachronic, heavily researched account of the progression of Blake's printing process. Viscomi argues, in contrast to prior assumptions, that in Blake's printing process, "page designs were not preconceived. For more on the mechanistic engraving practices Blake dislikes, see also Morris

Eaves's *The Counter-Arts Conspiracy: Art and Industry in the Age of Blake* (1992).
17. Johanna Drucker argues for the need to reverse "a common assumption ... that the visual dimension of writing is ornamental, decorative, extrasemantic—a matter of design, not signs that matter" (xi).
18. The logic of Blake's hand-drawn typeface is rooted in both style and efficiency, for it is also possible that italic script was quicker for Blake to write, saving him time and energy.
19. Blake's use of italics reminds one of Emily Dickinson's line, "Tell all the truth but tell it slant."
20. Mulvihill writes, "Students of Blake's media-reflexivity read *The Marriage of Heaven and Hell*, with its binaries of energy and reason, 'the Prolific' and 'the Devouring,' as an enactment of Blake's material practice as an artist, thus stressing the fundamental identity of his production techniques ... with his ontology of the inseparability of body and soul, spirit and incarnation" (124).
21. Saree Makdisi argues that "Blake's method works ... by erasing, burning, corrosives – revealing, among other things, the gaps and spaces between the words as much as the words and images themselves. The words and images are given shape from out of the background in which they are contained" (*Reading William Blake* 88).
22. Numerically, it is also interesting that the Song of Solomon has eight chapters, evoking a doubling of the fourfold structures found throughout Blake's poetics.
23. *The Holy Bible*, ed. Benjamin Blayney (Oxford: T. Wright and W. Gill, 1769).
24. It is not clear to me whether these are Swedenborg's unique practices or English printing practices of the time in general. See also Emanuel Swedenborg, *A Treatise concerning Heaven and Hell and of the wonderful things within* (1784).
25. The other two are the complete version of twenty-seven plates and copy K, the four plates right before "Song of Liberty," which is also a stand-alone pamphlet version. Cf. Makdisi, *Reading William Blake* (2015) and *The William Blake Archive*.
26. For more on Blake's etching method see Joseph Viscomi's *Blake and the Idea of the Book*.
27. Mitchell echoes Bloom's distinction between "the *Marriage* as in itself dialectical and the dialectic it attempts to present" ("Dialectic in the Marriage of Heaven and Hell" 501), by arguing that the struggle between poem and picture in "the total design of his illuminated pages continually reaffirms the ultimate identity of poem and picture by displaying a continuity between

the most abstract linear patterns and the most representational forms" (*Blake's Composite Art* 75). He argues, "At one extreme, visual form is constructed in accord with . . . (language); at the other extreme, the picture is designed as an immediate, synaesthetic presentation of primitive sensory elements" (75).

28. Mitchell, *Blake's Composite Art*.
29. For example, Mitchell names Blake's "more comprehensive idea of the 'Human Form Divine'" (*Blake's Composite Art* 34).
30. See also Eynel Wardi's, "Space, the Body, and the Text in *The Marriage of Heaven and Hell*," p. 253. She writes of the *Marriage*'s "poetics of expansion" using three foregrounding concepts: "space, the body, and textuality."
31. For more on the structures of *Jerusalem*, see Stuart Curran's work in *Blake's Sublime Allegory* (1973).
32. Cf. Morton D. Paley's authoritative reading in *The Continuing City: William Blake's Jerusalem*.
33. The amended transcription is taken from David V. Erdman's work in *The Complete Poetry and Prose of William Blake*.
34. As Makdisi points out, "The all-important prophetic figure of Los (who in certain of his incarnations stands for Blake himself) is a blacksmith, and the feverish poundings of his hammer and anvil boom continually in the background of *Jerusalem*" (*Romantic Imperialism* 164). For more on similarities between Shelley and Blake as philosophical idealists, see Terence Allan Hoagwood's *Prophecy and the Philosophy of Mind*.
35. On an early proof of the frontispiece that has been erased, Blake writes above the depicted archway, "There is a Void, outside of Existence, which if enter'd into / Englobes itself & becomes a Womb, such was Albions Couch" (*CPP* 144).
36. Karl Kroeber, "Delivering Jerusalem."
37. Kroeber, "Delivering Jerusalem" 363.
38. For more on rhizomatic theory, see Gilles Deleuze and Félix Guattari's *A Thousand Plateaus*.
39. Like Wheatley's emancipatory "On Imagination" ending in a "lay"/song, this work also ends in "song." In addition to their implicit critique of systems of enslavement, the orality and distinction between listening and reading in both works is something that Wheatley and Blake share.
40. Clare A. Simmons notes how "the human figures are not, as they had been in some earlier plates, dwarfed by the temple, but stand powerfully in front of it" (*Popular Medievalism* 55).
41. The principle reads, "PRINCIPLE 7th As all men are alike (tho' infinitely various) So all / Religions & as all similar have one source / The true Man is the source he being the Poetic Genius" (*CPP* 2).

Conclusion

Disorientation, v.
1. deviation from the eastward position.
2. The condition of having lost one's bearings; uncertainty as to direction.
Oxford English Dictionary

If orientations point us to the future, to what we are moving toward, then they also keep open the possibility of changing directions and of finding other paths, perhaps those that do not clear a common ground, where we can respond with joy to what goes astray.
Sara Ahmed, *Queer Phenomenology*

I began this book by proposing the poetics of orientation as a critical mode of reading Romantic poetry and the rise of Orientalism. A poetics of orientation traces the centrality of the poet, relational subjectivities, the dominance of the imagination, the lack of a coherent "Other," dislocated setting and/or time period, and plurality amidst universalism. The Scottish writer Hugh Blair argues in his 1763 dissertation on Ossian, "What we have been accustomed to call the oriental vein of poetry, because some of the earlier poetical productions have come to us from the East, is probably no more oriental than occidental; it is characteristical of an age rather than a country . . ." (4). In truth, this book has shown that what was often called "oriental" during the Romantic era represented British writers' attempts to write and envision themselves in a more global world. These writers represented cultural difference via the "Orient," remaking their own forms and styles in the process. "Characteristical" of their own aesthetics, the styles, subjects, and settings of Orientalism are indissolubly linked to the consolidated white subjectivity of the Romantic poet and an overwhelming imagination delinked from the colonial and imperial reality of British sovereignty.

This book has deployed multiple orientations—cultural, geographical, aesthetic, racial, and gendered— through which to situate Romantic poetics. In doing so, it has focused on the Orientalist sites, subjects, and settings commonly deemed "bad," unimportant, or marginal to the development of Romantic poetry. No longer marginal, the rise of the "Oriental" subject is essential to understanding the rise of the post-Romantic lyric subject as we understand it today. Starting with William Jones's call to turn to the East for expressive art, this book has surveyed Percy Bysshe Shelley's idiom of shapes, Byron's cosmopolitan "East," Felicia Hemans's affective poetics, William Blake's queer orientations, and detoured through the poetics of Wheatley, keeping open the possibility of changing directions.

Changing directions has also enabled me to better confront the whiteness of the lyric subject, its antiblackness, and how "Oriental" subjects are not alone in the racial hierarchy of the period. This "not alone" reflects the global project of white supremacy, but also opens up an opportunity for the non-white world to form collectives and solidarity amongst us, perhaps even "respond with joy to what goes astray" (Ahmed *Queer Phenomenology* 178). Returning to the important mission of the Bigger 6 Collective, this book shows that Romanticism is

> not a matter of diversification, of "going global," of adjusting the boundaries of Romanticism in the name of inclusiveness. Rather, it is a call to make our field in the image of those whose access to Romanticism has long been and continues to be actively restricted. Black Romanticisms, Feminist Romanticisms, Subaltern Romanticisms, Queer Romanticisms, Trans Romanticisms, Crip Romanticisms, Indigenous Romanticisms—these are not sub-fields or "special interests" within an unqualified Romanticism. (Bigger Six 140)

Through new orientations, changing directions, and moving away from the "Bigger Six," this book joins these collective efforts. It excavates an inheritance of poetry centering on white male subjects and reorients our imaginations toward an image of the world that includes the silenced, the marginalized, and those from the actual "East," including a woman like me.

I turn to my own positionality now with trepidation. As an Asian American woman who has been called "Oriental" too many times, I came to this project affectively—in response to the accrual of my own feelings upon hearing and reading the word throughout my life. I first encountered the liberatory and revolutionary imaginations of Shelley, Byron, and Blake as a college student, and their words gave me hope. Later in my studies, however, I found cultural references to the "East" and the "Orient" throughout their works that disenchanted and troubled me. Manu Chander writes in *Brown Romantics* that he loves the works of writers like Coleridge, Keats, Wordsworth, and Byron, but he is "incapable of forgetting that they would not have loved me in return" (105). These writers, I know, would not love me but fetishize, objectify, and misunderstand me and my very personhood as an English-speaking woman of color. It is from this unreciprocated and ambivalent space that this book germinated—the tension between my own literary appreciation and the urge to critically respond to the chasm between me and these writers.

While writing this book, the stakes of Orientalism heightened even further due to the COVID-19 pandemic. The word "Oriental" has taken on new, dangerous, and deadly iterations today particularly due to this global pandemic. "Oriental" forms and figures of aesthetic ambiguity, objectification, and inscrutability of representation undergird today's newly activated "Yellow Peril" rhetoric in response to China's association with the origin of COVID. The centrality of Orientalism to Donald Trump's "Kung-flu" and "China virus" usage is irrefutable. The idea of the Asian body of presumed Chinese descent has, for many people around the world, turned into a hyper-visible signifier of virus, infection, and contagion. The rise in anti-Asian racism, discrimination, and attacks around the world shows the heightened precarity of the Asian body. This precarity illustrates how today's Orientalism has taken root within the phenomenological space of the human body.

While the COVID-19 crisis is fundamentally epidemiological, the continuous idea of the "human" is more uncertain than ever. It is the task of the public intellectual to trace and make visible the historical formation of cultural human subjects like the "Oriental" to disrupt the furthering of anti-Asian targeting, racism, and discrimination. Rather than the normalized forgetting of "bad" words in the service of enforced civility, we must revisit our shared histories and discard useless words. We must disorient—turn away from fixed directions, disconcert, lose our bearings, and be open to uncertainty.

This openness is why I will end by bringing in the words of Wang Fang, the well-known Chinese writer who is writing from her home town of Wuhan, China, the early epicenter of COVID-19. Wang, who writes under the pen name "Fang Fang," is a lifelong resident of Wuhan and prolific writer of poems and fiction on urban working-class life. In turning to Wang, I shift the anglophone Western perspective and seek a more inclusive poetic future. One of the most famous examples of Chinese pandemic writing, Wang's *Wuhan Diary* is a sixty-entry daily diary that starts on 25 January 2020, at the beginning of the first lockdown in Wuhan. Wang chronicles her daily life in an honest, critical account that vividly records life in Wuhan. For me, reading Wang's diary throws into stark relief the semi-autobiographical impulses behind some of the poems I have studied in this book. For example, in Chapter 1 I noted Shelley's purpose behind writing *The Revolt of Islam*: "I felt the precariousness of my life, and I engaged in this task, resolved to leave some record of myself" (*Letters* 1, 577). Shelley wants to leave a record of his life, and he chooses to do so in an unnamed "Eastern" city "without much attempt at minute delineation of Mahometan manners" (*Letters*, I, 563–4). In contrast, Wang's record rebuts Shelley's incoherent, fictive use of the unnamed "Eastern" city and responds with a subjectivity of real political force and rebellion against the Chinese government. In an interview on her work, Wang asserts, "If authors have any responsibilities in the face of disaster, the greatest of them is to bear witness . . . I've always cared about how the weak survive great upheavals" (*New York Times*, 14 April 2020).

Bearing witness, Wang's "diary of a closed city" details her and her fellow residents' anxieties, frustrations, fears, and hopes during eleven weeks of lockdown. She records deaths, infections, and the daily experience of living in Wuhan in vivid detail. Though often censored by the Chinese government, the diary remains unflinchingly honest. Wang decries how the government is mishandling the pandemic and misleading the public. In meticulous detail, she records anonymous interviews with other city residents. In a 31 January entry, Wang describes her conversations with vegetable sellers at the streetside market: "I asked the storekeeper whether or not she was afraid of getting infected by staying open during the outbreak. She answered frankly: 'We've got to go on living; so do you!' That's right, they have to carry on, and we all have to carry on; that's simply all we can do!" (27). She feels "a strange sense of security" by these interactions and ends the entry describing streets "almost completely empty. Yet even then there would always be at least one sanitation worker out there, meticulously sweeping the streets" (27). Seeing these workers, Wang finds comfort.

By March, Wang details how her diary is not only censored but receiving hate from anonymous people accusing her of fomenting anti-government and anti-Chinese sentiment. Wang persists, however, rebuking condemnation and continuing to advocate for her truthful account online. She writes, "most diaries are never preserved, but these thousands of collective curses and attacks will ensure that my diary will last forever" (290). She is proven right, as her diary is now a book, published and translated into English with more translations to come.

After Wuhan announces the end of the first lockdown, Wang writes in the last entry, "Just because this is my last installment, that doesn't mean that I will stop writing . . . Even if I have to etch out one character at a time, I will carve their names on history's pillar of shame" (352–3). Wang's writing and activism continue today with her ongoing call to end internet censorship in China. In an afterword in the book version of the *Diary*, Wang recounts Wuhan's dynastic history:

> If you go back to an earlier time, Wuhan was once part of the Kingdom of Chu, which is why Wuhan residents like to refer to

> this place where they live as "the Land of Chu." People in Wuhan really worship the Chu. That is because the people of Chu were known for their military spirit; they had an unbridled *romanticism* and a strong will, which are both qualities that Wuhan natives appreciate. (355, emphasis mine)

Wang brings us back to romanticism, and her voice reflects a revolutionary, liberatory spirit that reflects, too, the highest ideals of the Romantics in this study. Her words forge an Asian woman's lyric subjectivity that speaks back to an anglophone literary tradition that has for too long excluded us from carving our names on "history's pillar." I hope her words have invited you, my reader, to imagine new, radical orientations that foster an "unbridled romanticism" for us all.

Works Cited

Abrams, M. H. *The Mirror and the Lamp: Romantic Theory and the Critical Tradition*. New York: Oxford University Press, 1953.
Ahmed, Sara. "Affective Economies." *Social Text* 22.2 (79) (Summer 2004): 117–39.
———. *The Cultural Politics of Emotion*. Edinburgh: Edinburgh UP, 2004.
———. "Orientations: Toward A Queer Phenomenology." *GLQ: A Journal of Lesbian and Gay Studies* 12.4 (2006): 543–74.
———. "A phenomenology of whiteness." *Feminist Theory* 8.2 (2007): 149–68.
———. *Queer Phenomenology: Orientations, Objects, Others*. Durham, NC: Duke UP, 2006.
Alexander, Meena. "Shelley's India: Territory and Text, Some Problems of Decolonization," in *Shelley: Poet and Legislator of the World*. Edited by Betty T. Bennett and Stuart Curran, pp. 169–78. Baltimore: Johns Hopkins UP, 1996.
Anderson, Benedict. *Imagined Communities: Reflections on the Origin and Spread of Nationalism*. London: Verso, 1991.
Aravamudan, Srinivas. *Enlightenment Orientalism: Resisting the Rise of the Novel*. Chicago: U of Chicago P, 2011.
Arnold, Matthew. *Poetry of Byron*. London: Macmillan & Co, 1888.
Attar, Samar. *Borrowed Imagination: The British Romantic Poets and Their Arabic-Islamic Sources*. Lanham, MD: Lexington Books, 2014.
Balfour, Ian. "Genres of the Sublime: Byronic Tragedy, *Manfred*, and 'The Alpine Journal' in the Light of Some European Contemporaries." *Université de Moncton Review* (2005): 3–25.
Balfour, Lawrie. "Reparations After Identity Politics." *Political Theory* 33.6 (2005): 786–811.
Bari, Shahidha. "Listening for Leila: The Re-direction of Desire in Byron's *The Giaour*." *European Romantic Review* 24.6 (2013): 699–721.

Bennett, Paula. "Phillis Wheatley's Vocation and the Paradox of the 'Afric Muse.'" *PMLA* 113.1 (1998): 64–76.

Bernstein, Charles. *Figuring the Word*. New York: Granary Books, 1998.

Bhattacharya, Nandini. *Slavery, Colonialism, and Connoisseurship Gender and Eighteenth-Century Literary Transnationalism*. London: Routledge, 2018.

The Bigger Six Collective. "Coda: From Coteries to Collectives." *Symbiosis* 23.1 (2019): 139–40.

Bigwood, Carol. "Seeing Blake's Illuminated Texts." *The Journal of Aesthetics and Art Criticism* 49.4 (1991): 307–15.

Blackstone, Bernard. *English Blake*. Cambridge: Cambridge UP, 1949.

Blair, Hugh. *A Critical Dissertation on the Poems of Ossian, the Son of Fingal*. London: T. Becket and P. A. De Hondt, 1763.

Blake, William. *Blake's Poetry and Designs: Authoritative Texts, Illuminations in Color and Monochrome, Related Prose, Criticism*. Edited by Mary Lynn Johnson and John E. Grant. New York: Norton, 1979.

———. *The Complete Poetry and Prose of William Blake*. Edited by David V. Erdman with commentary by Harold Bloom. Berkeley: U of California P, 1982.

———. *The William Blake Archive*. Edited by Morris Eaves, Robert N. Essick, and Joseph Viscomi. University of North Carolina at Chapel Hill and the University of Rochester. www.blakearchive.org/.

Bloom, Harold. *Blake's Apocalypse: A Study in Poetic Argument*. Garden City, NY: Doubleday Anchor Books, 1965.

———. "Dialectic in the Marriage of Heaven and Hell." *PMLA: Publications of the Modern Language Association of America* 73.5 (1958): 501–4.

Bly, Antonio T. "'ON *Death's* Domain Intent I Fix My Eyes': Text, Context, and Subtext in the Elegies of Phillis Wheatley." *Early American Literature* 53.2 (2018): 317–41. *JSTOR*, www.jstor.org/stable/90022194.

Bourdieu, Pierre. *Distinction: A Social Critique of the Judgement of Taste*. Cambridge, MA: Harvard University Press, 1984.

Brown, Garrett Wallace, and David Held, eds. *The Cosmopolitanism Reader*. Cambridge: Polity Press, 2015.

Bruder, Helen P., and Tristanne J. Connolly, eds. *Queer Blake*. Basingstoke: Palgrave Macmillan, 2010.

Butler, Judith. *Bodies That Matter: On the Discursive Limits of Sex*. Abingdon: Routledge, 2011.

———. *Gender Trouble: Feminism and the Subversion of Identity*. New York: Routledge, 1990.

———. *Precarious Life: The Powers of Mourning and Violence*. New York: Verso Books, 2006.
———. *Undoing Gender*. New York: Routledge, 2004.
Butler, Marilyn. "The Orientalism of Byron's *Giaour*," in *Byron and the Limits of Fiction*. Edited by Bernard Beatty and Vincent Newey. Liverpool: Rowman & Littlefield, 1988.
Byron, George Gordon, Lord. *Byron's Letters and Journals*. Edited by Leslie A. Marchand, 12 vols. Cambridge, MA: Harvard University Press, 1973–81.
———. *Complete Poetical Works*. Edited by Jerome McGann, 7 vols. Oxford: Clarendon Press, 1980–93.
———. *The Major Works: Including Don Juan and Childe Harold's Pilgrimage*. Edited by Jerome J. McGann. Oxford: Oxford UP, 2008.
———. *The Works of Lord Byron*. Edited by Rowland E. Prothero, vol. 11. London: J. Murray, 1904.
Carretta, Vincent, ed. *Phillis Wheatley: Complete Writings*. New York: Penguin Books, 2001.
Chander, Manu S. *Brown Romantics: Poetry and Nationalism in the Global Nineteenth Century*. Lewisburg, PA: Bucknell UP, 2017.
Chatterjee, Ronjaunee, Alicia Mireles Christoff, and Amy R. Wong. "Undisciplining Victorian Studies." *Victorian Studies* 62.3 (Spring 2020): 369–91.
Chaucer, Geoffrey. *The Complete Works of Geoffrey Chaucer, Vol. 4: The Canterbury Tales*. Edited by Walter W. Skeat. 2nd ed. Oxford: Oxford UP, 1900.
Cheeke, Stephen. *Byron and Place: History, Translation, Nostalgia*. Basingstoke: Palgrave Macmillan, 2003.
Chen, Mel Y. *Animacies: Biopolitics, Racial Mattering, and Queer Affect*. Durham, NC: Duke UP, 2012.
Chichester, Teddi Lynn. "Shelley's Imaginative Transsexualism in *Laon and Cythna*." *Keats-Shelley Journal* 45 (1996): 77–101.
Christensen, Jerome. *Lord Byron's Strength: Romantic Writing and Commercial Society*. Baltimore: Johns Hopkins UP, 1993.
Chuh, Kandice. *The Difference Aesthetics Makes: On the Humanities After "Man."* Durham, NC: Duke UP, 2019.
Clark, Steven H. *Sordid Images: The Poetry of Masculine Desire*. London: Routledge, 1994.
Cohen-Vrignaud, Gerard. *Radical Orientalism: Rights, Reform, and Romanticism*. Cambridge: Cambridge UP, 2015.
Coleman, Deirdre. "The 'dark tide of time': Coleridge and William Hodges' India," in *Coleridge, Romanticism and the Orient: Cultural Negotiations*. Edited by David Vallins, Kaz Oishi, and Seamus Perry. London: Bloomsbury, 2013.

Coleridge, Samuel Taylor. *Collected Letters of Samuel Taylor Coleridge*. Edited by Earl Griggs, vol. 1. Oxford: Clarendon Press, 1956–71.

———. *The Collected Works of Samuel Taylor Coleridge*. Edited by J. C. C. Mays, vol. 2. Princeton: Princeton UP, 2001.

———. "Fears in Solitude." 1798. *Samuel Taylor Coleridge: The Major Works including Biographia Literaria*. Edited by H. J. Jackson, pp. 92–8. Oxford: Oxford UP, 2008.

———. "Kubla Khan," *The Norton Anthology of English Literature*. 5th ed. Vol. 2, pp. 353–5. London: Norton, 1986.

———. "Mahomet." 1799. *Every Day in the Year: A Poetical Epitome of the World's History*. Edited by James L. Ford and Mary K. Ford. New York: Dodd, Mead, 1902.

———. *The Major Works including Biographia Literaria*. Edited by H. J. Jackson. Oxford: Oxford UP, 2008.

Collins, Patricia Hill. "Learning from the Outsider Within: The Sociological Significance of Black Feminist Thought." *Social Problems* 33.6 (1986).

Cottingham, Myra. "Felicia Hemans's Dead And Dying Bodies." *Women's Writing* 8.2 (2001): 275–94. *MLA International Bibliography*. Web. 11 October 2014.

Craciun, Adriana. "Citizens of the World: Émigrés, Romantic Cosmopolitanism, and Charlotte Smith." *Nineteenth-Century Contexts* 29.2–3 (2007): 169–85.

Culler, Jonathan D. *Theory of the Lyric*. Cambridge, MA: Harvard UP, 2015.

Curran, Stuart. *Poetic Form and British Romanticism*. New York: Oxford UP, 1986.

Curran, Stuart, and Joseph Anthony Wittreich, Jr., eds. *Blake's Sublime Allegory: Essays on The Four Zoas, Milton, Jerusalem*. Madison: U of Wisconsin P, 1973.

Deleuze, Gilles, and Félix Guattari. *A Thousand Plateaus: Capitalism and Schizophrenia*. Translated by Brian Massumi. Minneapolis: U of Minnesota P, 1987.

Diaby, Bakary. "Black Women and/in the Shadow of Romanticism." *European Romantic Review* 30.3 (2019): 249–54. *JSTOR*.

Drew, John. "'Kubla Khan' and Orientalism," *Coleridge's Visionary Languages: Essays in Honour of J. B. Beer*. Edited by Tim Fulford and Morton D. Paley, pp. 42–7. Cambridge: Brewer, 1993.

Drucker, Johanna. *Figuring the Word: Essays on Books, Writing, and Visual Poetics*. New York: Granary, 1998.

Eaves, Morris. *The Counter-Arts Conspiracy: Art and Industry in the Age of Blake*. New York: Cornell UP, 1992.

Ellison. Julie. *Cato's Tears and the Making of Anglo-American Emotion*. Chicago: U of Chicago P, 1999.

———. "The Politics of Fancy in the Age of Sensibility," *Re-Visioning Romanticism: British Women Writers, 1776–1837*, pp. 228–55. Philadelphia: U of Pennsylvania Press, 1994. *MLA International Bibliography*. Web. 2 December 2014.
Fang, Fang. *Wuhan Diary*. New York: HarperCollins, 2020.
Felski, Rita. *The Limits of Critique*. Chicago: U of Chicago P, 2015.
Flanzbaum, Hilene. "Unprecedented Liberties: Re-Reading Phillis Wheatley." *MELUS: The Journal of the Society for the Study of the Multi-Ethnic Literature of the United States* 18.3 (Fall 1993): 71–81.
Ford III, James Edward. "The Difficult Miracle: Reading Phillis Wheatley Against the Master's Discourse." *New Centennial Review* 18.3 (2018): 181–224.
Foster Damon, S. *A Blake Dictionary*. Lebanon, NH: Dartmouth College Press, 2013.
Franklin, Michael J. *Orientalist Jones: Sir William Jones, Poet, Lawyer, and Linguist, 1746–1794*. Cambridge: Cambridge UP, 2011.
Frye, Northrop. *Fearful Symmetry: A Study of William Blake*. Boston: Beacon Press, 1947.
Fulford, Tim. "Plants, Pagodas and Penises: Southey's Oriental Imports," in *Robert Southey and the Contexts of English Romanticism*. Edited by Lynda Pratt. Farnham: Ashgate, 2006.
Fulford, Tim, and Peter J. Kitson. *Romanticism and Colonialism: Writing and Empire, 1780–1830*. Cambridge: Cambridge UP, 1998.
Garber, Frederick. *Self, Text, and Romantic Irony: The Example of Byron*. Princeton: Princeton UP, 2014.
Garcia, Humberto. *Islam and the English Enlightenment, 1670–1840*. Baltimore: Johns Hopkins University Press, 2012.
Gates, Amy L. "Fixing Memory: The Effigial Forms of Felicia Hemans And Jeremy Bentham." *Women's Writing* 21.1 (2014): 58–73. *MLA International Bibliography*. Web. 11 October 2014.
Gephardt, Katarina. "The Occidentalist Costume: Lord Byron and Travelers' Perspectives on Eastern Europe," in *The Idea of Europe in British Travel Narratives, 1789–1914*. Abingdon: Routledge, 2014.
Glissant, Édouard. *Poetics of Relation*. Translated by Betsy Wing. Ann Arbor: U of Michigan P, 1997.
Gottlieb, Evan, editor. *Global Romanticism: Origins, Orientations, and Engagements, 1760–1820*. Lewisburg, PA: Bucknell UP, 2014.
Green, Matthew J. A. "'That lifeless thing the living fear'; Freedom, Community and the Gothic Body in *The Giaour*," *Byron and the Politics of Freedom and Terror*. Edited by Matthew J. A. Green and Piya Pal-Lapinski, pp. 15–32. Basingstoke: Palgrave, 1998.

Gutschera, Deborah A. "The Drama of Reenactment in Shelley's 'The Revolt of Islam.'" *Keats-Shelley Journal* 35 (1986): 111–25.

Haddad, Emily A. *Orientalist Poetics: The Islamic Middle East in Nineteenth-Century English and French Poetry*. Aldershot: Ashgate, 2001.

Hallaq, Wael. *Restating Orientalism: A Critique of Modern Knowledge*. New York: Columbia UP, 2018.

Hamilton, Paul. "Byron, Clare, and Poetic Historiography," in *Rethinking British Romantic History, 1770–1845*. Edited by Porscha Fermanis and John Regan. Oxford: Oxford UP, 2014.

A Hand-book of English Ecclesiology. London: J. Masters, 1847. *Google Books*. Web.

Hartman, Saidiya. *Scenes of Subjection: Terror, Slavery, and Self-Making in Nineteenth-Century America*. Oxford: Oxford UP, 1997.

Harvey, David. *The Condition of Postmodernity: An Enquiry into the Origins of Cultural Change*. Oxford: Wiley-Blackwell, 1989.

Hazlitt, William. *Characters of Shakespeare's Plays*. London: J. M. Dent, 1915.

Hegel, Georg W. F., and John S. Kedney. *Hegel's Aesthetics: A Critical Exposition*. Chicago: S. C. Griggs & Co, 1885. HathiTrust Digital Library.

Hemans, Felicia. *The Domestic Affections, and Other Poems*. London: T. Cadell and W. Davies, 1812.

———. *Felicia Hemans: Selected Poems, Letters, Reception Materials*. Edited by Susan J. Wolfson. Princeton: Princeton UP, 2000.

———. "The Indian City," *Records of Woman: With Other Poems*. Edited by Mary Mark Ockerbloom, pp. 83–96. 2nd ed. Edinburgh: William Blackwood. *A Celebration of Women Writers*. Philadelphia: U of Pennsylvania, 1994. Web. 5 October 2014.

———. *Tales and Historic Scenes, In Verse*. London: John Murray, 1819.

———. "Woman on the Field of Battle," *Songs of the Affections: With Other Poems*, pp. 123–7. Edinburgh: W. Blackwood, 1830. *The Internet Archive*. Web.

Hoagwood, Terence Allan. *Prophecy and the Philosophy of Mind: Traditions of Blake and Shelley*. Tuscaloosa: University of Alabama Press, 1985.

Hogsette, David S. "Eclipsed by the Pleasure Dome: Poetic Failure in Coleridge's 'Kubla Khan.'" *Romanticism on the Net* 5 (1997).

hooks, bell. *Feminist Theory from Margin to Center*. Boston: South End Press, 1984.

Horta, Paulo Lemos. *Marvellous Thieves: Secret Authors of the Arabian Nights*. Cambridge, MA: Harvard University Press, 2017.

Jackson, Virginia. "Lyric," *The Princeton Encyclopedia of Poetry and Poetics*. Edited by Roland Greene and Stephen Cushman. Princeton: Princeton UP, 2012.
Javadizadeh, Kamran. "The Atlantic Ocean Breaking on Our Heads: Claudia Rankine, Robert Lowell, and the Whiteness of the Lyric Subject." *PMLA* 134.3 (May 2019): 475–90.
Johnson, Mary Lynn, and John E. Grant. *Blake's Poetry and Designs: Authoritative Texts, Illuminations in Color and Monochrome, Related Prose, Criticism*. New York: Norton, 1979.
Johnson, Samuel. *The History of Rasselas, Prince of Abissinia*. Originally titled *The Prince of Abissinia: A Tale*. London: R. and J. Dodsley, and W. Johnston, 1759.
Jones, Frederick L. "Canto I of *The Revolt of Islam*." *Keats-Shelley Journal* 9.1 (Winter 1960): 27–33.
Jones, William. *Poems, Consisting Chiefly of Translations from the Asiatick Languages: To Which Are Added Two Essays*. Oxford: Clarendon Press, 1772.
——. "A Hymn to Narayena." 1785. *The Norton Anthology of English Literature*. 8th ed. New York: Norton, 2010. Norton Topics Online. Web.
——. "Hymn to Surya," in *The Collected Works of Sir William Jones*. Edited by Garland Cannon. New York: New York UP, 1993.
Kaiwar, Vasant. *The Postcolonial Orient: The Politics of Difference and the Project of Provincialising Europe*. Leiden: Brill, 2014.
Kant, Immanuel. *Critique of Judgment*. 1790. Translated by James Creed Meredith. Oxford: Clarendon Press, 1973.
——. *Political Writings*. Edited by H. Reiss. Cambridge: Cambridge UP, 1991.
——. *Toward Perpetual Peace: A Philosophical Sketch*. 1795. Translated by Ted Humphrey. Indianapolis: Hackett, 2003.
Kaplan, Cora. *Salt and Bitter and Good: Three Centuries of English and American Women Poets*. London: Paddington Press, 1975.
Knezevich, Ruth. "The Empire of the Page: Footnotes in Byron's *The Giaour*." *Essays in Romanticism* 24.1 (2017): 35–52.
Koretsky, Deanna. *Death Rights: Romantic Suicide, Race, and the Bounds of Liberalism*. New York: SUNY Press, 2021.
Kroeber, Karl. "Delivering *Jerusalem*." *Blake's Sublime Allegory: Essays on The Four Zoas, Milton, Jerusalem*. Edited by Stuart Curran and Joseph Anthony Wittreich, Jr., pp. 347–67. Madison: U of Wisconsin P, 1973.
Larrissy, Edward. "Blake's Orient." *Romanticism* 11.1 (2005): 1–13.
Leask, Nigel. *British Romantic Writers and the East: Anxieties of Empire*. Cambridge: Cambridge UP, 1992.
Leonard, Garry M. "'Without Contraries There Is No Progression': Cinematic Montage and the Relationship of Illustration to Text in

William Blake's the [First] Book of Urizen." *University of Toronto Quarterly* 80.4 (2011): 918–34.

Lindgren, Agneta. *The Fallen World in Coleridge's Poetry*. Lund: Lund UP, 1999.

Lloyd, David. *Under Representation: The Racial Regime of Aesthetics*. New York: Fordham UP, 2018.

Lootens, Tricia. *The Political Poetess: Victorian Femininity, Race, and the Legacy of Separate Spheres*. Princeton: Princeton UP, 2017.

Loving, MaryCatherine. "Uncovering Subversion in Phillis Wheatley's Signature Poem: 'On Being Brought from AFRICA to AMERICA.'" *Journal of African American Studies* 20.1 (2016): 67–74.

Lowe, Lisa. *Critical Terrains: French and British Orientalisms*. New York: Cornell UP, 1991.

———. *The Intimacies of Four Continents*. Durham, NC: Duke UP, 2015.

Lowes, John Livingston. *The Road to Xanadu: A Study in the Ways of Imagination*. New York: Vintage, 1959.

Luu, Helen. "Fantasies Of 'Woman': Hemans's Deconstruction Of 'Femininity' in Records of Woman." *Women's Writing* 21.1 (2014): 41–57. *MLA International Bibliography*. Web. 11 October 2014.

McDayter, Ghislaine. *Byromania and the Birth of Celebrity Culture*. New York: SUNY Press, 2010.

McGann, Jerome J. *Byron and Romanticism*. Edited by James Soderholm. Cambridge Studies in Romanticism Series. Cambridge: Cambridge UP, 2002.

McKay, Michele, and William J. Scheick. "The Other Song in Phillis Wheatley's 'On Imagination.'" *Studies in The Literary Imagination* 27.1 (1994): 71–84.

Makdisi, Saree. *Making England Western: Occidentalism, Race, and Imperial Culture*. Chicago: U of Chicago P, 2014.

———. *Reading William Blake*. Cambridge: Cambridge UP, 2015.

———. *Romantic Imperialism: Universal Empire and the Culture of Modernity*. Cambridge: Cambridge UP, 1998.

Makonnen, Atesede. "'Even in the Best Minds': Romanticism and the Evolution of Anti-Blackness." *Studies in Romanticism* 61.1 (Spring 2022): 11–22.

Mandell, Laura, ed. *Romanticism on the Net*: "The Transatlantic Poetess," Special Issue. 29–30 (February–May 2003).

Mason, Nicholas. "Building Brand Byron: Early-Nineteenth-Century Advertising and the Marketing of *Childe Harold's Pilgrimage*." *MLQ: Modern Language Quarterly* 63.4 (December 2002): 411–40.

May, Cedrick. *Evangelism and Resistance in the Black Atlantic, 1760–1835*. Athens: U of Georgia P, 2008.

Melnyk, Julie. "William Wordsworth and Felicia Hemans," *Fellow Romantics: Male and Female British Writers, 1790–1835*. Edited by Beth Lau, pp. 139–58. Farnham: Ashgate, 2009.

Merleau-Ponty, Maurice. *Phenomenology of Perception*. Translated by Donald A. Landes. London and New York: Routledge, 2014.

Meyer, Eric. "'I Know Thee not, I Loathe Thy Race': Romantic Orientalism in the Eye of the Other." *ELH* 58 (1991): 657–99.

Milton, John. *Paradise Lost*. 1st ed. London: Samuel Simmons, 1667.

Miranda, Omar F. "The Global Romantic Lyric." *The Wordsworth Circle* 52.2 (Spring 2021): 308–27.

Mitchell, W. J. T. *Blake's Composite Art: A Study of the Illuminated Poetry*. Princeton: Princeton UP, 1978.

———. *Picture Theory: Essays on Verbal and Visual Representation*. Chicago: U of Chicago P, 1994.

Mohanty, Chandra Talpade. *Feminism without Borders: Decolonizing Theory, Practicing Solidarity*. Durham, NC: Duke UP, 2003.

Morris, David B. "Dark Ecology: Bio-anthropocentrism in *The Marriage of Heaven and Hell*." *Interdisciplinary Studies in Literature and Environment* Spring 19.2 (2012): 274–94.

Morrison, Toni. "Unspeakable Things Unspoken: The Afro-American Presence in American Literature." The Tanner Lectures on Human Values. Ann Arbor: University of Michigan, 7 October 1988.

Mulvihill, James. "Blake's *The Marriage of Heaven And Hell*." *Explicator* 56.3 (1998): 124. *Academic Search Complete*. Web. 3 November 2012.

Nayar, Pramod K. "The Imperial Picturesque in Felicia Hemans' 'The Indian City.'" *Journal of Literary Studies* 31.1 (2015): 34–50.

Needler, Harold. "'She Walks in Beauty' and the Theory of the Sublime." *The Byron Journal* 38.1 (2010): 19–27.

Nersessian, Anahid. *Utopia, Limited*. Cambridge, MA: Harvard UP, 2015.

O'Gorman, Marcel. *E-crit: Digital Media, Critical Theory and the Humanities*. Toronto: U of Toronto P, 2007.

Osman, Sharifah A. "'Mightier than death, untamable by fate': Felicia Hemans's Byronic Heroines and the Sorority of the Domestic Affections." *Romanticism on the Net* 43 (2006). Web.

Ouejian, Naji B. "Orientalism: The Romantics' Added Dimension; Or, Edward Said Refuted." *Romanticism in Its Modern Aspects: Review of National Literatures and World Report*. Edited by Anna Paolucci and Virgil Nemoianu, pp. 37–50. Wilmington: Council on National Literatures, 1998.

Paley, Morton D. *The Continuing City: William Blake's Jerusalem*. Oxford: Clarendon Press, 1983.

Pechey, Graham. "*The Marriage of Heaven and Hell*: A Text and Its Conjuncture." *Oxford Literary Review* 3.3 (1979): 52–76.

Perry, Seamus. *Coleridge and the Uses of Division*. Oxford: Clarendon Press, 1999.

Richards, Phillip M. "Phillis Wheatley and Literary Americanization." *American Quarterly* 44.2 (1992): 163–91. MLA International Bibliography. Web. 10 December 2014.

Richardson, Donna. "'The Dark Idolatry of Self': The Dialectic of Imagination in Shelley's 'Revolt of Islam.'" *Keats-Shelley Journal* 40 (1991): 73–98. Web.

Riede, David G. *Allegories of One's Own Mind: Melancholy in Victorian Poetry*. Columbus: Ohio State UP, 2005.

——. *Oracles and Hierophants: Constructions of Romantic Authority*. Ithaca, NY: Cornell UP, 1991.

Robinson, Jeffrey C. *Unfettering Poetry: Fancy in British Romanticism*. London: Palgrave Macmillan, 2006.

Saglia, Diego. "Locating Byron: Languages, Voices, and Displaced Utterances." *Philological Quarterly* 86.4 (Fall 2007): 393–414.

——. "Words and Things: Southey's East and the Materiality of Oriental Discourse," in *Robert Southey and the Contexts of English Romanticism*. Edited by Lynda Pratt. Farnham: Routledge, 2006.

Said, Edward W. *Orientalism*. New York: Vintage, 1979.

Sandler, Matt. *The Black Romantic Revolution: Abolitionist Poets at the End of Slavery*. London: Verso, 2020.

Schwab, Raymond. *The Oriental Renaissance: Europe's Rediscovery of India and the East, 1680–1880*. New York: Columbia UP, 1984.

Sedgwick, Eve Kosofky. *Epistemology of the Closet*. Berkeley: U of California P, 1990.

Shaffer, Elinor S. *"Kubla Khan" and The Fall of Jerusalem: The Mythological School in Biblical Criticism and Secular Literature, 1770–1880*. Cambridge: Cambridge UP, 1975.

Sharafuddin, Mohammed. *Islam and Romantic Orientalism: Literary Encounters with the Orient*. London: I. B. Tauris, 1994.

Sharpe, Christina. *In the Wake: On Blackness and Being*. Durham, NC: Duke UP, 2016.

Shelley, Percy Bysshe. *The Complete Poetry of Percy Bysshe Shelley*. Vol. 3. Baltimore: Johns Hopkins UP, 2012.

——. *Laon and Cythna, or The Revolution of the Golden City*. Edited by Anahid Nersessian. Ontario: Broadview, 2016.

——. *The Letters of Percy Bysshe Shelley*. Edited by Frederick L. Jones, 2 vols. Oxford: Clarendon Press, 1964.

——. "On Love." *Romantic Circles*. University of Maryland, 1997. Web.

——. *Poetical Essay on the Existing State of Things*. London: B. Crosby, 1811. Bodleian Libraries. Web.

——. *Shelley's Poetry and Prose: Authoritative Texts, Criticism*. Ed. Donald H. Reiman and Neil Fraistat. New York: Norton, 2002.

Shields, John C. *Phillis Wheatley and the Romantics*. Knoxville: U of Tennessee P, 2010.
Simmons, Clare A. *Popular Medievalism in Romantic-Era Britain*. New York: Palgrave Macmillan, 2011.
Simpson, David. "The limits of cosmopolitanism and the case for translation." *European Romantic Review* 16.2 (2005): 141–52.
Sitter, Zak. "William Jones, 'Eastern' Poetry, and the Problem of Imitation." *Texas Studies in Literature and Language* 50.4 (2008): 385–407. Project MUSE. Web. 4 August 2016. https://muse.jhu.edu/.
Sklar, Susanne M. *Blake's Jerusalem as Visionary Theatre: Entering the Divine Body*. Oxford: Oxford UP, 2011.
Spence, Joseph. "An essay on Pope's Odyssey in five dialogues." London: R. Dodsley, 1747.
Spivak, Gayatri Chakravorty. "Can the Subaltern Speak?" *Marxism and the Interpretation of Culture*. Edited by Cary Nelson and Lawrence Grossberg. Urbana: U of Illinois P, 1988.
Swedenborg, Emanuel. *A Treatise concerning Heaven and Hell and of the wonderful things within*. London: R. Hindmarsh, 1784.
Trumpener, Katie. "Afterword: The World Viewed," in *Global Romanticism: Origins, Orientations, and Engagements, 1760–1820*. Edited by Evan Gottlieb. Lewisburg, PA: Bucknell UP, 2014.
Viscomi, Joseph. *Blake and the Idea of the Book*. Princeton: Princeton UP, 1993.
——. "Blake's Invention of Illuminated Printing, 1788." *Branch Collective*. Edited by Dino Felluga. n.p., n.d. https://branchcollective.org/?ps_articles=joseph-viscomi-blakes-invention-of-illuminated-printing-1788.
Walker, Cheryl. *The Nightingale's Burden: Women Poets and American Culture Before 1900*. Bloomington: Indiana UP, 1983.
Walsh, Megan. *The Portrait and the Book: Illustration and Literary Culture in Early America*. Iowa: U of Iowa P, 2017.
Wardi, Eynel. "Space, the Body, and the Text in *The Marriage of Heaven And Hell*." *Orbis Litterarum: International Review of Literary Studies* 58.4 (2003): 253–70. MLA International Bibliography.
Warren, Andrew. *The Orient and the Young Romantics*. Cambridge: Cambridge UP, 2014.
Watkins, Daniel P. *Social Relations in Byron's Eastern Tales*. Rutherford, NJ: Fairleigh Dickinson UP, 1987.
Watson, Alex. *Romantic Marginality: Nation and Empire on the Borders of the Page*. London: Pickering & Chatto, 2012.
Watt, James. *British Orientalisms, 1759–1835*. Cambridge: Cambridge UP, 2019.

Weir, David. *Brahma in the West; William Blake and the Oriental Renaissance*. New York: SUNY Press, 2003.

Wheatley, Phillis. *The Collected Works of Phillis Wheatley*. Edited by John C. Shields. New York: Oxford UP, 1989.

———. "On Imagination." 1773. *Unchained Voices: An Anthology of Black Authors in the English-Speaking World of the Eighteenth Century*. Edited by Vincent Carretta, p. 64. Lexington: U of Kentucky P, 2004.

Wilkes, Joanna. *Lord Byron and Madame de Staël: Born for Opposition*. Abingdon: Routledge, 2018.

Wittreich, Jr., Joseph Anthony. "Opening the Seals: Blake's Epics and the Milton tradition," in *Blake's Sublime Allegory: Essays on The Four Zoas, Milton, Jerusalem*. Edited by Stuart Curran and Joseph Anthony Wittreich, Jr. Madison: U of Wisconsin P, 1973.

Wolfson, Susan J. "'Something must be done': Shelley, Hemans, and the Flash of Revolutionary Female Violence," *Fellow Romantics: Male and Female British Writers, 1790–1835*. Edited by Beth Lau, pp. 99–122. Farnham: Ashgate, 2009.

Wordsworth, William. *The Poetical Works of William Wordsworth*. Edited by Ernest De Selincourt and Helen Darbishire, vol. 5. Oxford: Clarendon Press, 1949.

———. *William Wordsworth*. Ed. Stephen Gill. Oxford: Oxford UP, 2012. *Twenty-First Century Oxford Authors*.

Yao, Xine. *Disaffected: The Cultural Politics of Unfeeling in Nineteenth-Century America*. Durham, NC: Duke UP, 2021.

Youngquist, Paul. "Reading the Apocalypse: The Narrativity of Blake's *Jerusalem*." *Studies in Romanticism* 32.4 (1993): 601–25. JSTOR. www.jstor.org/stable/25601035.

Zafar, Rafia. *We Wear the Mask: African Americans Write American Literature, 1760–1870*. New York: Columbia UP, 1997.

Zuroski, Eugenia. *A Taste for China: English Subjectivity and the Prehistory of Orientalism*. Oxford: Oxford UP, 2013.

Index

Abrams, M. H., 21, 22, 50
aesthetics
    aesthetic "East" in Eastern Tales, 63–4, 68–9, 71
    aesthetic perception, 52
    Blake's handwriting choices, 123
    geoaesthetics of *The Revolt of Islam*, 50–1
    Orientalism within Romantic aesthetics, 2, 4–7, 9–10, 16, 29, 56–7, 159–60
    personal subjectivity and aesthetic value, 18, 19
    Shelley's aesthetics of shapes, 38, 39, 40–1, 42, 43–4, 154, 160
    time-space compression, 42–4
affect/affective, 92, 102–5, 110, 114, 142, 146
affection, 87, 92, 100, 102–3, 114
Ahmed, Sara
    on disorientation, 154, 159
    on emotions, 92, 102
    on feminism, 113
    on the futurity of Orientalism, 93
    object/subject relationship, 37
    on orientation, 1, 49, 88, 93
    phenomenology of whiteness, 77
    queer phenomenology, 88–9, 154
    term queer, 120
Arabian Nights, 31

Beckford, William, 61
Bigger 6 Collective, 14, 160
Bigwood, Carol, 126

Black studies, 12
Blake, William
    Biblical narratives, 119, 121, 130–2, 142–3
    culturally heterogeneous mythologies, 121, 136–7
    disruption of the East/West binary, 119, 120, 121, 143, 150–1, 154–5
    the East as a site of self-discovery, 119, 122, 127, 150–5
    figure of Jerusalem, 121, 148–9, 153
    four cardinal points, 121–2, 143, 149
    fourfold structures of *Jerusalem*, 143–4, 146, 149–50, 154
    gender-fluid bodies, 119–20, 122–3, 138, 139–41, 144, 146–7, 151–3, 154, 160
    handwriting choices, 123–33, 137–9, 141
    italic script, 123, 126–8, 129–30, 131
    italic script's communicative function, 133–7, 141
    italics/roman juxtapositions, 127, 128, 129, 132, 133–4, 139
    Jerusalem, 118, 122–4, 131, 142–54
    The Marriage of Heaven and Hell, 119, 121, 122–3, 125–42, 152
    Milton, 132
    Miltonic themes, 130–1, 132
    modular/modularity, 14, 120–1, 126, 128, 133, 141, 149, 154
    multimodal use of image and text, 119, 120, 123–6, 133, 134, 138–9, 141, 142

Blake, William (*cont.*)
  poetic representation in *Jerusalem*, 144–6, 147–8
  printing processes, 124–6, 134–5
  prophetic works, 119, 120, 121, 142
  queer futurity, 120, 122–3
  Songs of Innocence and of Experience, 126–7
bodies
  the Asian body, 161–2
  Black embodiment in Wheatley's works, 104–5
  gender-fluid bodies in Blake, 119–20, 122–3, 138, 139–41, 144, 146–7, 151–3, 154, 160
  precarity and bodily injury, 38–9
  Shelley's aesthetics of shapes, 38, 39, 40–1, 42, 43–4, 154, 160
  as taking shape, 49
Bourdieu, Pierre, 52
Butler, Judith, 38–9, 98, 99
Butler, Marilyn, 62–3
Byron, Lord
  within the anglophone poetic tradition, 61–2
  celebrity figure of, 57, 60, 62, 70, 71
  Childe Harold's Pilgrimage, 7, 56, 57–8, 61, 62, 71, 72, 95
  Don Juan, 78
  Hemans's Byronic heroine figure, 95, 96–9
  influence on Black studies, 12
  Jones's influence on, 26
  Lara, 7
  on national identity, 70
  as an Orientalist, 30, 56–7, 58, 59–60, 70, 78
  oriented/relational subjectivity, 60
  poetic subjectivity of, 57, 62, 70, 72
  self-fashioning as a poetic figure, 12, 71–3
  see also Eastern Tales (Byron)

Chander, Manu, 4, 58, 161
Chaucer, Geoffrey, 8, 24–5
Cohen-Vrignaud, Gerard, 46–7, 59
Coleridge, Samuel Taylor
  the active and passive imagination, 27–8, 30–1, 107
  on fancy, 28, 30–1, 32, 33, 107
  figure of the poetic genius, 27
  Jones's influence on, 26
  "Kubla Khan," 19, 29–30, 31–5, 118
  "Mahomet," 19, 35–7
  principle of unity, 28–9, 30–1
  The Rime of the Ancient Mariner, 66
  theories of poetry, 26–7
cosmopolitanism
  the cosmopolitan "East" in Eastern Tales (Byron), 56, 58, 59, 63, 70, 71, 73–4, 160
  ideal of in *Childe Harold's Pilgrimage*, 57–8, 62
  Kant's model of, 11, 58, 59, 74
  whiteness of, 5, 58, 59
COVID-19 pandemic, 161–2
culture
  ambiguous cultural representation in Eastern Tales, 60–1, 63, 64–7, 68–70
  cultural generalizations in Orientalist poetics, 59–60
  cultural logic of aesthetic perception, 52
  ethics of representation, 87

Diaby, Bakary, 90
disorientation, 121, 143, 154, 159

Eastern Tales (Byron)
  aesthetic of Orientalism, 63
  ambiguous cultural representation, 60–1, 63, 64–7, 68–70
  The Bride of Abydos, 57, 58, 67–70, 71
  Byron's corrections and edits to, 67–8, 69
  Byron's poetic subjectivity, 57, 62, 70, 72
  The Corsair, 57, 58, 70–3
  the cosmopolitan "East," 56, 58, 59, 63, 70, 71, 73–4, 160
  creation of an imagined "East," 57, 58–9, 60–2, 65, 70, 73, 78
  the Eastern sublime, 74–7
  female agency, 67–8, 69, 73, 76
  geographies of, 62–3
  The Giaour, 57, 58, 62–7, 71

Lara, 12, 57, 58, 71, 72, 73–7
 narrative fragmentation in *The Giaour*, 62, 65, 66, 67, 68
 the Oriental subject, 59, 70, 72, 74–5
 popular success of, 57, 61
 women as sexualized objects, 63–4, 68–9, 71, 73
Eaves, Morris, 124, 131
Ellison, Julie, 105, 107, 108
emotions
 Ahmed on, 92, 102
 feeling vs unfeeling, 103
 racial and sexual politics of, 103
 tropes of emotions and affect in Hemans's work, 92, 99–100, 102–3, 113, 160
 in Wheatley's works, 103
ethics of representation, 9–10, 87

fancy
 Coleridge's theories of, 28, 30–1, 32, 33, 107
 in Hemans's works, 108
 "Memorable Fancy" (Blake), 126, 129–30, 134, 137
 in Orientalist poetry, 28, 32, 33
 in Wheatley's works, 87, 106–10, 134
feminist criticism, 89, 90, 91, 103, 110, 113
Fulford, Tim, 17, 33

Garcia, Humberto, 35, 36
gender
 gender norms in Hemans's works, 98
 gender performativity, 98–9
 gendered Orientalism, 25, 78, 87
 gender-fluid spiritual bodies in Blake, 119–20, 122–3, 138, 139–41, 144, 146–7, 151–3, 154, 160
 narratives of becoming, 98–9
 in *The Revolt of Islam*, 38, 45–6, 48
 see also women
geography
 cosmopolitan ideal of *Childe Harold's Pilgrimage*, 57–8, 62
 of the Eastern Tales (Byron), 62–3
 geoaesthetics of *The Revolt of Islam*, 42–4
 Hemans's use of Orientalist settings, 94–5, 96–7, 98, 113
 imaginative geography, 57, 79 n.7
 imagined geography of "Kubla Khan," 33–4, 36, 48
 in "Mahomet," 36
 Romantic place- and world-making, 118–19
 time-space compression in *The Revolt of Islam*, 39–40, 43
 travel narratives, 34, 59
Glissant, Édouard, 104–5, 113
Godwin, William, 38

Haddad, Emily, 9–10, 59, 60
Hallaq, Wael B., 6
Hazlitt, William, 99
Hegel, Georg Wilhelm Friedrich, 23, 28
Hemans, Felicia
 the Byronic heroine figure, 95, 96–9
 emotions and affect in, 92, 99–100, 102–3, 113, 160
 ethnic and racial logics, 87
 on fancy, 108
 gender norms in her works, 98
 "The Indian City," 92, 93, 94–9, 102–3, 113
 Orientalism of, 93, 94–5, 102–3
 within the "Poetess" tradition, 87, 89–90, 91, 103
 proto-white feminism, 89–90
 racialized female figures, 87, 92, 99, 102–3, 113
 Records of Woman, 87, 91, 92–3, 94–6
 as a Romantic woman writer, 86–7
 Songs of the Affections, 91, 92, 100
 universal white womanhood, 87, 91–3, 96, 99, 102, 113
 use of Orientalist settings, 86–7, 94–5, 96–7, 98, 113
 warrior woman, 96–7, 100–2
 "Woman on the Field of Battle," 92, 98, 99–102, 103, 113
hooks, bell, 110, 115 n.2
Hunt, Leigh, 30

italic script
  Blake's use of italic script, 123, 126–8, 129–30, 131
  italic script's communicative function in Blake, 133–7, 141
  italics/roman juxtapositions in Blake, 127, 128, 129, 132, 133–4, 139
  in Wheatley's works, 104, 112–13

Javadizadeh, Kamran, 4, 22
Johnson, Samuel, 53 n.6
Jones, Sir William
  cultural impact of, 17
  on the expressive in lyric poetry, 20, 21–2, 23–4, 26, 27, 41, 56–7, 60, 147, 160
  "Hymn to Surya," 118
  influence on the Romantics, 26, 37, 41
  on the lyric subject, 17–18, 22
  on Orientalist poetics, 20–6
  Poems, Consisting Chiefly of Translations from the Asiatick Languages, 17, 20
  poetics of orientation, 17–18
  "Solima, an *Arabian* eclogue," 23–5
  "translations," of, 18, 20, 21, 24, 25–6, 29
  valorization of classical studies, 20–1, 25–6

Kant, Immanuel, 2, 11, 58, 59, 74
Kaplan, Cora, 89, 106

Lalla Rookh (Moore), 67, 71, 79 n.9, 80 n.15
Livingston Lowes, John, 34
Lootens, Tricia, 87, 89, 103, 106
Lowe, Lisa, 6, 13, 88
lyric poetry
  the global lyric form, 118
  Hegel's Oriental lyric unity, 23, 28
  "Kubla Khan," as Orientalist lyric, 29–30, 31–5
  as a paradigmatic expressive form, 20, 21–2, 23–4, 26, 27, 41, 56–7, 60, 147, 160
  of the Romantic period, 22–3

lyric subject
  antiblackness, 13, 90, 93, 111–13, 114, 160
  within discussions of Orientalism, 3, 160
  in Jones's theories, 17–18, 22
  new Orientalist lyric form, 16, 29
  as a site of contestation, 3, 4
  the white lyric subject, 3, 22, 23, 37, 78, 89

Makdisi, Saree, 59, 61, 133
Merleau-Ponty, Maurice, 10
Milton, John, 130–1
Miranda, Omar F., 29, 118
Moore, Thomas, 30, 58, 67, 70, 71
Morrison, Toni, 82 n.24
Murray, John, 67, 74

Orient, term, 1
orient, term, 8–9
Oriental subject
  cultural erasure, 18
  in Eastern Tales (Byron), 59, 70, 72, 74–5
  invention of, 3, 18, 19
  Jones's representation of, 18
  in "Mahomet," 36–7
Orientalism
  within the aesthetics of Romanticism, 2, 4–7, 9–10, 16, 29, 159–60
  during the COVID-19 pandemic, 161–2
  as an eighteenth-century field of study, 29–30, 52 n.2
  as ideological construction, 6
  as literary concept, 5–6, 87
  Occident/Orient distinction, 23
  orientation and, 2
  during the Romantic period, 2–3
  as scholarly field, 6
  term, 9
  and the white lyric subject, 3, 22, 23, 37, 78, 89
  of women Romantic authors, 86
Orientalist poetry
  devices and motifs, 59–60
  East/West binary in *The Revolt of Islam*, 38, 40–1, 42

fancy in, 28, 32, 33
genre, 4, 19
Jones on Orientalist poetics, 20–6
"Kubla Khan," as, 29–30, 31–5
of the Romantic period, 18–19
orientation
  as an action, 8
  the orient within, 1, 2
  religious iconography and, 8
  term, 1, 7–8, 88
Osman, Sharifah A., 93–4
otherness
  creation of the self in opposition to, 7, 10, 16
  hemispheric divisions and, 2
  self/other and the East/West binaries, 38, 40–1, 42, 65
  term, 4

Peacock, Thomas, 85 n.52
Perry, Seamus, 30
place *see* geography
poetics of orientation, concept, 3, 11, 13, 18–20, 51, 59, 78, 89, 118, 159
poetry
  Coleridge's theories of, 27–9, 30–1
  the "Poetess" tradition, 87, 89–90, 91, 103
  turn towards the expressive, 19, 20, 21–2, 23–4, 26, 27, 41, 56–7, 60
  Wordsworth theories of, 26–7
  see also lyric poetry; lyric subject
politics
  the Orient as political metaphor, 37, 38–41
  precarity and, 38–9
Poole, Thomas, 30, 31
precarity, concept, 38–9
printing processes, 124–5, 134–5
Purchas, Samuel, 34

race
  antiblackness and the lyric subject, 6, 13, 90, 93, 111–13, 114, 190
  non-white opacity, 104–5, 113
  the phenomenology of whiteness, 3, 5, 77–8

racialization of the poet/poetess as white, 87
racialized female figures in Hemans's poetry, 87, 92, 99, 102–3, 113
in Romantic studies, 6, 90
universal white womanhood in Hemans's poetry, 87, 91–3, 96, 99, 102, 113
Wheatley's Black poetic imagination, 87
Wheatley's black self-making of, 104–5, 113
white supremacist logics within Romantic studies, 3, 4, 5, 88, 90, 96
whiteness of the lyric subject, 3, 22, 23, 37, 78, 89
see also Oriental subject
Republic of Scholars, 125
Revolt of Islam, The (Shelley)
  feeling before action, 42
  gender identity and expression, 38, 45–6, 48
  metaphors of political revolution, 37, 38–9, 41–2, 46–7, 94, 154
  Orientalist East/West binary, 38, 40–1, 42
  Orientalist representations, 50–1, 64
  shapehood as a structuring motif, 26, 39, 40, 42–3, 44–5, 46–50, 64, 69, 76, 154, 160
  Snake/Eagle scene, 42–4
  time-space compression, 39–40, 43
  universalized Orientalism, 19, 37
  woman as "Shape," 44–5
Romantic imagination
  as both active and passive, 27–8
  in Coleridge, 27–8, 30–1, 107
  emergence of, 4–6
  the expressive turn, 20, 21–2, 23–4, 26, 41, 56–7, 60, 147, 160
  figure of the poetic genius, 27
  in "Kubla Khan,," 32–3, 36
  tropes of imagination and fancy in Wheatley, 87, 106–10, 134
  Wheatley's Muse figure, 106
Romanticism
  the lyric form and, 22–3

Romanticism (cont.)
  Orientalism within Romantic aesthetics, 2, 4–7, 9–10, 16, 29, 56–7
  white supremacist logic within Romantic studies, 3, 4, 5, 88, 160–1

Saglia, Diego, 61, 76
Said, Edward
  imaginative geography, 79 n.7
  representations of the Orient, 52 n.2, 64, 77
  the Romantic pilgrimage, 81 n.20
  term Orientalism, 6, 9
Schwab, Raymond, 30
Shaffer, Elinor, 31
Sharpe, Christina, 90
Shelley, Mary, 26, 42, 86
Shelley, Percy Bysshe
  aesthetics of shape, 38, 39, 40–1, 42, 43–4, 154, 160
  A Defence of Poetry, 37, 42, 43, 45
  Jones's influence on, 26, 37, 41
  the Orient as political metaphor, 37, 38–41
  The Triumph of Life, 50
  see also *Revolt of Islam, The* (Shelley)
Sitter, Zak, 21, 24
slavery
  Christian theology and, 112–13
  singularities of slavery and antiblackness, 90–1
  in Wheatley's works, 104, 112–13
Southey, Robert, 26, 30, 35, 61
Swedenborg, Emanuel, 130, 133, 134

Wang Fang (Fang Fang), 162–4
Warren, Andrew, 40, 61
Wheatley Peters, Phillis
  black self-making of, 104–5, 113
  emancipation, 90
  emotion in the writing of, 103
  on imagination and fancy, 87, 106–10, 134
  "To Maecenas," 105–6
  the muse figure, 105–6
  "On Being Brought from Africa to America," 112–13, 118
  "On Imagination," 106–7, 108–10
  "On Recollection," 108
  in opposition to political and bodily slavery, 104, 112–13
  Poems on Various Subjects, 88
  and the "Poetess" tradition, 88, 89–90, 103
  poetic expression beyond the white world, 90–1, 104–5, 106, 110–11, 113, 118, 160
  as a Romantic poet, 88–9, 90, 104, 105, 113
  "To S. M. A Young *African* Painter, On Seeing His Works," 110–11
  transnationalism of, 111–12
  typographical choices, 104, 112–13
  white supremacist logics, 90, 106
Wilkins, Charles, 29
Wolfson, Susan, 93, 94
women
  female agency in Eastern Tales, 67–8, 69, 73, 76
  female agency in *The Bride of Abydos*, 67–8, 69
  Hemans's Byronic heroine figure, 95, 96–9
  the Orientalized woman, 23–5
  Romantic authors, 86
  as sexualized objects, 63–4, 73
  as sexualized objects in Eastern Tales, 63–4, 68–9, 71, 73
  solidarity and a politics of difference, 91
  universal white womanhood in Hemans poetry, 87, 91–3, 96, 99, 102, 113
  woman as "Shape," in *The Revolt of Islam*, 44–5
Wordsworth, William
  on feeling before action, 27, 42
  Preface to *Lyrical Ballads*, 26–7, 42
  The Prelude, 5, 131
  theories of poetry, 26–7
  "Tintern Abbey," 29

EU representative:
Easy Access System Europe
Mustamäe tee 50, 10621 Tallinn, Estonia
Gpsr.requests@easproject.com

www.ingramcontent.com/pod-product-compliance
Lightning Source LLC
Chambersburg PA
CBHW051127160426
43195CB00014B/2376